Banking and Finance

The Nature of Management
2nd Edition

by

Gerald J. Cohen

Senior Lecturer, City of London Polytechnic

Graham & Trotman

First published in 1985
Second edition published in 1988 by
Graham & Trotman Limited
Sterling House
66 Wilton Road
London SW1V 1DE

Graham & Trotman Inc.
101 Philip Drive
Assinippi Park
Norwell
MA 02061, USA

ISBN 1 85333 030 2 (softcover)
      0 86010 582 2 (hardback)
      0 86010 920 8 (series)

British Library Cataloguing in Publication Data

Cohen, Gerald J.
   The nature of management.—(Banking and
finance series)
   1. Management
   I. Title   II. Series
   658.4   HD31

   ISBN 0-86010-582-2
   ISBN 1-85333-030-2

Typeset in Great Britain by Acorn Bookwork, Salisbury, Wiltshire
Printed in Great Britain at the Alden Press, Oxford

Contents

Series Foreword

The *Banking and Finance Series* has been written for students who are preparing for the Associateship of the Institute of Bankers. The structure of the series follows the syllabus closely. Although the emphasis is on the Institute of Bankers' examinations the series is also relevant to students for the kinds of other professional examinations such as the different Accountancy Bodies, Chartered Secretaries, Diploma in Public Administration, undergraduate business courses, BTEC, BEC, HND, DMS, Stock Exchange courses, Association of Corporate Treasurers, Institute of Freight Forwarders, Institute of Export.

March 1985

Brian Kettell
Series Editor

Preface

This book has been written primarily for students who are preparing for the Associateship of the Institute of Bankers. It is however equally relevant to Building Society "Management" and "Personnel Management", to the Organisational Behaviour, Personnel Administration, and Management Principles & Practice exams of the ICSA, and to the "Management" subject of CIMA, ACCA and ACA. In writing it the author has tried to meet a number of their needs. First and foremost is the need of students to be fully prepared for their examinations and this has determined the scope of the book. Management is such a wide field that a book of this size cannot deal thoroughly with every aspect. The syllabus of the Institute of Bankers has been covered but the topics chosen for thorough presentation are mainly those on which students are likely to be examined. The author has only gone outside the syllabus when additional or background knowledge is necessary for a full understanding of the main topics.

The author has been teaching full-time, evening and day release students, in the Management subjects for many years. His experience has determined the order in which the subject matter has been developed. The amount of explanation devoted to various topics reflects the comparative difficulty that students have had in comprehending them.

A further consideration in the choice of material has been the desire to make it relevant and interesting to young people in, say, their first ten years of employment. The management concepts have therefore been discussed with reference to those aspects of the business which readers are likely to experience themselves, or with which they are likely to be in contact. Concepts applicable to senior levels in the management hierarchy have been left for more advanced treatises.

It has been found that many students have difficulty with the management terminology that is often used loosely in general conversation. A special effort has therefore been made to define the terms used, to differentiate between them, and to use them consistently throughout the book.

Most research into management theory and practice has been into manufacturing industry and the resulting literature naturally has the same bias. The need to relate such work to service industries does not appear to have been properly met and the author hopes that his presentation will make management theory and practice much more easily comprehensible to those working in the service industries. To this end all the examples, illustrations and diagrams are for the first time specifically taken from, or refer to, the banking sector.

Keeping the material fully up to date and relevant has only been possible due to the help received from colleagues and friends at City of London Polytechnic, in the Clearing Banks, in other Banks, at the Institute of Bankers and other institutions in the City. The author wishes to express his appreciation to all of these and the Chief Examiner for "Nature of Management", for their help and advice. Special thanks are due to Desmond Fitzgerald for contributing several examples and to John Plenderleith for his thorough reading of the draft and the many useful suggestions.

Throughout the book the masculine sense equally applies to the feminine and vice versa. The feminine tense has been intentionally introduced to reflect a neutral attitude. The choice of topics for either gender is completely random and has no specific implication.

Thanks are also due to the Institute of Bankers and the Institute of Cost and Management Accountants for permission to use past examination papers and to the following for permission to publish extracts from their publications and documents.

Bank of England.
Hay MSL Consulting Group
IBRO
Committee of London Clearing Banks
Confederation of London Clearing Bank Employees

Gerald J. Cohen
March 1987

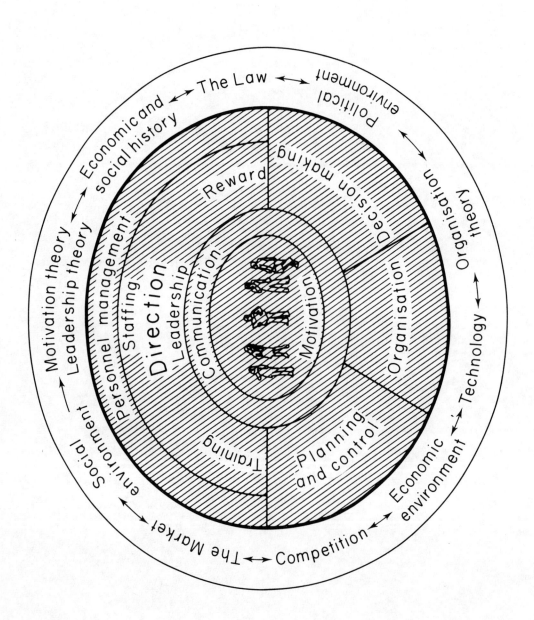

HOW TO STUDY FROM THIS BOOK

The diagram on p. xviii represents the firm within society. It also illustrates the relationship of management's functions to each other. This relationship is more fully explained at the beginning of each chapter.

STUDY AIDS

The author hopes that this book will make interesting reading and will help young managers to perform well. However, the majority of readers will, no doubt, use the book to help them in their studies for an examination. It must be emphasised that to pass examinations, knowledge and skill must be combined.

(A) Acquiring knowledge	READ	textbooks journals newspapers
(B) Apply the knowledge	VIEW	the environment your workplace people
	RELATE	knowledge and experience
(C) Remember knowledge and experience	RECORD	make notes do exercises apply concepts in your job
(D) Convince the examiners	PASS	Revise practice answer writing develop examination technique.

This book has several features to help you in your efforts.

(1) *Inter-relationship of topics*. The diagram and description at the beginning of each chapter helps you understand how the topic fits into the general pattern.

(2) *References* within the text remind you how the subject matter fits in with material in other parts of the book.

(3) *Notes.* At the end of each period of study you should *write* down a short summary of what you have read. Some readers may have a photographic memory, but for the vast majority making notes is an essential part of the learning process.

(4) *Practice exercises.* After each chapter, exercises have been suggested which will help you relate what you have read to what happens at work. Apart from being useful, these exercises are often very interesting. Again *write down* your findings, for learning and revision. You may find it useful to put each question at the head of a sheet of paper which you take with you to work.*

(5) *Progress check.* At the end of each chapter there is a list of what you should have learnt. Test yourself by writing down a summary of each item. Then go back to the text to confirm that your summary is correct. If not, re-read the material, repeat any relevant exercise and re-test yourself on a future occasion. Repeat this process until you are sure of your knowledge. (You may have a friend to check your work, if you do not trust yourself.)

(6) *Index.* A comprehensive index enables the reader to look up any particular item.

(7) *Further reading.* References in the text refer the reader who requires more detail to specialist literature. Students should also keep up to date by reading the professional journals and relevant material in the press.

Examination Questions and Model Answers

To help students prepare specifically for the AIB "Nature of Management" and similar examinations, a sister manual to this book is being published. It contains nearly fifty recent examination questions, case study questions, with full model answers. Topic summaries are also included. Advice on writing answers is also included.

---

*If you are not in a job at present you can do many of the exercises by observing conditions in stores, garages, post offices or banking halls.

Section A

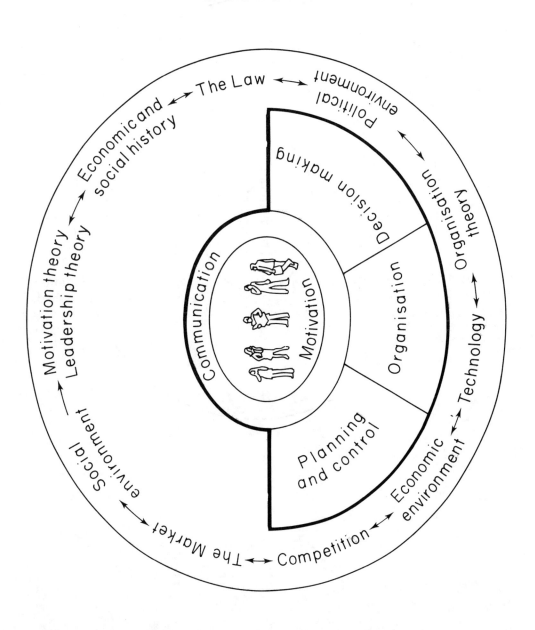

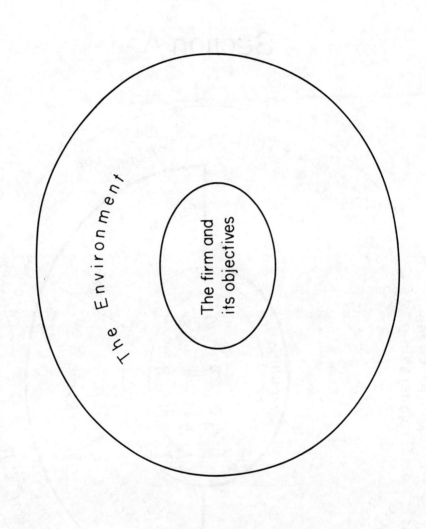

Chapter 1

Introduction

SUMMARY OF CHAPTER 1

The *Mission* comprises   An economic objective
                                 A market identification
                                 A time horizon

A *system of business and functional objectives* is established through analysing the strengths (S) and weaknesses (W) of the enterprise in relation to the opportunities (O) and threats (T) from the environment.

Forecasting is an essential element of the SWOT analysis. A *hierarchy of objectives* is used to transmit corporate objectives to other levels.

Policy   = guide to action or decision making.
                 May be implied or specific.

Rule   = instruction how to act/decide.

Procedure   = a sequence of rules.

Constraint   = limitation to action/decision.
                 May be formal/informal or external/internal.

Bureaucracy = system of management based on rules and procedures;

	it is	safe	inflexible
		stable	demotivating
		consistent	cumbersome.

The first part of the chapter sets the scene and defines the terms for the rest of the book.

N.B. The material on bureaucracy is particularly relevant to Chapters 3 and 4.

AIB Syllabus "Purpose and Nature of Management".

ENTERPRISES

This book is about enterprises in the finance sector. An enterprise is regarded as a group of individuals combining to achieve a common purpose. The principles to be discussed will be the same for a small or large enterprise, and whether it is private or publicly owned. The way these principles are put into practice will, of course, vary with the nature of the enterprise.

OBJECTIVES

For an enterprise to be successful the primary need is for the "common purpose" to be defined. This "common purpose" is variously known as the "Primary Objective", "Corporate Objective" or "Mission".

A misson will have several objectives, which should include at least:

> An Economic Objective
> A Market Identification
> A Time Horizon

The mission is usually a fairly general statement but unless it includes the above components it is unlikely to be effective in creating a common purpose for the enterprise. An example of the mission of a clearing bank is:

> "To be a profitable and prudent private sector, national and international bank." *Chairman's address — Barclays Bank PLC Annual Report 1985*.

It will be noted that this provides a criterion against which any proposed new activity may be judged.

The components of the mission must then be refined to provide realistic objectives for top management.

THE ECONOMIC OBJECTIVE

This is also sometimes known as the "survival" objective. It is now generally accepted that any enterprise, whatever its size or the nature of its owner-ship, must be economically viable to survive. In a small business (for instance an insurance broker working from home), the economic objective will be a minimum regular income. In a company where capital is provided by shareholders a certain "Return on Invested Capital" must be reached. This is the interest which is available on the investors capital. In public companies investors, i.e. the shareholders, seldom take part in the manage-ment of the company, provided that they receive a satisfactory return on investment. If this is not received they will certainly not be prepared to invest additional funds in the company and they may well vote existing

Directors out of office at Annual Meetings and replace them with more successful managers.

The shareholders may alternatively accept offers for their shares from more profitable companies. In this way many well known companies, including banks, whose return on investment has been inadequate, have been taken over and have disappeared as separate entities.

The financial sectors include many enterprises whose capital is provided from different sources. The National Giro is funded by the government, while the Co-operative Bank and the Building Societies are owned by their members. The economic objective will be different in these cases. In the case of clearing banks "post-tax return on shareholders funds" and "post-tax returns on average assets" may be the principal measures of profitability. The National Giro Bank Target for 1985/8 is "22% Annual return on mean assets, before interest on long term loans."

Whatever the economic objective is, the important point to remember is that the owners of an enterprise, whether they are private shareholders, pension funds, governments or depositors, will not, in the long run support the enterprise unless it gives value for money – i.e its economic aim is achieved.

FULFILLING A MARKET NEED

All enterprises in both public and private sector depend for their survival on providing services which are in demand. The great ocean liners providing a five day "express" service across the Atlantic have disappeared, as has the village blacksmith, because their services are either not required by present day society or they are required in a different form. A company must therefore firstly identify a market and secondly identify the services required in that market and then decide which of the services it is capable of providing profitably.

An alternative approach to this component of the mission can be used by companies which have unusual or high levels of technological expertise. In this case the company might decide to provide any service in any market where its technology might profitably be applied. The clearing banks might be considered to have such expertise in the field of data storage and transmission. A recently suggested market for this technology has been the matching of managerial vacancies in industry and commerce with personal customers of the bank who are looking for jobs, or wishing to change their jobs.

The "Corporate objective" may combine both the market and technology, and usually also determines the geographical boundaries of the enterprise. Smaller Building Societies operate only in certain local areas, The National Giro Bank in the UK only, and the Clearing Banks throughout the free world.

TIME HORIZON

The corporate objective should also clarify the period for which the enterprise is expected to operate. In the case of enterprises such as the clearing banks or accepting houses, the time horizon is in practice indefinite and implied rather than stated. This is not necessarily so. It is not unusual for consortia of banks to be formed to back a particular project, for instance a syndicated loan or to support a government for a specific time, and in many private businesses or partnerships the time horizon is the working life of the owner or the main partners.

A major point that arises from the foregoing is that companies operating in the same business sector will often have different missions or purposes. The Building Societies and Clearing Banks as deposit takers are a good example. The starting point of a different mission or corporate objective will lead to different policies and strategies and management in any one company should be aware of, and allow for, the objectives of the other companies in the industry.

A SYSTEM OF OBJECTIVES

The primary corporate objective described can be considered a focus for the activities of an enterprise, but in itself it is of little value to managers in determining their individual duties. This applies even to senior managers. For instance the "Group Treasurer" or "General Manager, Computers" who would find little to guide their decision making in a perfectly valid corporate objective of the bank to "increase profits by 10%".

Each of the components of the Primary Corporate Objectives have, therefore, to be subdivided into "business objectives" for subsidiaries of the group or into "functional objectives" for managers of "functions" such as "computing" or "finance". The sub-division may take place in different ways, depending on the organisational structure of the group but whichever way is chosen they must:

(a) contribute to the achievement of a corporate objective
(b) be unambiguous in their meaning and preferably measurable
(c) be attainable.

In order for these objectives to have the support of managers and be compatible with each other it is advisable to search for and adopt objectives in a systematic way which involves all the managers concerned. Their involvement ensures that they are aware not only of their own problems and contributions within the company, but also of the problems and contributions of others. A systematic approach should convince managers that the objectives set are the correct ones, and obtain their support even if the objectives are not in line with their personal views or preferences.

A simple example of such an approach is shown in Fig. 1.1.

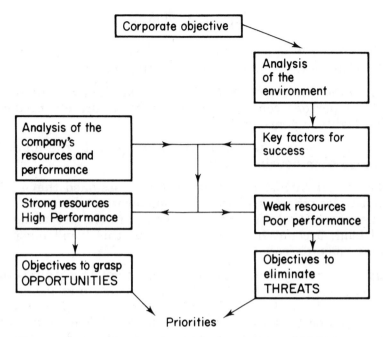

Fig. 1.1 Example of a systematic approach to setting objectives

ENVIRONMENT ANALYSIS

Any business, banking or otherwise, is part of its wider environment – part of the society in which it operates. It is this society which provides the market for its services. The types of services that will be in demand depend on the needs and desires of the society served and it is only by studying this society that the services needed can be identified and properly designed.

The main resources used by the financial community are money and staff. Both these are drawn from the society in which it operates. To ensure that adequate recruits of appropriate calibre can be found, the careers of employees will have to be designed on the basis of society's standards. To ensure an adequate supply of money the needs of depositors and strategies of competitors have to be investigated.

Other factors which will affect banks are the *state of the economy, government influence, and developing technology.*

Corporate and business objectives are set with a view to being achieved in three, five, or even ten years time. In analysing the bank's environment, one is, therefore, concerned with the future, rather than the present. The present provides, of course, the most easily accessible information about the world around us, and is, therefore, the basic source of information about the future, but it is essential to anticipate changes which may occur to prepare realistic forecasts as to future environment.

FORECASTING

The details of forecasting are a topic outside the scope of this book, but it is useful to be aware of three important forecasting methods:

(a) *Predicting the future from known facts about the past:* for example the number of persons coming of age can be accurately predicted from "births" eighteen years previously;

the number of new flats and houses coming on to the market can be determined from housing starts.

(b) *Analysing past trends.* It can generally be assumed that a trend will continue unless there is a specific reason for it not doing so. To take one example, there has been a steady increase in the proportion of people with a bank account in recent years, but this trend must stop once everyone has an account.

(c) *Identifying change points.* Trends, rather than cease altogether, may change in an important respect. A stable condition is one example of a "trend". It is obviously very useful to identify any factors which may cause a trend or a stable condition to change. For instance the change from a rising trend in oil prices to a downward trend has had dramatic effects on the economies of a number of countries and their credit-worthiness.

KEY FACTORS FOR SUCCESS

A complete analysis of the environment results in a massive amount of information. From this it is necessary to identify those factors which will be of greatest significance to the strategy of one's company. Examples of factors which might be considered "Key Factors" during the late 1980s might be:

Up to date communication technology
Automation
Speed of decision making
Industrial relations
Plastic card technology
Availability of services

Once the key factors have been identified they are compared to the relevant resources and performances of the company. The extensive branch network of the banks may be regarded as providing a ready base for automatic cash tills. This is a STRENGTH which represents an OPPORTUNITY.

The formal procedures of some clearing banks may on the other hand be considered a WEAKNESS in relation to the need to make quick corporate lending decisions. The THREAT thus posed by quicker competitors may need to be met.

In relation to the quality of service to the less highly educated depositor the simple deposit and withdrawal facilities of some building societies and their informal and friendly atmosphere are STRENGTHS, whereas in relation to the same key factor the "formal" atmosphere of banks is a WEAKNESS.

In each case an appropriate objective has to be formulated.

In most cases a number of objectives will be identified by this systematic approach. This often creates problems such as the following:

(1) More than one major objective may overload individual managers.

(2) Some of the objectives will conflict.

(3) Objectives may have different time scales.

The first two problem areas require top management to determine priorities for the objectives. An objective of improved personal service to high income individuals, e.g. by having managers and staff available who are fully acquainted with the customers' accounts and circumstances, and qualified to deal with their requests, may conflict with an objective of cost reduction. Which should have first call on cash available for investment – new branches in California or Automated Teller machines in the UK? In each case a clear statement of priorities will prevent managers in different locations, or who are responsible for different aspects of the same activity, from taking up conflicting positions.

CONCENTRATION

P. F. Drucker and others recommend a policy of "concentration" in management. Concentrating on those activities which will most contribute to success. This applied to "objective setting" means that each manager should only have one priority objective and all his other activities are secondary.

THE HIERARCHY OF OBJECTIVES

The set of Business Objectives described above provides targets for the General Managers of the various divisions of the bank. It then becomes necessary for the General Manager to sub-divide these objectives to give each of the managers at different levels within the division an appropriate goal. Figure 1.2 shows a simplified example:

Objective   Mortgage advances, net of repayments, outstanding at end of
                 year (£1000)

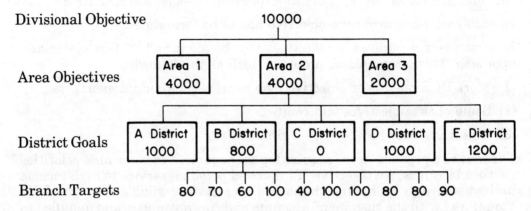

Fig. 1.2 Example of a hierarchy of objectives

Note two very important points

(1) The sum of the targets at each level is the same as the next higher level
    goal.

(2) At any one level the targets vary from, say area to area, or branch to
    branch, according to the local potential, competition and other factors.
    This meets the requirement of being "attainable".

The apparently simple short-cut of dividing a goal by the number of sub-
divisions to get a lower level target is a recipe for failure because some of
these arbitrary targets will be too high and therefore ignored by the managers concerned because they are resigned to not being able to meet them,
while others will be too low and opportunities will be lost. In both cases they
will be ridiculed by lower management who may lose faith in the competence of their superiors.

POLICIES, PROCEDURES, RULES

DEFINITIONS

A *policy* is a "guide to decision making" or a "guide to action". An employee
is, therefore, perfectly in order not to act according to policy, provided he can
subsequently justify the way he acted. Even if he cannot do so he should not
be penalised, although constantly going against, say, departmental policy,
will obviously brand him as a bad team member.

Rules are instructions as to how to act or make decisions in given circumstances. They differ from policies in that employees may not use their discretion. Transgressing a rule normally carries a penalty, the severity of which depends on the importance of the rule.

Procedures. Prescribed methods of carrying out a task, or of reaching a decision. In effect they are series of rules and therefore carry penalties for not keeping to them.

The way in which policies, procedures and rules are handled has an important effect on the managerial style. A bureaucracy is a type of organisation where most of the activities of managers and staff are governed by rules and procedures. (Max Weber: *Essays in Sociology*, Routledge & Kegan Paul, 48.) Some other features of a bureaucracy are:

- Rational basis for activities.
- Jobs clearly defined, in writing and in detail, describing duties and position in hierarchy.
- Each person has exclusive authority within his sphere and no authority in other areas.
- Promotion on a strictly impersonal basis e.g. by achievement of standards or length of service.
- Defined career and salary structures.
- Predictable salary progression.
- Job security and pensions.

ADVANTAGES OF BUREAUCRACY

The main advantages of a bureaucracy are that such a system of management is safe, stable and consistent in its decision making.

From the point of view of the employees they can look forward to a lifetime career with a predictable promotion pattern and increase in standard of living. With modern educational screening most people can even assess how far up the ladder they will go. There will be little need to exercise judgement and take risk, because rules and procedures are laid down.

For customers and suppliers safety and stability means they know exactly what to expect – the quality, availability and reliability of the service and how they will be treated.

It will be noted that safety and stability may be of paramount importance to depositors and borrowers of money.

For managers the advantages of bureaucracy lie in the close control it gives them over the decisions and activities of the staff. This may be particularly important where mistakes can lead to considerable expense for the company as is the case in banking and insurance.

The consistency aspect of bureaucracy is especially important when an organisation is accountable to society for its decisions. This is one of the reasons why bureaucracy predominates in government departments and public bodies.

A further theoretical advantage of a bureaucracy is that it *should* be relatively cheap to run. The advantages of a safe and stable career attract reliable staff without the need for very high salaries, particularly as lower and middle management does not need high levels of ability to make independent decisions – they are all predetermined. Furthermore the specialisation of work and consistence of roles should result in economies in training, purchasing of equipment and materials, and elimination of mistakes should further reduce costs.

DISADVANTAGES OF BUREAUCRACY

The biggest disadvantage of a bureaucracy lies in its very stability. Stability may be perfectly acceptable in a service which permanently remains constant, for instance the payment of pensions, where over a long period the only variation is an annual change in the amount to be paid. It becomes a major problem however in a situation where new technology, competition, government influence and the changing requirements of customers require a company to modify existing services frequently, withdraw from some markets, and introduce new services rapidly (i.e. where there is a need for flexibility).

It may have been noted that many of the advantages quoted for bureaucracy depend on the circumstances of the business and the point of view of the individual. Many people do not wish to have a career in which their progress is absolutely predictable and may feel bored and unsatisfied in such an environment. In practice people in bureaucratic organisations tend to do what is required of them with little interest. They are *trained* not to take decisions and any non-routine matter is therefore ignored or referred upward. All rules and procedures have to be observed so that even normal decisions may take a long time. Customers may have considerable difficulty if their requirements are non-standard and mistakes by the organisation may take a long time to rectify. The concept of consistency becomes an excuse for not making decisions in difficult cases. Consistency theoretically ensures that everybody, staff and clients are treated fairly. This presupposes that staff or clients are all alike. In practice staff and clients are made up of individuals who differ in their abilities, attitude, enthusiasm, needs and desires. Treating them all alike is as likely to *create* unfairness as not, and often results in bitterness and friction.

Because all procedures and rules have to be followed, and controls are applied to all activities, rather than relying on the judgement of people, a tremendous amount of paperwork may be created, even on minor routine tasks. Thus the potential cost savings of a bureaucracy are more often than not swamped by expenses which are not incurred in a different type of organisation.

The effect of bureacracy has been analysed in some detail at this stage because a bureaucratic organisation may be intentionally designed for a specific purpose, but it can also be created inadvertently by the indiscriminate introduction of large numbers of rules and detailed procedures. It is essential for managers organising work even in quite a small department to be aware of the effect of these rules and procedures on the way the department operates.

POLICIES

A less restrictive organisation is created by replacing procedures with policies. An employee then knows what he is expected to do in normal situations, but is at liberty to use his judgement in special cases. It is, of course, not necessary to give any guidance at all. A completely decentralised organisation is one where individuals are given a task and left to their own devices as to how to carry it out. In the same way as the number of rules and procedural details determine how bureaucratic an organisation becomes, so the extent to which top management *guides* the decisions of its subordinates determines the degree of centralisation. The "lending policy" of a bank is a "guide to lending managers on how to achieve the lending objective". If no policy is specified a manager has complete discretion how to reach his target. A *specific policy* may give guidance on the risk which should be incurred, the order of preference for sectors and types of loan, guidance on preferred size of advance, rates of interest, and length of loan, and on advances to be avoided. The more guidance given, the more restrictive the management style becomes. It will be noted that a decentralised role means a greater challenge to individuals and probably requires a more able individual to fill it successfully. It also is more adaptable to unexpected situations and offers more scope for trying out new ideas. In practice a company will have a mixture of policies, rules and procedure. English clearing banks tend to be fairly bureaucratic and are certainly more so than their American counterparts. At the other end of the spectrum some of the merchant banks operate on a very freewheeling or "organismic" basis.

IMPLIED POLICIES

When a policy has been formulated and conveyed to those responsible for applying it, it should be put in writing or recorded for reference. This is one way of avoiding the misunderstandings which often arise from *implied policies*. If the outcome of a series of similar decisions is always the same e.g. if a number of applications for mortgages from police officers are turned down repeatedly in a particular area, a newly appointed manager may assume it is the business's policy not to lend to policemen. In fact the particular individuals may not have been regarded as creditworthy. If all genuine policies can be referred to in the company manual, a manager can readily distinguish between policy and coincidence. Many personnel misunderstandings arise from assumptions about, e.g. promotion, salary, training or retirement policy.

CONSTRAINTS

A constraint is defined as a limit on the discretion of managers. A constraint may be either *formal* or *informal*. Formal constraints are stated limitations on the decision making power of managers, while informal constraints arise indirectly, often from a lack of the resources which a manager needs. These include

Money in the form of cash, capital or credit which frequently prevents equipment etc. from being acquired or chosen.

Staff. A manager may be unable to investigate one of a number of alternative projects because of a lack of investigating staff.

Knowledge. It often takes a long time to get information, it may be expensive, and is sometimes unobtainable – e.g. the future plans of competitors.

An alternative course of action may therefore be excluded by lack of information.

Skill. The rate of installation of new equipment may be inhibited by the availability of skilled operators.

Equipment. Output targets depend on mechanised equipment being available.

Space. Installation of ATMs may be prevented by lack of space.

Time. Many opportunities are of a transient nature and it may not be possible to get decisions quickly enough. This is one of the arguments for decentralisation and a reduction in bureaucracy.

Cultural or societal practices, such as the long lunch break in Mediterranean countries, or the objection to alcohol in Moslem countries may also be important informal constraints, as is the attitude of staff, e.g. their willingness to work at night or on Saturday mornings.

FORMAL CONSTRAINTS

Formal constraints may be external (at international, national or local level) or internal. The main *external constraints* are at national level in the shape of the Law, government regulations and codes of practice, applying either to the whole nation or to particular industries. Examples of such constraints limit the ability of commercial companies to become banks, of Bank directors to decide on reserve ratios, on personnel managers to discriminate against one of the sexes. In more local terms the Bank of England constrains the operations of the financial sector and Local Authorities limit the choice of sites for branch offices. Nowadays there are also more and more International constraints such as those applied during the Falklands war, or the limitations on foreign banks in many countries.

INTERNAL CONSTRAINTS

These are imposed by management itself. As opposed to policies, which guide managers in what they do, or rules which tell them what they *must* do, constraints tell managers what they *must not* do. In this sense the internal constraints are more important to management than the external ones, because they are controllable, while the external ones have to be accepted, at least in the short term. Clearly constraints play a similar part to rules and policies in determining the ethos of an enterprise. They are usually used to ensure concentration of effort and to eliminate overlap between roles. To achieve an "organismic", flexible, adaptable and progressive enterprise, constraints should be as few as possible. The more constraints are imposed, the less opportunities there will be to try new ideas and the less progressive the enterprise is likely to be.

Practice Exercises

(1) Obtain the annual report of the company for which you work. From it try to work out the mission, economic objective, market orientation and time horizon of the business.

(2) Think of an event which, barring disasters, is certain to happen in 2005.

(3) What could change the present trend of "privatisation"?

(4) Explain the following terms: advertising "policy"
    disciplinary "rules"
    selection "procedure"

(5) What constraints are there on the actions of your departmental manager?

(6) Identify an activity which is bureaucratically run. Is bureaucracy suitable for the situation you have identified? Why? (Or why not?)

From Chapter 1 you should have learnt:

The meaning of Mission, Time horizon and Market identification.

The difference between a "system" and a "hierarchy" of objectives.

The differences between corporate, business and functional objectives.

A method of deriving business objectives and their priorities.

Three forecasting concepts.

The differences between policies, rules, procedure and constraints.

The definition of policies, rules, procedure and constraints.

The meaning of bureaucracy, its advantages and disadvantages.

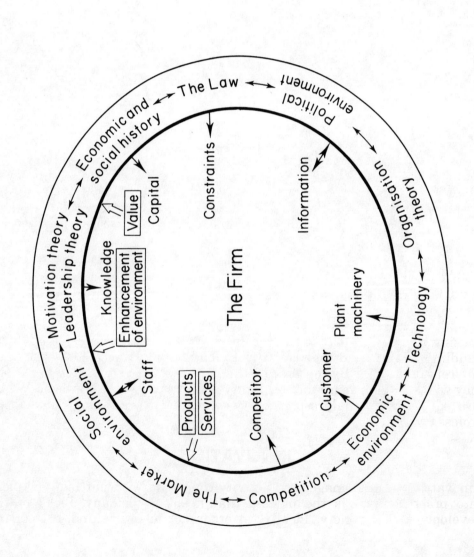

Chapter 2

The Banking Environment

In Chapter 1 the importance of the environment for any business was stressed, particularly in order to help top management choose the correct long-term objectives for their enterprise. Apart from this any enterprise must adapt its objectives, policies and strategies as society changes. The larger the enterprise the longer it will take to implement any change. So although the process of adaptation is always important, a large organisation can only keep up to date by *anticipating change*. This means constantly monitoring the environment, recording information, identifying trends, working out the future effect of current and recent events, and whether they may cause trends to be changed. Certain interesting change points can be identified in Fig. 2.1.

In addition to this the strategies of large companies may themselves cause changes in the environment. Banks, by their policies on lending, interest rates, staff conditions and strategies in fields in which they are influential may cause such changes. For instance, by moving their chargecard and computer centres away from the City of London changes in employment, housing and travel patterns are caused. The mortgage rates charged by building societies and their attitude to lending may affect house prices in different categories. By considering the impact of their strategies on society they will not only ensure the continuity and prosperity of their markets but also satisfy the social responsibility which nearly all senior managers profess to feel.

INNOVATION

Innovation is the management activity concerned with putting new ideas into practice. This is the process that keeps a company ahead of the developments in society. Ideally, in order not to lag behind, a company

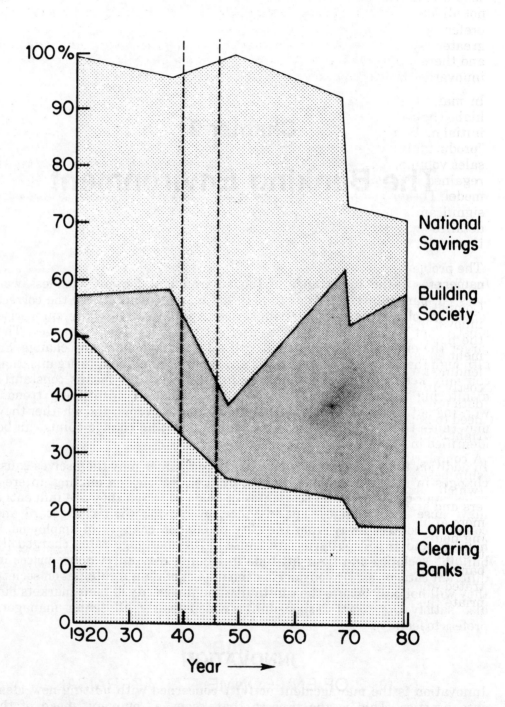

Fig. 2.1 Percentage shares of interest bearing deposits of UK main financial institutions

should lead in innovation and always be ahead of its competitors. Because not all ideas necessarily work out profitably or successfully some companies prefer not to be in the vanguard of innovation. These companies run a greater risk of being left at a disadvantage compared to their competitors and therefore have an even greater need to watch the environment for any innovation which may now or in the future be of relevance.

In many manufacturing industries the cost of innovation is dangerously high. The cost, in terms of design, setting up factories, building up stock, and initial marketing of a new car such as the Ford Sierra is so high that a single "product failure", in the sense of a design which does not reach its predicted sales volume, may be disastrous even for the largest companies. Ford never regained its dominance over General Motors after the failure of its Edsel model. The development costs are so high, that even if the new product is not significantly different from existing ones – as in the case of most new cars – detailed market research and accurate forecasting are possibly the most important management activities.

The problem is even greater in the case of completely new products, e.g. 3D cameras.

Compared with innovation costs in manufacturing the cost of product innovation in financial services is relatively low. After their rapid entry into the house-mortgage market the banks were able to reduce their commitment equally rapidly and without significant cost when they reached their lending targets. Process innovation in the finance industry is however very costly. In 1986 Barclays Bank announced planned expenditure on electronic data processing equipment of £500 million over five years. Other companies need to make similar investments and it is essential that they invest in the right equipment.

A complicating factor when investigating the environment is the relationship between many of the trends and events. Is increased car ownership (which is relevant to banking because of the travel patterns of both customers and staff) due to a relative reduction in the cost of cars or because of a more affluent society? Do social attitudes create a demand for shorter working hours, or do shorter working hours spark an increased interest in leisure? In the survey which follows, the various factors which make up the banking environment are grouped for clarity, recent trends are demonstrated and assessments are made of the foreseeable future. Where appropriate the relationship to other groups has been indicated.

THE MARKET

SCOPE OF ENVIRONMENTAL APPRAISAL

There must obviously be some limit as to how much of the environment can and should be monitored. This limit is normally defined by the corporate objectives of a company, either on the basis of the market it considers itself to be in, or on the basis of its special technical excellence. The clearing banks, for instance, have an outstanding expertise in money transmission and any activities involving money transmission within this country should therefore be within their scope. Building Societies have special expertise in housing, and any of the requirements of housebuyers should be of interest to them.

It is necessary for students to appreciate the ramifications of the market and structure of the financial sectors and how these may change before they can understand the way the companies in the industry are managed.

If the market is taken as the basis, various *segmentations* are possible. The limits may be set:

Geographically
By industry
By size of customer
By nature of customer
By type of revenue
   (e.g. fee or interest).

In the financial community the primary division of markets is usually:

(a) Multinationals

Here the customers are companies operating or having shareholders in more than one country. The removal of exchange controls has widened this market considerably for British Banks who had previously only been able to provide limited services to companies owned or operating in other countries. Environmental factors on a much wider geographical area have to be considered. This is the most competitive sector, because multinationals are at liberty to seek their suppliers of services anywhere in the world. Their importance in some countries is such that they may be able to obtain more favoured treatment.

(b) The British corporate sector

This sector covers the whole range of customers who use finance for the purpose of their business, be it manufacturing, distribution, retailing or the provision of services. Customers vary in size from the one-man business to large public companies, and in addition each customer's needs will alter whenever an environmental change occurs – e.g. an increase in petrol tax.

(c) The Public Sector

This comprises:

The government, who spend large sums not only on administration and governmental activities such as tax collection, but also on research, the defence forces etc.

Local authorities, whose involvement in providing services and even products, e.g. housing, has steadily increased.

Nationalised Industries.

Statutory Authorities, such as the water boards.

Foreign Governments.

This sector is obviously an enormous market for a whole range of money transmission and financial services. At the same time this sector favours the Post Office who are one of the private banks' main competitors and who have a monopoly, for instance in payment of pensions, and transmitting National Savings.

It should be noted that it is the declared intention of the present government to achieve a 1% per annum reduction in public spending. This would represent a drastic change in trend, the consequences of which would require careful analysis.

(d) Financial Institutions

Among these Building Societies, Pensions Funds, Foreign Banks and Life Insurance companies have shown the largest growth, but while these companies are an important market, particularly in money transmission, e.g. of pension payments, they are also major competitors.

More important is the wholesale market – e.g. hire purchase, leasing, finance and factoring companies, who effectively retail the bank's money. To be successful in this market involves also monitoring the spheres of operation of these companies.

(e) The Personal Sector

These are the "consumers" of finance, i.e. they want finance for their "personal" needs rather than for business purposes. One of the distinctions between this sector and those previously mentioned is the sheer number involved – potentially the whole adult population – all having very small value transactions, compared to comparatively few large transactions, in the market segments described above.

The distinction calls for both different organisations, e.g. the branch network with cash dispensers and Chequepoints, and different management-techniques such as consumer research.

It should incidentally be noted that in this country over the last ten years the proportion of account holders in the adult population has increased from 40% to 61% compared to over 90% in the USA and most of continental Europe. While this may partly be due to the pre-occupation of British Banks with other areas of expansion, the existence of a strong Building Society system favoured by tax legislation, and social attitudes to weekly cash wages, there is little doubt that the market penetration abroad is largely due to successful marketing effort of the "direct credit" concept by the banks to the corporate and public sectors.

The overall picture of account holding masks a considerable disparity in the pattern of account holding between England and Wales on the one hand and Scotland on the other. Current accounts are held by only 44% of the adult population in Scotland compared with 63% in England and Wales but deposit/savings accounts by 50% as against only 30% in England/Wales. However, overall bank account holding in Scotland, at 77%, outstrips that in England and Wales at 72%.

Although recent years have seen the introduction of several types of budget and special accounts, the proportion of adults with any of these is still tiny compared with the possession of ordinary current accounts, amounting to some 2% of all adults with a budget account and much fewer than 1% with a special account.

Growth in current account holding has not taken place evenly over the population. Owing to changes in the structure of the population, both in terms of socio-economic groups and age, it is perhaps simplest to look at categories. As might have been expected, the greatest growth has been amongst the lower socio-economic groups (essentially blue collar worker families). (See Fig. 2.2.)

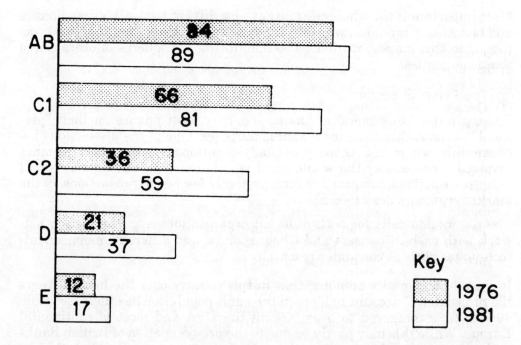

Fig. 2.2 Who has a current account? Social class percentage with a current account

The consumer market is more affected by social trends than the corporate market. The increasingly highly educated population of the future is more likely to question decisions of financial institutions regarding, for example, interest rate differentials, the interest rates themselves, the basis of charges and lending decisions. This attitude will probably create a trend to more "open" services, with a more frequent and critical interface between customer and branch manager, thus requiring a greater number of adequately qualified appointed staff. Together with pressure of costs this will accelerate the division between such activities and routine services which will continue to become less personal and more mechanised. Such consumer attitudes are also undermining customer loyalty. It used to be very rare for private individuals to change their bank or building society, whereas it is now becoming much more common.

The need to deal with local problems and react quickly to competition in the personal sector is greatest in the segment dealing with wealthy individuals who are connected with the corporate sector, or who are candidates for starting new businesses. The technological developments involving computer terminals will make it easier for banks to decentralise – and thereby speed up – the decision making process, because local managers will have immediate access to centrally or regionally held information. Central management conversely will have direct access to local records. This simplifies control of decentralised activities.

NEW MARKETS

In considering new markets which may become available, one enters the difficult area of economic forecasting. There are however several established trends which are likely to continue.

(1) Growth rates in the third world will continue to be higher than in developed countries. The rate will vary as between oil producers and users, but until some sort of balance between the two parts of the world is established, there will be more scope in the less well developed countries.

(2) In the developed countries the new markets will mainly be in the service industries – education, health, entertainment, travel and in *their* supporting industries. In addition completely new industries are emerging as a result of the new technology as well as other environmental pressure. The ones most significant in this country are:

   Energy conservation – e.g. double glazing

   Alternative energy sources in addition to the oil sector which has already become a major part of British Industry

   Microelectronics

   Communications

Biotechnology

Material Sciences

Franchising

(3) The development of the EEC offers opportunities for British financial institutions to extend their markets. The development of ECU based products is the result of this and barriers to insurances services are being dismantled.

(4) These new markets will be in different geographical locations from the old. The off-shore oil industry is centred on Aberdeen and parts of Scotland which did not previously house any significant industry. The companies in the four high-technology industries mentioned are mainly concentrated in what has become known as "the technological triangle" – basically the Thames Valley with Oxford, Swindon and Winchester as its extremities. "Science parks", the future equivalent of industrial estates, are being developed close to most Universities. Cambridge, hitherto mainly a market town apart from the University, now contains nearly 500 science based enterprises.

An important point for banks is that the existing branch networks were located to serve the old industries. Banks have to ensure that attractive facilities are made available for the new industries, whilst avoiding what may be unjustifiable costs of expensive branches in areas where they are no longer needed.

The deregulation of financial markets is creating a "global financial village". This is providing a whole range of opportunities for foreign currency dealing, options and futures.

Which new markets a company chooses to enter will depend on:

(1) The constraints imposed by its mission, e.g. whether it is willing to go outside certain geographical boundaries, or provide services which are not strictly financial.

(2) The demands of its economic objectives. One of the economic trends is towards discontinuity – in the present context, for instance, sharp fluctuations in interest rates. To counteract this banks will be searching for fee-based markets.

(3) Its technical and human expertise. The main human expertise among bankers is their skill in interviewing and evaluating clients. By combining this with their technical expertise in data collection, storage, transmission and speedy retrieval, the banks potentially can offer useful services by matching people to homes, hotels, theatres, jobs and even other people! New markets have already been entered by the clearing banks who are matching people, homes and mortgages through estate agency subsidiaries, or through co-operation with estate agents.

subsidiaries, or through co-operation with estate agents. Building Societies' expertise at present is mainly in the housing market. New potential for them lies in conveyancing, surveying and speculative building.

(4) Under-utilised Resources. The resources involved in the financial sector which are most likely to be under-utilised are branches and computer capacity. Both of these would be useful for the services mentioned in (4) above. The switch to computerised accounting by the Building Societies has effectively created money transmission systems for them. These are linked to each other through nationwide systems such as "LINK" so that cash withdrawal, cheque accounts, traveller cheques and other retail banking products can be provided to compete in the traditional markets of the clearing banks.

MARKET AND MARKETING RESEARCH

The correct design of a service and the appropriate means of marketing it can only be determined by research in the appropriate field.

Market research covers research into the size, potential composition of a market and the presence in it of competition.

Field research is that part of market research carried out by direct contact with customers.

Desk research consists of gathering and analysing information from publications and statistics.

Consumer research is specifically concerned with consumer markets and because of the numbers involved requires specialised techniques such as sampling.

Motivation research enquires into the reason for the decisions of customers.

Marketing research investigates the success and effect of different marketing methods.

STRUCTURE OF THE INDUSTRY

THE SAVINGS AND DEPOSIT MARKET

Historically one of the principal retail markets is the safe keeping of customer valuables, e.g. jewellery and documents, for which there is not much competition, but above all the depositing of money. Money being kept for customers in current accounts or on "deposit" is also an important source of funds for lending and therefore doubly valuable.

The competitors for personal deposits are:

      National Girobank
      National Savings
      Building Societies
      Clearing Banks
      Life Insurance Companies
      Pension Companies
      Retail Organisations

ACCOUNT HOLDING

A trend that has occurred over recent years has been the rapid growth in current account holding. This has been matched by the growth in the proportion of people with building society accounts. Only 15% of adults have no account of any kind.

Figure 2.1 illustrates the competition for deposits in the UK. These figures should be looked at in conjunction with Fig. 2.4 which shows the trend in the overall value of deposits. It will be noted that the total amount on deposit has increased tremendously, so that the present value of interest-bearing deposits held by the clearing banks is much greater than it was in 1920. This example highlights the importance of analysing and interpreting statistics about the environment with care.

Figure 2.1 demonstrates several trends:

(a) the growth in market share held by Building Societies (clearly inter-rupted during the 1939–45 war when housing was not regarded as a safe investment);

(b) the growth in the market share of other institutions, mainly the pension funds; after the war tax concessions by the government and perhaps also a greater sense of responsibility by society in general, encouraged their growth.

Apart from the two "change points" already noted, i.e. the beginning and end of the war, the main change points are

in 1967 – a jump in Bank Rate;
in 1970 – the first "oil shock".

Withdrawal facilities are required by depositors and savers. With-drawals from savings accounts with retailers are made indirectly through purchases. The clearing banks, including the TSB, the Co-operative Banks and now some of the large foreign banks, provide transfers from accounts by means of direct debits and other transfers. Cheque withdrawals are provided by the above, and also by the major Building Societies.

Cash withdrawals are available through traditional bank and Building Society branches, supplemented by an extensive network of cash dispensers. The table on page 37 shows the relative development of these two facilities.

As a result of competition a great variety of "new products" have been created, each directed at a specific market segment.

Specialist firms such as stockbrokers and Unit Trusts have created money and currency funds for wealthy investors. At the other end of the scale are children's saving accounts. The clearing banks and Building Societies attempt to cover the whole range.

THE LENDING MARKET

The structure of this market varies according to the segment being considered. Some important segments are:-

CORPORATE FINANCE

This market segment requires products such as overdrafts, long term loans, development finance and equity capital. In addition to the traditional contenders for this business, i.e. the clearing and merchant banks, and the international banks, which entered the market after the relaxation of exchange controls and have captured a significant part of the business, de-regulation has encouraged the formation of large international financial conglomerates which are a new source of competition. The establishment of 100 Corporate Banking Centres in the U.K. by National Westminster Bank is probably in response to such competition, as is their development of corporate business throughout the United States.

HOUSING FINANCE

Both because of the growth of the population and their attitude this market is expected to grow substantially for the rest of this century.

In 1985 77% of the loans for private house purchases were provided by the 190 Building Societies, of which over half was accounted for by the five largest societies. The smallest 170 societies have about 15% share of the above, and may be considered as regional rather than national competitors.

Nearly all the remaining loans were provided by the clearing banks. Since then the TSB has entered the market and novel products are being offered by a number of international institutions. Proposals to harmonise housing finance in the EEC may provide both threats and opportunities in the longer term. In the meantime the development of a variety of new products, e.g. pension/mortgages, for specific segments is certain.

ADVICE AND SERVICES

Many loans to and deposits by both consumers and corporate customers are made in connection with activities about which the customer requires advice and services such as insurance. Fees are usually charged for such services, and they may be offered, either as profitable activities in their own right, or to ensure that other business stays with the organisation. The competitors for these services are the same as for deposits, with the addition of:

    Solicitors
    Accountants
    Stockbroker

and other professional firms.

Among other competitors worth a mention are:

Companies providing a specialised service – e.g. *Diners Club* or *American Express*.

The Co-op Bank with its special relationship with an important section of society.

The Post Office as an agent for government as illustrated by the recent development of issuing "stamps" to save for licences etc.

METHODS OF COMPETITION

In any industry competition does not only derive from businesses and other organisations offering the same service, but also from the way in which the service is offered. The factorw which customers will consider in choosing to whom to give their business are:

    Standard of Service
    Style of Service
    Safety
    Pricing Strategy
    Accessibility
    Confidentiality
    Tradition/Novelty

Advertising
Special Promotions.

STANDARD OF SERVICE

This can be sub-divided into efficiency, reliability, speed and the attitude of staff. Efficiency in this context relates to the amount of effort a customer has to make to obtain the service he desires. The complexity of application forms and the detail required on them are relevant, but probably the most important factor is waiting time. This is one of the reasons for the popularity of ATM's and the introduction of "Quick Service" positions.

Reliability is a quality which banking customers value highly. The quality and training of bank staff and banks' procedural systems make reliability one of their strengths, particularly in relation to competitors such as accountants and solicitors. On the other hand the same systems are something of a draw-back when speed of response to customers, special requests are concerned. This conflict may well lead to organisational separation of services requiring a different emphasis.

STYLE OF SERVICE

Major differences in style of service are the alternatives of "mechanical" or "personal" service, as in automatic or manned tills. To a large extent customers preferences depend on their personal attitudes and both types of service are therefore likely to continue to be in demand. In addition older customers tend to prefer personal service partly because they have not grown up, like the younger generation, with mechanical and electronic devices and partly because time spent with a cashier, or even waiting in a queue with other people is regarded as a boon rather than a waste.

Building Societies have, in the past, provided a less formal and more friendly service to depositors at their branches than the clearing banks. The latter are now trying to match this.

One major clearing bank sent all management and staff in contact with customers on courses providing comprehensive attitude and skill training during 1985/6.

Another aspect of the style of service is the surroundings in which the service is provided. To the established bank customer the traditional banking hall is a safe and reasonably efficient environment. To many of the unbanked it is comparable to social security and other official establishments which are to be avoided. This feeling is accentuated by the traditional way in which banking staff dress. To established clients this characterises reliability, but it creates a gulf between the staff and people accustomed to less formal clothes.

All the clearing banks now have experimental branches with open plan banking halls and, on the basis of experience here and in other countries this closer contact with customers is likely to be extended. Casual dress is being used on Saturday opening when customers who prefer informality are most likely to come.

As far as corporate customers are concerned, the remoteness of branch managers (who in the past were are frequently only available after overcoming the resistance of several junior staff and a secretary and then only by appointment) is a notably different style to, for instance, the insurance agent who will initiate contact with a prospective client and offer to visit him at his home at any time including evenings and Sundays. Several clearing banks are creating "accounts executives" to match such service.

PRICING STRATEGY

The cost of a service to customers is obviously a factor in their choice, but three important points should be noted:

(a) Price is not necessarily the most important or even a major factor. It will probably be the determining factor in "undifferentiated services", i.e. those services which are identical in every way. Automatic teller machines might be an example. In other cases reliability, speed or ease of access may be much more important.

(b) Customers have an "expectation" of what prices should be – for example an affluent customer will expect to pay more for his personal overdraft than for an overdraft for the company of which he is a director, although both on a cost and creditworthiness basis this may not be logical. Departure from expected pricing strategies may be treated with suspicion and resistance. At the same time innovative pricing may result in considerable competitive advantages for the firm introducing it. The growth of supermarkets in retailing is partly due to a departure from traditional selling margins.

(c) Cross-subsidisation plays an important part in price considerations. The customer will consider the overall cost of his "shopping basket" of services, including such non-price costs as one-stop shopping which takes account of the expense of travelling and the value of time. Any associated benefits will also be taken into account. A guarantee of a mortgage at some time in the future, or the ready availability of short term overdrafts to cover emergencies, are examples.

There is a definite trend for customers to be more price conscious, and to object to what may be considered arbitrary charges, i.e. those which the customer cannot work out for himself.

Price competition in the savings market, notably from unit trusts and merchant banks through money market funds, and from National Savings has caused all institutions to provide a whole range of high interest accounts.

Free current account banking is widely offered by clearing banks to compete with building society accounts.

ACCESSIBILITY

The ease with which a service is available, both from the point of view of time and place may well be the basis of a customer's choice. Most branches of banks were located with this in mind – in High Streets and near railway stations – both easily accessible by public transport, which was the main form of transport when the branch network was built up. Unfortunately many railway stations are now disused, and "shopping centres" have developed away from High Streets, but even where this has not taken place the High Street is very often avoided by the typical car owning bank customer and more so by corporate customers who put a high value on time. The smaller customers of the Building Societies are less affected. For present or potential customers who are employed during the normal working week, the accessibility to a service outside these hours may be of paramount importance. Saturday opening by Building Societies has virtually forced banks to provide services outside traditional banking hours at selected branches on Saturday mornings or through the medium of automatic teller machines. The trend to greater accessibility will almost certainly continue to influence the marketing of services, e.g. some Scottish banks open until 6 p.m. on certain days and Lloyds Bank has introduced full Saturday opening at some branches, and out-of-hours, out-of-the-weather deposit and withdrawal facilities in the lobbies of some branches.

TRADITION/NOVELTY

In undifferentiated services, such as the conventional current account, people do not normally change without some special reason (usually poor service). The basis of choice for most people with their first current account is the bank their parents use. Influencing this choice is therefore very important. It is the basis of many special promotions directed at students and young people, and the reason for providing childrens' accounts and savings accounts.

People may be divided into those with a conservative outlook and those known as innovators, which are a much smaller proportion. Traditionalists are very reluctant to try any new service, whereas the importance of innovators as a market is that they are prepared to try out new services, and that they act as unpaid salesmen. The traditional customer is more likely to change to a different service by being told about it by a satisfied "innovator" than for any other reason. As customers become more sophisticated due to the spread of education and information they will demand services which match their requirements more clearly. On the deposit taking side Building Societies are setting the pace with a great variety of accounts suiting most requirements for amounts, length of deposit and withdrawal facilities. This trend towards greater variety is likely to continue.

ADVERTISING AND SPECIAL PROMOTION

The traditional banking services were well known to the limited sector of society which used them. As more of the less sophisticated parts of society join the ranks of customers and the range and variety of services increases, a key to increased market share is to ensure that customers are aware of what is available to them. This may be done by using all the modern communication media including direct mail, television advertising for services with mass consumer appeal, advertising in magazines and newspapers and seminars or conferences on specialised topics such as small business finance. It will undoubtedly be necessary for all sections of the financial sector to make greater use of the communications media.

TRENDS ATTRIBUTABLE TO COMPETITION

Competition in the financial sector has been greatly increased over the last two decades by the removal of exchange controls, the interest cartel of banks and Building Societies, the removal of the banking "corset", and dual capacity on the Stock Exchange, and most recently The Building Society Act, 1986. The overall effect of these changes is to eliminate traditional lines of demarcation between different firms. Technical developments have at the same time made it easier for firms to combine new services with their existing ones. Overseas banks and other international financial conglomerates have been able to enter the U.K. market without having to bear the cost of an extensive branch network.

Major trends arising out of this competition include:

● entry of non-banking companies e.g. retailers into financial services
● diversification of banks, Building Societies and "single product" companies into other fields
● amalgamations creating financial conglomerates
● provision of services such as ATMs and EFTPOS jointly with other organisations.
● diversification overseas. Examples of this are the co-operation with overseas banks on the EUROCARD System, as well as direct expansion abroad.

A new idea which may herald an important future source of competition for both deposit taking and lending is "Fund Swapping" between companies. This applies to those companies who have a seasonal demand for funds. Firms in Christmas oriented business have to build up stock in the early part of the year, building up a large demand for advances during the summer for settlement in winter when the firms may have surpluses. These surpluses could be directly loaned to companies having a complementary seasonal demand – e.g. holiday camp operators. The same system can also be applied to cyclically complementary companies – i.e. over a longer period, although such trade cycles are not as predictable as seasonal variations. In overseas trading "barter" is an old idea now being revived.

INDUSTRY FEATURES

It was seen in the first chapter that a way of determining the strategies of organisations is to judge their STRENGTHS and WEAKNESSES against the trends in the environment. It must be borne in mind that a particular feature of a business may be a strength when considered against one trend and a weakness when considered against another. One of the major features of the sector is London being a major financial centre due to its position in the time zones, and its good communications. This is a strength for most companies operating in London, but being located elsewhere may be a weakness.

Other general features in the financial sector are:

- Extensive branch networks
  strength – in relation to availability of consumer services
  weakness – overall costs
- Large customer base
  strength – introducing new services
  weakness – speed and cost of change
- Membership of high technology money transmission system
  strength – in relation to nearly all financial services
- Loyal and experienced staff
  strength – defence of existing markets against new competition
  weakness – if markets are declining
- Standing and reputation
  strength – in defending existing and developing new business

Further strengths and weaknesses will be identified for different sectors of the industry as environmental trends are studied in the rest of this chapter. OPPORTUNITIES arise when a business has strength in relation to a trend. THREATS arise when it has a weakness.

POLITICAL AND GOVERNMENT INFLUENCE

Many of the environmental trends which follow are originated or influenced by governments or political events. Government influence is felt at three levels. Firstly through its general management of the country. Monetary, credit, and interest rate policies, while they may be of particular interest to the financial services industry, have a much wider impact on consumers (e.g. the savings ratio) and industry (e.g. capital spending), as do policies on housing, welfare regional development, defence. Nearly half the U.K.'s expenditure is directed by the public sector. The public sector therefore largely determines where change will take place and how quickly.

A serious, hopefully short term, trend is to protectionism.

In this respect overseas exposure may well be a weakness.

Secondly governments pass laws which, while not specifically aimed at the financial sector, affect it in common with the rest of industry. Major legislation of this type in recent years concerned:

    Health and Safety at Work
    Equal Opportunity
    Dismissal procedures and minimum notice
    Sickness pay procedures
    Freedom of information

The impact of such legislation is gradual over a long period. While it does not normally represent a major opportunity or threat, it may have considerable effect on company policy or practice.

Midland Bank have set up an Equal Opportunity Steering Committee, and have introduced a Retainer scheme to enable men and women pursuing a long term career to have one unpaid break of up to five years to provide pre-school care for their children.

Thirdly there are laws and regulations directly at the financial services industry. Significant examples currently affecting the industry are:-

    The Financial Services Bill
    The Building Societies Bill
    Deregulation of the Stock Exchange

The general effect of these Bills is to dismantle traditional boundaries between different segments of the industry, and to increase competition. Firms in the industry will tend either to specialise or to provide a wide range of services, depending on whether their strength lies in specialist experience and knowledge, or in capital backing.

On the other hand the Polarisation rules of the Securities and Investment Board mean that people who sell life assurance and unit trusts must clearly identify themselves as either independent intermediaries or as representatives of a particular company. This clearly affects the branch operations of Building Societies and Banks. They will have to revise their policies, and possibly re-organise some of their activities to meet the requirements.

The possession of specialised skills and experience is a strength in this situation.

A relatively new development which may become a trend is the harmonisation of regulation between the financial markets of different countries. This will benefit reputable companies because it will weaken those who take unfair advantage of differing regulatory environment.

In relation to this development companies who have made profits through "sailing close to the wind" will be in a position of weakness.

ECONOMIC ENVIRONMENT

STANDARD OF LIVING

Since the 1930s the standard of living in the UK has been steadily rising. A rising standard of living normally brings with it:

Firstly an *increased investment in consumer durables,* e.g. household goods, care and housing, all of which provide a market for loans.

Secondly an *increased spending on luxuries*, providing a similar market.

Thirdly, in conjunction with social trends, an *increase in leisure activities*. Apart from reinforcing the first two factors, this has created the travel market, including the provision of travel facilities, foreign exchange dealing, opportunities for expansion overseas, as well as the need to widen the money transmission networks.

Car ownership has resulted in changes of travel patterns which means that the location of many high street branches is no longer satisfactory for either customers or staff. At the same time new branches or retail outlets are needed in locations such as hypermarkets, shopping precincts, factories and industrial estates.

CONCENTRATION

Since 1950 there has been considerable concentration in British Industry. This has resulted in a reduction in the number of autonomous companies and headquarters operating locally, thus concentrating the need for corporate services and advice on a much smaller number of customers, while at the same time affecting the type of service and advice required. (See Fig. 2.3.)

Fig. 2.3 Effects of concentration

	1970	1980
Number of retail co-operative societies	477	270
Number of building societies	481	273

In parallel with the above the demand for money transmission, such as remitting cash takings or paying wages, between the units of large organisations has increased.

Concentration is an opportunity for flexible organisations with low overheads, e.g. subsidiaries of foreign banks, and for those with strong money transmission systems. It is a threat to organisations with large branch networks, some of which may be redundant.

HOUSING

Partly following from the above there has been a dramatic differentiation of house prices in the U.K., with prices in the south rising to what many consider to be untenable levels, while in some parts of the north owners may have difficulty in recovering their investment. Combined with intensive competition in this market a trend to more mortgage repayment failures has emerged. This may become much more serious if the trend to higher prices is suddenly reversed, as has already happened in the U.S.A. and Germany.

AGRICULTURE

The drive for more efficient food production, particularly in the EEC has now led to overproduction. This is leading to economic difficulties for many farmers. Change of land use is being encouraged. More land may well become available for housing in areas where at present the demand cannot be met. This will change the demand for services in the areas affected.

These developments will create opportunities for organisations with both local knowledge and staff who either have experience of the replacement activities or the skill to assess the potential and risk of innovation.

Such international expansion is however very uneven, largely due to the fluctuating price of oil. High prices favour some countries and low prices others. Overexpansion by those doing well leads to serious bad debt problems. Relative changes in exchange rates, and particularly the falling dollar, compound these problems.

The international situation represents opportunities for those who have the knowledge, skills and flexibility to take advantage of them, and whose strength lies in assessing and controlling risk.

INTERNATIONAL FACTORS

Due to the increasing demand for energy and other natural resources, the balance of economic power has shifted from industrialised countries to the "third world". This means that many of the latter are achieving very high growth rates, while the increase in the standard of living referred to above has slowed down in developed countries and in some, notably the UK is actually declining.

THE TECHNOLOGICAL ENVIRONMENT

We are sometimes said to be living during a technological revolution because of the number of technological changes which are taking place. In each branch of technology there is steady progress punctuated by significant developments. As new technologies are added, the frequency of major innovation accelerates. Companies in all industries must therefore look not only to keeping abreast of knowledge in their own field of excellence, but even more so in other fields which may affect them and their customers.

TRANSPORT

A feature of progress in technology is that it generally leads to a reduction in cost of the end product or service. Nowhere is this more apparent than in private motoring, sea ferries, containerised freight and air transport. The effect on local and international travel has already been explained. It will also be realised that whole new industries have emerged, e.g.

Caravan and Camping Sites and Equipment
Container manufacture and leasing.

Furthermore the reduced relative cost of transport has modified world-wide trading patterns, leading to major expansion in services such as

Bills of Exchange
Export Credit

for both home-based and foreign companies.

MICROELECTRONICS

The features of this new technology are that it makes mechanisation and automation much less expensive and smaller. The problem of size was in the past a major barrier to development of equipment. Microelectronics is an enormous expanding market for the banks, and it affects all other customers – corporate or personal – of banks in ways which must be monitored. In addition it has revolutionised most banking processes.

MECHANISATION

Among the machinery made possible are:

Cash dispensers
Cash issuing terminals
Cheque printing equipment
Mechanised document sorting, folding and mailing.

COMPUTERS AND DATA-PROCESSING

The reduced cost of data storage and retrieval has led to the centralisation of records and more ready availability, particularly to corporate customers, of a wide range of financial information about their own operations.

Improved and cheaper transmission of information has facilitated such systems as:

Bankers Automated Clearing System (BACS)
The Electronic Interbank Payment System for Abroad (SWIFT)
Company Information (EXTEL)
Visual display units for immediate access to data stores
Linking banking facilities with retailers and customer (PRESTEL)
Clearing House Automated Payment System (CHAPS)

ELECTRONIC FUNDS TRANSFER/POINT OF SALE

An example of new technological development is the national point-of-sale electronic payments system (POS).

The system which will involve installing electronic terminals in shops and garages connected directly to banks, could eventually revolutionise shopping in the high street.

EFT/POS will work rather like the existing bank cash dispensers. However, it will allow customers to pay for goods in shops with a plastic card and the money will be debited directly from their bank accounts, the retailers' accounts being credited (EFT = Electronic Funds Transfer).

The big English and Scottish clearing banks are involved as well as the Co-op Bank, National Giro and Trustee Savings Bank. The bank of England is also on the 12-bank policy committee.

There are several pilot schemes in action already, although major issues on control, ownership and funding of the system have still to be sorted out. The terminals which will have to be installed in shops are expected to cost up to £800 each and retailers have been arguing with the banks over who should pay for these. Both the Government and the Bank of England are likely to take a keen interest in how the system is owned and managed. The Office of Fair Trading has been following developments closely and is expected to have lengthy discussions with the banks on the subject to ensure that the big clearing banks do not assume a too dominant role in running the system.

For their part, the banks are likely to argue that since they will be carrying much of the cost of the system, they should be able to run it.

British Telecom will also be involved in supplying link-ups between retail outlets and the banks.

BACSTEL

The growth in Micro Computers and Cash Management Systems for Corporate Companies are a parallel example.

BACSTEL allows the customer to send his payroll instructions, his direct debit lists or his purchase ledger trade payment instructions over the telecommunications system, direct from his computer.

Previously BACS has had to ask its customers to submit data in the form of tape, disk or cassette.

A further refinement means that data can be transmitted at any time the customer chooses, not just at pre-booked times or by short on-demand messages.

Big users include building societies making interest payments and firms paying out dividends and pensions.

DEVELOPMENTS IN PLASTIC

These have made "credit cards" possible, with their implications for security and, in conjunction with the other developments referred to, progress towards a cashless society.

COMMUNICATION

Developments in communication, largely based on optical fibres, when taken in conjunction with microprocessor developments, may well have the biggest impact on changes in the way companies in the financial services sector are run during the next decade. Branch Processors are being installed which carry much more customer data than is currently stored on the accounts of central computers. Through Branch Interface Equipment these processors can be connected to Digital Integrated communication Networks centred on regional data bases. These DINs are also connected to each other, making access to all the locally held information possible.

These technical developments greatly enhance the importance of "management services" and "systems" departments and require new solutions to issues of control and of organisational design and culture. The opportunities for decentralising decision making to local managers, or conversely to centralise to specialists will also be increased.

In insurance, for instance, senior underwriters have access to a vast amount of information on all types of risk, virtually at the touch of a button, provided they have the technical skill to retrieve and analyse it.

Thus, organisational issues as well as retraining of existing staff will have to be dealt with. Due to the high demand for staff with computer skills, there will be a greater risk of labour turnover. Recruitment and industrial relations policies will have to be reviewed accordingly.

Existing bureaucratic structures, and conservative staff and cultures are weaknesses in relation to technical trends. Profitability and large capital bases, and technical expertise, are strengths.

SOCIAL ENVIRONMENT

During the Industrial Revolution there was a very definite attitude towards work and self reliance. These attitudes have been gradually changing and the process is still continuing.

ATTITUDE TO WORK

Work, as well as "Self Reliance" was regarded as a virtue in itself. This excluded the necessity, even the desirability, of making it interesting or enjoyable. Because enjoyment and pleasure were generally frowned upon, there was no point in having "free" time. This attitude to work spawned the classical approach to management.

As peoples' attitudes have changed, the importance of "interesting work" has been recognised by investigators such as Maslow, Herzberg and Vroom. Rising standards of living also enable people to develop personal interests outside their work. Together these changes have resulted in a growing demand for leisure time combined with increasing value being put on giving up such leisure time. This source of pressure for a shorter working week, longer holidays and earlier retirement can be expected to continue in the foreseeable future. Some banks have already lowered the normal retiring age for staff to 60 – both for men and women.

SELF-RELIANCE

Part of the attitude referred to above was self-reliance. This has gradually given way to growing dependence on society for provisions for old age, sickness and unemployment. This in turn has required greater taxation. As all taxes distort trade in one form or another, banking will inevitably be affected. There are signs that the proportion of people's income going on these "transfer payments" has reached a level which cannot be sustained.

Consumer Protection and legislation by government are further examples of the trend away from self-reliance. The appointment of Banking and Building Society Ombudsmen are examples of this, as are all the self regulatory bodies under the umbrella of the Securities and Investment Board.

ATTITUDE TO CREDIT

The same moral approach meant that it was unacceptable to enjoy the fruits of one's labour before it had been earned. Thus many people now are still reluctant to make use of credit facilities. The rate of change of this attitude is however becoming more rapid.

OTHER CHANGES

Among other important social changes are:

Education. The increased sophistication of society requires much higher levels of education, and what is perhaps more important, re-education at intervals.

Sex equality means that as many women now have current accounts in their own right as men. This largely new market for the banks often requires a different approach from the male market. It also means that women among bank staff are now more interested in a long term career.

EFFECT ON STAFF

As a result of economic changes, staff:

are likely to live further from town centres;

place a higher value on leisure time – demanding shorter working hours and working weeks, less travelling time and longer holidays;

have higher material expectation from their salaries and from fringe benefits, particularly those peculiar to the financial sector, such as cheap housing loans.

Cost pressures on the Industry and the need to cope with growth dictates a strategy of mechanisation. This results in reduced demand for staff and reduced security.

Social and technological factors reinforce these effects and in addition:

The technological effect on jobs has created a greater differential between "career" and "non-career" staff. The former will be expected to have higher qualifications, either in specialisms such as programming or statistics, or in marketing, inter-personal, or management skills. For non-career staff, entry qualifications are likely to be lowered. The ratio of career to non-career staff in insurance, banking and Building Societies has dropped from 60:40 ten years ago to 50:50 and it is becoming more difficult to switch. Within the non-career stream the proportion of part time staff is generally increasing.

Understanding information technology and being able to use it will be essential for all staff.

Staff will have to adapt to changes in their jobs more frequently.

They will have to be prepared to up-date their knowledge and retrain accordingly.

As the restructuring of the industry proceeds, staff will have to accommodate cultural changes.

EFFECT ON CUSTOMERS

When designing services or determining strategies it will be necessary to take into account how customers are affected by environmental changes. Examples can be listed:

Car ownership often determines which branch is the most convenient for customers.

Increased value of leisure time penalises queueing systems and favours banks with large numbers of retail points, whether manned or unmanned.

The demand for credit facilities of a variety to suit purchases ranging from a few pounds to large sums and from long term to convenience credit cards.

Availability of the widest range of services including travel facilities from one source.

Corporate customers require services from the banks to help them meet the requirements of their own customers and staff due to the same economic factors. The provision of banking facilities convenient to staff and customers of corporate clients is an important example.

EFFECT ON BANKING STRATEGY

Growth from the various factors identified has indicated the need for alternative methods of cash handling and money transmission, hence the continuing switch to:

Cash dispensers   direct credits
"Cashpoints" and similar unmanned outlets   standing orders
teletransmission of information   credit cards
direct debits

The need to obtain economies of scale in some activities and re-location of customers calls for the continuous adaptation of the organisation of a bank.

For instance, the impact of the progress of electronic banking on the banks' branch networks is a reduction in what otherwise would have been the use of branch services. Instead services will be provided by alternative and probably new delivery systems. The table below projects the future situation in Britain.

Branch Outlets in Britain	1971	1981	1990	2000
High Street Banks	19,440	19,231	?	?
Post Offices	24,514	21,756	?	?
Building Societies, Money Shops, etc	2,261	6,573	?	?
TOTALS	46,215	47,569	47,000	Less than 40,000
ATMs		2,590	7,300 ⎫	
Point of Sale and other terminals		–	10,000? ⎬	millions

The increased use of the fully automatic direct deposit, direct debit and standing order services of the Automated Clearing House will displace costly payments activity from branches. The use of ATMs, POS and home banking terminals could have a similar effect; indeed the development of ATMs and POS will depend on that being the case. Furthermore, the development of systems interfaces and business terminals will reduce the need for corporate customers to rely on conventional branch services.

The impact on the banks will depend on whether or not they are operating in a saturated market. Fortunately for the UK banks they do not. This allows some scope to expand the banking habit and absorb the growth of new business without requiring a damaging contraction of the branch network.

Technological needs will require more careful manpower planning to avoid redundancies and an ever greater emphasis on training to maintain efficiency and acquire different skills. This will apply to managerial and non-managerial staff.

Support services will have to be adapted to advise operating management on complex issues. This will have to be accompanied by more specialised operating functions, particularly those requiring a high marketing input.

RESISTANCE TO CHANGE

Whilst society is changing in many ways all the time, any individual change is slow to start and it only gradually gathers momentum. Managers who identify changes early have plenty of time to adapt their enterprises. It is only when managers and/or staff refuse to accept the need for change, that its gathering speed leaves them behind and often leads to the decline and perhaps even the demise of their firm.

Practice Exercises

(1) Make a list of services provided by your department/branch.

(2) At which market segment/s is each service aimed?

(3) Who are the main competitors for each service?

(4) What shops/factories have closed or opened in your area in recent years? What caused these closures/new developments?

(5) What effect have the following had (a) on you, (b) on the employees?

    (i) computerisation of petrol pumps
   (ii) automatic ticket machines in buses/stations
  (iii) automated tellers through bank walls

(6) If any new equipment has been installed in your office/branch what effect has it had?

    (a) on you;
    (b) on other staff;
    (c) on the manager.

(7) Ask older members of your office/department what effect the sex discrimination and maternity legislation has had on employment in your firm.

From Chapter 2 you should have learnt:

The meaning of market segmentation.

The main market segment for banking services.

The trends in the market and competition.

The main competitors in the banking sector.

The main economic trends and social trends.

Major economic developments.

The impact of environmental trends on

(a) banking staff;
(b) the managers in banks;
(c) the bank's customers.

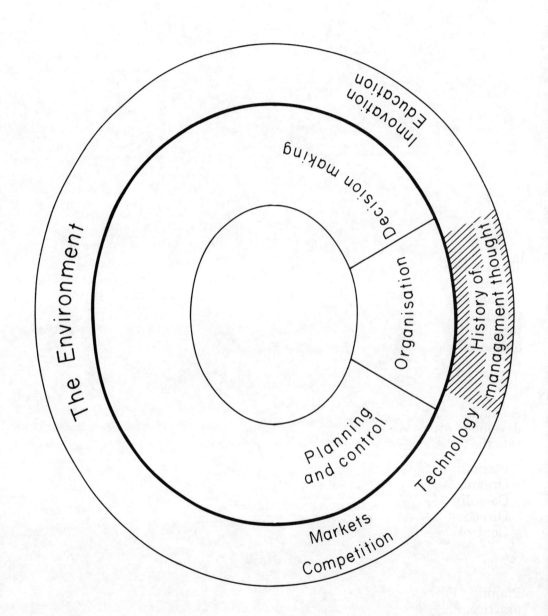

Chapter 3

Theories of Management

MANAGEMENT

There are many definitions of management. Drucker has called it the "specific organ" of the enterprise. A perhaps clearer statement is that: "Management activates the wealth producing resources of an enterprise." One may have buildings, machinery, people and money, but they will not produce "wealth" – i.e. goods or services in demand – unless they are co-ordinated and activated in an efficient manner.

ELEMENTS OF MANAGEMENT

As management theory is a relatively new discipline it is still in a state of development. For the purposes of this book it may most usefully be divided into the following elements:

Planning
Organisation
Co-ordination
Direction
Control

PLANNING

Planning is the preparation of a pre-determined course of action, and is, in practice, inevitable. In any enterprise senior management must have some concept of what they intend to do, or expect to happen in the future. There is however a great deal of variation in the formality, detail and thoroughness with which plans are made and for how far ahead. The need for planning is least in small enterprises such as local Building Societies where the main members have a comprehensive knowledge of all its activities and are in close and frequent contact with each other. It becomes of critical importance in large groups where individuals are, in practice, concerned with only their own activities, know very few of their colleagues, and even less of their activities.

ORGANISATION

This is concerned with the "structure" of an enterprise. It involves ensuring that there is a correct place, known by everyone concerned, for all articles and persons in the enterprise. It also establishes the relationships between them.

DIRECTION

The original term used for this element of management was "command". It is specifically concerned with people and with "directing" their activities. There was a trend in recent years to revise the terminology yet again and replace "direction" by "motivation" – i.e. self-direction. This is a very important concept which will be dealt with more fully in later units. Yet it must be realised that however well motivated a person may be – i.e. however interested in his work and the success of the enterprise, he will still need to be guided in his activities, and instructed as to specific tasks which may have to be undertaken. It has also been established that all people prefer, at some times, to be given clear "orders" rather than have to make decisions themselves, and large numbers of people prefer this as a general rule, rather than as an exception.

CONTROL

This is concerned with:

   measuring results
   comparing with expectations
   taking corrective action.

It will be noticed that control is impossible in the absence of objectives and/or planning. Further consideration will show that planning is, in practice, meaningless without a degree of control. Planning and control therefore become very closely linked, and are by some management theorists regarded as one combined activity.

CO-ORDINATION

This is concerned with ensuring that all the activities within an enterprise proceed at a common pace. At an early stage in the development of management this was regarded as a major element in management. This is still so in unplanned activities, such as, for instance, dealing with an unexpected emergency, or in what is known as "crisis" management.

As organisations have become larger, and planning more important, as well as more sophisticated and accurate, the need for co-ordination has been reduced to the extent that it now normally only arises where plans fail, or while they are being adjusted to cope with a large proportion of the contributors to a plan falling out of line. While co-ordination is therefore still a part of every manager's duty it has ceased to be regarded as a major element except in the cases quoted above.

HENRI FAYOL — GENERAL PRINCIPLES OF MANAGEMENT

These principles have survived almost unaltered since their original publication in France in 1916 and they still provide the basis of management according to the Classical approach. Most of them are retained in the other approaches as well. (*General Industrial Management*, Pitman, 49.)

(1) *Division of work* – the idea of specialisation as initiated by F. W. Taylor. ("Shop Management", reprinted in *Scientific Management*, Harper, 47.)

(2) *Authority and Responsibility* must be congruent cf. Chapter 8.

(3) *Discipline* – to a reasonable extent is necessary in any organisation.

(4) *Unity of Command* – any employee must have only one boss.

(5) *Unity of Direction* – there must be a common objective for the organisation as a whole, and for its constituent parts.

(6) Subordination of Individual Interest to General Interest.

This must be accepted by the employees of the firm.

(7) *Remuneration of Personnel* – must be fair and give satisfaction to both employer and employee.

(8) *Centralisation* – is said to be inevitable to a greater or lesser extent according to the type of organisation.

(9) *Scalar Chain* – this principle insists that when looking at organisation charts there should be a single, unambiguous path from each employee to the Chief Executive.

(10) *Order* – there must be a designated place for all persons or objects within the company, where they can be quickly found.

(11) *Equity* – This results from a combination of justice and kindliness in dealing with employees.

(12) *Stability of Tenure of Personnel* – unnecessary switching of staff from job to job is undesirable.

(13) *Initiative* – The management style should be such that initiative is encouraged at all levels.

(14) *Esprit de Corps* – Developing a team spirit requires teams not to be split up, and written communication to be limited.

ALTERNATIVE APPROACHES TO ORGANISATION

Four alternative approaches to designing the structure of an organisation are generally recognised:

The Classical Approach
The Human Relations Approach
The Systems Approach
The Contingency Approach

CLASSICAL APPROACH

Based on the work of F. W. Taylor, and on the writings of Fayol, Sheldon and Urwick and others, the classical approach is task oriented. The steps involved in establishing an organisation structure are:

(1) Analyse the tasks to be carried out
(2) Group the tasks by the nature of activity
(3) Group to achieve economics of scale
(4) Establish realistic spans of control
(5) Group to achieve co-ordination
(6) Establish relationships for responsibility, reporting and information.

(1) ANALYSIS OF THE WORK TO BE DONE

Specialisation

F. W. Taylor is known as the "father" of Scientific management. His main contribution was the idea of specialisation. He postulated that by training people thoroughly in one limited activity, very high rates of output could be achieved. This concept could be further improved by careful selection of people so that simple work at relatively low rates of pay could be allocated to those with limited ability, whilst highly paid craftsmen concentrated on work only they were capable of. The importance of fair pay based on performance was intrinsic to this system.

Method Study

Taylor's work was followed by F. B. & L. Gilbreth who developed Work Study – the forerunner of Industrial Engineering in manufacturing industry and O & M in service departments and the service industries. Method study (the M in O & M) is concerned with analysing activities into their component parts and deriving from this the best way of doing the job. It is thus a very detailed extension of Taylor's concept of specialisation. O & M, together, attempt to arrive at the best way of combining a number of activities.

A second part of Work Study is Time Study. When activities have been divided into very small elements, standard times for such elements, e.g. grasping a pen or tool, can be established. By combining all these times, the overall time for a job can be theoretically "synthesized" and subsequently checked by actual timing. Such a time can be used as a standard, and to put pressure on employees to increase output. This has created fear and resentment among employees when badly handled, but the primary purpose of time study is to establish the time and staff required for given activities. This information is essential as a basis for estimating, scheduling and designing an organisation structure. It is through O & M that the number of people needed in each specialised activity is found.

(2 and 3) GROUPING FOR TYPE OF WORK AND ECONOMIES OF SCALE

In designing a structure by means of the scientific approach, the analysis of the task, combined with O & M, finds the number of operatives required for each speciality. An example of this would be opening letters in a large office, followed by distributing them. If this activity were grouped for co-ordination, mail would be distributed directly to addressees and opened by them. Through grouping for type of work considerable economies of scale can be achieved – in this case by using letter opening machines.

Once the total number of operatives needed for each speciality has been found, it is necessary to appoint managers to take charge of them. This may give rise to a number of "sections" each looked after by what is in management terms a "first line manager" or "first level manager". Several sections will be formed into a department which will be directed by a "second level manager".

(4) SPANS OF CONTROL

If there are many operatives of one type more than one manager may be needed to look after him. In order to decide how many managers are needed it is necessary to determine the span of control. This is the number of operatives for which one manager can effectively be responsible. The span of control may vary between 2–50; 4–6 is normal at management levels and 8–12 at operator level. Simple calculations will show that for a given number of operatives, the number of managers and the number of levels of management in an organisation structure increase as the span of control is reduced. This involves an increase in overheads as well as more cumbersome management. The span should therefore be as wide as possible.

Factors Limiting the Span of Control

Work Related Factors

The number of *different* jobs which have to be supervised
The extent to which the jobs change
The complexity of each job
The extent to which the work involves risk to personnel or others.

Organisational Factors

The location of the subordinates
The preferred managerial style – e.g. a desire for centralisation
Inefficient control systems
Cumbersome, slow or ineffective communication systems
The rate at which the organisation is changing
Insufficient specialist help for the manager.

Personnel Factors

The ability of the manager, and of his subordinates
The attitude of the manager, and his subordinates
How well the manager is trained
The volume of the manager's non-supervisory work.

It should be noted that the methods of increasing the span of control, e.g. better training, often involve considerable expenditure, which must be balanced against the higher overheads of narrower spans of control.

(5) GROUPING FOR CO-ORDINATION

If there are only a small number of operators in each type of work, they are grouped for co-ordination – a general term covering related activities, sequential activities and the reduction of physical movement between work stations. The counter-room of a large branch, responsible for incoming and outgoing money and documents, is such an example.

Grouping for co-ordination also takes place between large departments concerned with one function or product. These make up divisions or other large management units. Grouping at the higher levels is the final step in the scientific approach.

Two of the criteria for grouping of activities are economies of scale and co-ordination. There are however a number of other factors which have to be taken into account. These can be illustrated by looking at a typical lay-out for operations. Let us examine the case of a unit of a company which provides four different services, each of which involves:

Meeting customers to receive instruction, discuss problems and provide information (E = Editing)
Processing (P)
Checking (C)
Typing, records and back-up services (T)

In this simple situation the two main types of lay-out can be illustrated. Each letter represents a member of staff.

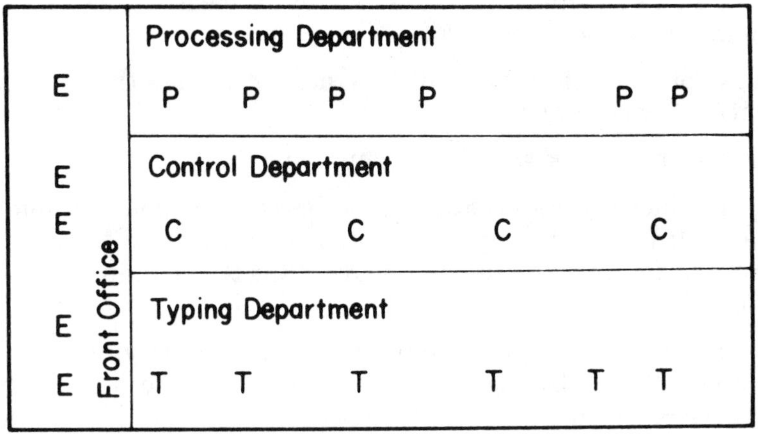

E	Front Office	Processing Department						
		P	P	P	P		P	P

E		Control Department			
E		C		C	C	C

E		Typing Department				
E		T	T	T	T	T	T

Fig. 3.1

Each letter represents a member of staff. This lay-out

- encourages the development of specialised skills
- facilitates training in specialised skills
- requires all purpose equipment to deal with the needs of several services
- allows staff, equipment and other resources to be applied to any service
- may give rise to friction between departments.

(2) Product Lay-out

Safe keeping		Documentary credits		Travel facilities		Money management	
E	T	E	R	E	T	E	T
R	T	E	C	P	C	P	T
C	T		T	P		P	C

Fig. 3.2

The number of staff in each speciality are the same but they are grouped so that each group is only concerned with one particular service.

Product lay-out:

- encourages interest in, and specialised knowledge of each service
- facilities the use of specialised equipment for each service. This normally results in lower operating costs
- enables departments to expand, contract, or change their methods independently of each other
- encourages teamwork within the department.

In general product lay-out is cheaper, has less management problems, and is preferable, *provided a high utilisation* can be guaranteed for the specialised equipment and facilities. This means also that the demand must be stable and predictable.

The same lay-out is used by some merchant banks, providing services to a number of customers, by arranging for one section to deal with a whole range of services but for one customer only.

The functional lay-out is better if the demand for each service fluctuates and/or is unpredictable.

Features of the Classical Approach

The classical approach to management and organisation tends to create a hierarchical management structure with maximum specialisation.

- Roles are clearly defined, and the authority of each role is limited by rational rules and regulations.
- Activities are whenever possible reduced to routine.
- Appointments and promotion are strictly on merit, the main criterion of performance being technical abilities in relation to the tasks to be carried out.
- The motivation of the employees is assumed to be purely economic.
- Communication is vertical along the lines of authority (and is usually downwards), i.e. a person will normally only communicate with other departments through his own manager.

Problems of the Classical Approach

As the classical approach was applied to businesses during this century, a number of problems were encountered which grew more serious as the techniques associated with the classical approach were developed. The detailed analysis, using O & M, of all the tasks in a business is a long and costly project. It may take several years and is therefore only practical if the ensuing structure can be used for a long time – in other words in stable conditions, or where there is a controlled market, or a service with an extended, predictable life. The approach is not suitable in unstable or unpredictable conditions.

Because of its complexity there are likely to be numerous imperfections in the structure derived from a scientific analysis. This leads to "informal organisation".

The vertical communication system has long channels of communications and is therefore slow.

Excessive specialisation and routine makes jobs, particularly at operating levels, extremely boring. Operators lose interest, the volume and quality of output drops. Labour turnover and absenteeism rise and industrial relations between the employers and alienated staff become difficult.

INFORMAL ORGANISATION

Part of organising is allocating work and defining roles. If work is not allocated accurately, it leads to work overload or excessive spare time. Work overload is bad because it may result in mistakes, discourteous or otherwise inadequate service, or some work not being done at all. Employees may become strained, ill, have accidents or leave. The main disadvantage of under-employment of staff is unnecessarily high costs, but all the problems associated with boredom may also arise. What tends to happen in both cases is that employees will *informally* try to correct the errors by leaving out work which they regard as unimportant, they will simplify processes by taking short cuts and transfer work to each other to even out the load. If roles are defined in considerable detail, but in a way that does not suit particular employees, transfer of work may take place between these employees, so that each of them has a greater proportion of work of a type which suits them. What has happened is that employees have reorganised themselves in a way which may well be more effective, but is certainly different from the organisation intended by management. There is a *formal* and an *informal* organisation.

Employees also create informal organisation to deal with temporary changes in work load. Such changes in work load may occur because of customer demand, because of special tasks or trainees assigned to a department, or because of some employees taking holidays.

The real problems of informal organisations are firstly, that it is different – and if it is acceptable for employees to arrange their own work, why spend a lot of money on the scientific analysis in the first place? Secondly, managers may lose track of what is actually happening in their departments. The proponents of the scientific approach argue that it is the manager's duty to monitor any informal organisation which develops in his command. If the development is an improvement, it should be incorporated into the structure. If the development is unsatisfactory, it should be stopped at once. Alternative approaches to management try to make informal arrangement part of the organisation structure.

«Authoritative Leadership, Ch. 11, p. 226»

THE HUMAN RELATIONS OR BEHAVIOURAL SCIENCE APPROACH TO ORGANISATION

The problems created by excessive rigidity, formality, overspecialisation and by slow communication in the scientific approach began to be a cause for concern after the first world war. Together with developments in Psychology as a scientific discipline this gave rise to the Human Relations School of Management Thought. It must be emphasised that this school of thought was concerned, just as was the classical one, with identifying the organisational and management techniques which would make the most successful organisations. The aims of all the approaches is to maximise the wealth produced by a given input of human and other resources, for the benefit of all.

The father of the human relations approach is Elton Mayo whose Hawthorne experiments are briefly described on p. 154 *et seq*. The major conclusions from these studies as they affect organisation are the *social role of the supervisor*, and the importance of *intangible factors in motivation*. Both these findings are quite contrary to the assumptions made in the classical approach.

The classical assumption was that people only worked for money, and the only way to improve output was by related piecework or wages, and there were deductions for bad work or absence. The Hawthorne experiments, and subsequent work described in Chapters 7, 8 and 9 of this book identified a whole range of factors which affected people's work, of which the most important was the impact of groups on the individual. Another finding was that, particularly with increased mechanisation, technical training of operators was better carried out by experts from outside a department, who also had the expertise to solve technical problems. Meanwhile the supervisor or operating manager could concentrate on the interpersonal relations within his department. Thus it is interpersonal relations skills which he needs rather than technical expertise.

THE MAN-MACHINE SYSTEM

Eric Trist, at the Tavistock Institute, developed the important concept of the man-machine, or socio-technical system. The earlier management researchers tried to improve efficiency by mechanisation and improving the technological environment. Faster and more accurate specialised machines led to mass production, and organisation and method study provided lay-out and tools to improve the output of operators. This was, and is still, valuable work. When a line can be completely run with robots, the ultimate in efficiency can be achieved. The fallacy in the scientific approach was that insufficient attention was paid to the role of the operator. The Tavistock Institute approach recalled the importance of the formula

$$E_O = E_M \times E_H$$

Where E_O = Efficiency of output; E_M = Efficiency of the machine; E_H = Efficiency of the operating staff.

A reasonably well-designed machine tends to work in the efficiency range of 80–95% (E_M = 0.9). Modern, microprocessor based machines such as word processors or the Stock Exchange Automatic Quotation system are even more efficient. The losses of time are due to setting up, cleaning, maintenance and breakdowns. Substantial further reductions in unit cost can usually only be achieved by economies of scale and greater specialisation.

The range of efficiency of the operating staff is much greater. A conscientious, motivated operator will be working 90% of the time. An alienated worker may be absent from work 2 days a week. When at work he may find reasons for not getting on with the job, and work slowly, so that his output may be halved. This can give a human efficiency as low as 30% (E_M = 0.3). Taking the output efficiency equation

$$E_O = 0.8 \times 0.3$$

it is evident that there is much more scope for improvement on the human than on the technical side of the equation.

The behavioural scientists attributed the low human efficiency in the mass-production systems designed by the followers of F. W. Taylor to "isolation". Psychologists had found that the majority of people are only at their best in company with others of their kind. For reasons detailed in Chapter 7, they need to work in a group rather than individually. The emphasis by productions engineers and "O & M" specialists on improving machinery and their lay-out meant that the operators were physically separated from each other. As conversation was not possible, the only way people could meet their needs to socialise was to interrupt their work in one way or another. Where management was able to prevent this, people stayed away as relief from the isolation at work. Whenever possible they found other jobs and mass production firms found they had to increase their wages well above prevailing levels to attract any employees at all. A typical example of man-machine system design is the lay out of desks in a large office, where clerks carry out routine work. Figure 3.3a shows a classic "functional" lay-out for minimum cost. Employees are isolated and can only talk to others by getting up from their work. In Fig. 3.3b the desks have been arranged to form groups of four.

Based on their investigations and theories, the behavioural scientists approached the establishment of an organisation through the following steps:

(1) Analyse the people in the organisation
(2) Group the people for social factors
(3) Establish spans of control based on the social needs of the staff and the interpersonal skills of the manager

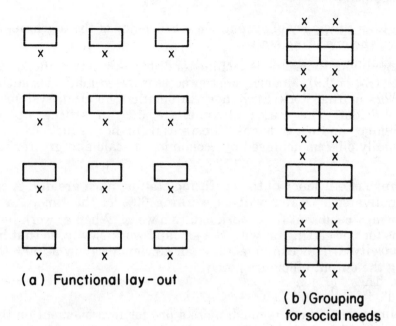

(a) Functional lay-out

(b) Grouping
for social needs

Fig. 3.3

(4) Group to achieve co-ordination
(5) Group to achieve economies of scale.

Features of the Human Relations Approach

The main feature of this approach is the preference given to human rather than technical factors. It will be noted that the same factors are taken into account but that the priorities and emphasis change.

In order to overcome the problems of an informal organisation structure which differs substantially from the formal one, tasks are, whenever possible, assigned to groups of people, who can organise the work within each group to suit the talents and inclinations of the members. Managers are appointed primarily for their interpersonal skills. The importance of non-economic factors in motivation are recognised and the reward system takes this into account. Communication between staff throughout a level in the business is encouraged, i.e. it is horizontal rather than vertical.

«Ch. 7, p. 155»

Problems of the Human Relations Approach

There is no doubt that the human relations approach improves motivation and morale, reduces industrial relations problems, and increases efficiency dramatically in some cases.

Unfortunately there are many instances where the savings made by mechanisation or mass production are so great that attempts to improve the satisfaction of the operators result in higher costs and uncompetitive products or services. For instance attempts made by Volvo in Scandinavia to improve industrial relations using socio-technological approaches were very successful in improving industrial relations, but had to be abandoned because the final cost of building a car was higher. In practice the Human Relations approach is rarely used exclusively to design an organisation structure. Its importance lies in the influence which it has had on those designing organisations in the traditional way.

THE SYSTEMS APPROACH

SYSTEMS THEORY

This is a method of analysis which can be applied to most areas of research and knowledge. It is based on the idea that it is more useful to look at groups of inter-related components rather than at the individual components themselves. These groups are called systems. Theoretically a system can be "closed". A closed system is completely self-contained and does not need anything outside itself for survival. In practice most systems are open systems which are defined by boundaries. They depend for their survival on "Inputs" and "Outputs" and can be diagrammatically represented as in Fig. 3.4.

All open systems are part of the Meta-system. At the same time open systems contain a number of sub-systems. Each of the sub-systems can again be regarded as a system with its own further sub-systems. Each system has boundaries. Banks, Insurance Companies, Building Societies etc. are all individual "systems" within the Financial System, which is part of the Economic System. Inputs enter the system and outputs are discharged from it. An organisation's boundaries are not physical. They cannot generally be seen, but are determined by corporate strategy. Some employees of organisations work regularly at these external boundaries. They are those concerned with sales and purchasing, and with acquiring or altering the resources of the organisation. One of the key features of an open system of this type is its dependence on the Meta-system or environment. This Meta-system has been examined in detail in Chapter 2.

The boundaries of the sub-systems are known as "interfaces", when they coincide with the boundaries of other sub-systems. Katz and Kahn differentiated between five *types* of sub-systems in organisations:

Supportive Sub-systems

These are the systems which procure the inputs and dispose of the outputs of the technical sub-systems.

Maintenance Sub-systems

These are concerned with the relative stability or predictability of the

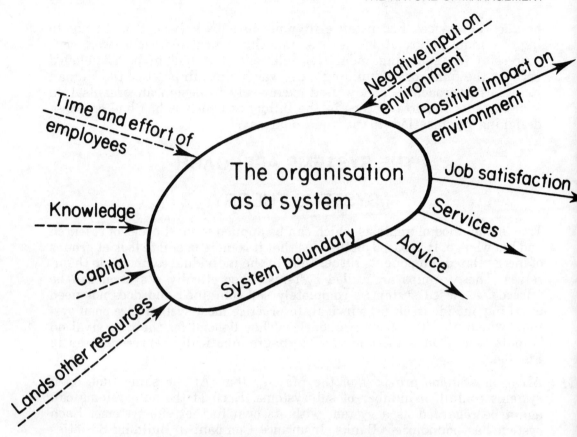

Fig. 3.4 The conversion process in systems theory

organisation. They provide for the rules, the roles and the rewards applicable to those who work in the organisation.

Technical or Productive Sub-systems

The subsystems which create the services offered by the system to the environment. Some of these sub-systems may only create part of a service, or components for several services.

Adaptive Sub-systems

These are the sub-systems which ensure that the organisation adapts itself to changes in the environment, and implement any changes in strategy determined by the organisation's stake-holders. The long-range planning department and R&D fall in this category.

Managerial Sub-systems

These sub-systems control and co-ordinate the activities of the total system. They deal with the resolution of conflict, and the definition of roles and authority within the organisation.

Illustration

Typical of technical sub-systems within a clearing bank are domestic branches. The boundary between a branch and the environment is very clearly defined. The input includes deposits from customers, labour from the working population, the output includes advice and loans. The interfaces between branches are also clearly defined on a territorial basis, with very few transactions across these interfaces. The boundaries between a branch and other sub-systems do not coincide so clearly.

From the personnel department there is an input of training, advice and services such as payment of wages. The output to the personnel department is information and training. Some decisions in the field of personnel are exclusively within the authority of the branch manager, e.g. allocation of work rotas for cashiers. Some decisions are exclusively within the authority of the personnel department, e.g. salary scales, but some are based on joint decision making – e.g. promotion within the branch. This joint area of responsibility is illustrated in Fig. 3.5 by the overlapping systems boundaries.

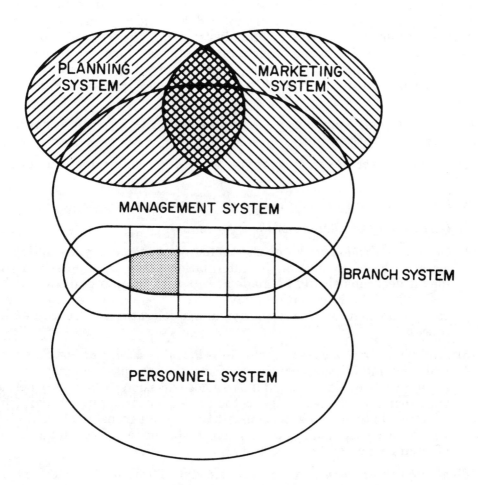

Fig. 3.5 Inter-relationship of some sub-systems of a clearing bank

Certain decisions, those appertaining to promotion policy, for instance, would also involve the management system. This area of decision making, where all three systems are involved, is shown dotted.

The diagram also shows that there is no direct interface between the branches and the marketing and planning systems.

The boundaries, inputs and outputs of the systems are based on where decisions are made, and on information flows rather than on physical movement of resources.

THE SYSTEMS APPROACH TO ORGANISATION

While some management researchers simply used the systems concept as an alternative method of analysing management problems, others realised that it had great potential for overcoming one of the main difficulties of the scientific approach, that of dealing with rapidly changing situations. In rapidly changing situations it is useful to determine any stable components. It has been found that in any given industry, while the scale of an operation, its duration, complexity and other components may vary, the decision making process may remain the same. This includes the type and sources of information needed, and the skills and experience required to make decisions.

Thus the systems approach is *decision* based. The steps in designing an organisation structure are:

(1) *Analysing the decision making process* to determine the decision required.

(2) *Determining the information needed to make the decisions.*

(3) *Determining the sources of the information.*

(4) *Grouping decision making* to establish management roles taking into account the economies of the information flows. In simple terms this means decisions should be made at the point in an organisation where the bulk of the information is available. This eliminates unnecessary, costly transmission of information and accelerates the decision making process.

(5) *Modifying the structure* to group for *skills of decision making*. Some staff, while having all the necessary information themselves, may not have the ability to evaluate it and make a good decision. Others may not have the experience needed to assess the consequences of alternative courses of action. In those cases, responsibility has to be transferred to a point at which the correct quality of decision can be made. It becomes a question of balancing cost against quality.

(6) *Modifying the structure* to take account of *risk and side-effects*. Any decision which has substantial impact on a number of sub-systems should be taken jointly or at a level at which the impact on these sub-systems is taken into account.

Illustration

A branch manager may gather all the information about a major lending application from a client. Because of the size of loan and the risk involved the impact on the rest of the business may be considered to be too high to allow a decision to be made by the branch manager. It is, therefore, re-allocated to a higher level.

A similar situation is a tax advice request, where the information gathered would be passed to a specialist, for him to prepare a proposal.

Features of the Systems Approach

The main advantage of the approach is that once established, preferably on a data processing base, it lends itself to designing structures for new projects or businesses very quickly. The same applies to adapting existing structures. The use of this approach frequently results in the establishment of Matrix type structures.

Another advantage is that because of its pre-occupation with inputs and outputs it is very outward looking and changes in the environment will be spotted early enough for positive action. This is in contrast to the concentration of the classical approach on internal matters, which may cause it of "fight yesterday's battles".

WORK STATIONS

An organisational layout derived from the systems approach, which has become common recently, is the "work station", as used by foreign exchange, money market and stock exchange dealers. All the information required for a deal is fed into a work station and enables the dealer to make an immediate decision, convey the details to his company's administrative departments, and inform the stock-exchange and regulatory authorites. The station includes a P.C. and terminals to all necessary information sources, as well as direct connections to clients and supplies. It may cost as much as £400 000.

Problems of the Systems Approach

The main problem of this approach to organisation is that it is conceptually difficult. The necessary analytical work requires specially trained systems analysts, who are less common than the production engineers and O & M specialists required in the scientific approach. Data processing capacity facilitates systems analysis, and as data processing equipment becomes part of more and more firms' infrastructure, the use of the systems approach will no doubt become more common.

THE CONTINGENCY APPROACH

During the 1950s Professor Joan Woodward carried out a series of investigations to determine the relationship between the success of companies and the approach to organisation which they had adopted. Her initial findings were that there was no direct correlation. These findings gave rise to the "Contingency" approach. The contingency approach recognises that there is no single approach to organisation which is appropriate to all situations. The approach which is most likely to lead to success depends on a number of variables.

The so-called Aston Group conducted a major study into the relationship between structure and other factors and concluded that the size of the organisation was an important determinant.

> Larger size tends to lead to:
> more specialisation
> more standardisation
> more formalisation
> but less centralisation

Burns and Stalker identified the rate of innovation in the firm's environment to be important.

Joan Woodward identified one of the variables as "The technology of production"

TECHNOLOGY OF PRODUCTION

The technology of production covers the operation necessary to create the services which a firm expects to sell to its customers, and which provide its revenue. There are four distinct types of these operational processes:

- Unit operations
- Batch operations
- Mass production operations
- Continuous operations

UNIT OPERATIONS

Unit Operations involve producing a one-off service or package. Unit operation is distinguished by

(a) limited planning (because the cost of planning in detail is not justified for a never to be repeated activity);

(b) close top management involvement, with current operations (because the lack of detailed planning often makes quick strategic decisions necessary);

(c) high quality staff at all levels, because absence of detailed plans forces them to use their discretion;

(d) good industrial relations, arising from (b) and (c).

The key to success in unit production is the controlling of the progress of projects. The role of the project manager is therefore significant.

In Banking unit production is usually confined to the merchant banking sector. Within the clearing banks experimental projects, or a move to a new head office block, or installation and commissioning of a new computer may be organised on this basis.

Batch Production

Batch production involves repeating the same operation a number of times. Batches may range from a few to many thousands. Batch production is distinguished by:

(a) *departmental conflict*, because those responsible for costs of output desire large batches, while those responsible for serving customers find small batches usually give a better service;

(b) *"service" departments* playing a large role – inspection, maintenance, personnel;

(c) few industrial relations problems, because *work tends to be varied and interesting*;

(d) *multipurpose machinery* and equipment;

(e) *functional lay-out* of operations.

The key to success is resolving the conflicts of interest between departments, and between operating and service departments. The role of middle management and communication is significant.

Illustration

Most of the operations in branch offices are of the batch type. At one end of the scale a manager will spend one morning analysing and evaluating lending proposals, and another interviewing subordinates for their annual assessment. The "batch" only contains a small number, and another batch will be dealt with in a few days time.

An example of a large "batch" is several thousand monthly statements, or a notification of an interest change, sent out by the area office.

Mass Production

The principle of mass production is to break a process up into standard time elements. For each time element the most efficient procedure and equipment is adopted. At the end of the time element, the partly produced "product" is transferred to the next work position. Mass production is only economic if the demand for the service is sufficiently large to absorb the high initial cost of setting up the process, and sufficiently stable to keep it working at a high capacity utilisation. Mass production is distinguished by:

(a) emphasis on *forward planning* to assess the demand for the service to be produced;

(b) the importance of *maintenance* departments to keep the service in operation;

(c) *unskilled operators*;

(d) *industrial relations problems* because of (c), and because the work is routine and boring. The personnel function is therefore also important;

(e) *process lay-outs*;

(f) *special purpose machinery* and equipment.

The key to success is keeping up output. This makes planning, marketing, maintenance and good personnel management most important.

Illustration

ATMs are examples of mass production equipment. Here is a high cost piece of equipment, able to carry out a small range of activities, very accurately and at high speed. Its cost means that it can only be installed in a location where the demand is high. If the demand changes – perhaps because access is blocked, it becomes a white elephant. It also depends for its success on good maintenance.

Continuous Operation

In some industries, notably those using heat and chemicals, the cost of halting an operation is prohibitive. Special processes have to be designed to obtain continuity. These industries tend to be highly mechanised and automated and use few unskilled employees. Hence they have few industrial relations problems. Apart from that they have similar characteristics to mass production industries. Continuous operation is seldom applicable to the financial sector.

Just in time

JIT is an approach to organisation developed by Toyota in Japan during the 1970's which is being adopted by quite a number of American and British companies. Although its features make it particularly attractive to manufacturing industries it is also applicable to service industries. The approach requires the use of multi-purpose equipment, such as branch processors which combine the ability to store and manipulate local information with access to central and regional data banks. The second main principle is that of multiple skills staff who are, for instance, expected to deal with more than one type of equipment, as well as with minor faults and routine maintenance.

Total quality control means that employees are expected to check their own work for correctness as opposed to the conventional assumption that everyone makes mistakes for which another person has to check.

If their own work is completed employees are expected to use their own discretion to switch to other work which is waiting to be done. Group bonuses related to company performance and individual merit awards at the discretion of the immediate management, are part of the JIT approach.

The advantages of the JIT approach are a reduction in unutilised time of equipment and staff, a reduction in indirect labour costs, and a large measure of job enrichment.

The initial disadvantages are that a change in organisational culture, including greater stress on the operators, and a completely new approach to training and reward systems may be required.

THE RATE OF INNOVATION

If a firm operates in a market which expects frequent changes of product, e.g. the fashion industry, the organisational climate must be organic, i.e. it must encourage creativity by having flexible roles and lateral rather than vertical communications. Communication should consist of information and advice rather than instructions and decisions. People should be committed to achieving objectives rather than keeping to the rules. The opposite conditions create a "mechanistic" structure – as in the pure classical approach – which is cheaper to run and suitable for long periods with little innovation.

STABILITY OF THE ENVIRONMENT

Where the demand for service of their life fluctuates rapidly, and particularly if these changes in demand cannot be predicted, the environment is said to be "uncertain". To succeed in such an environment it is necessary to monitor it closely and be ready to adapt quickly to any change. This requires managers differentiated by expertise in different fields; it is also necessary to have managers specialising in short term adaption, while others look ahead and try to anticipate the future – they are differentiated by their time horizons. At the same time it is also necessary to integrate the work of these differentiated managers. The resolution of managerial conflict is a key to success in such an environment.

Features of the Contingency Approach

The contingency approach does not propose new methods of designing organisations. It proposes that the approach used must take into account such factors as the technology of production, the rate of innovation, and the stability of the environment. No specific criteria for the choice of method have yet been determined. It is likely that in view of the range of variables, designers of organisations will always have to use their judgement. The other important contribution of the Contingency Approach is that even within one firm, and at different levels within the firm, different approaches may have to be used.

Illustration

In the clearing banks the scientific approach is still predominant because such good features as standardisation of service, promotion on merit and predictable career and salary projections outweigh any disadvantages.

Where innovation is required – as in marketing departments – a more human relations orientated approach is adopted. The same applies to, say, an economic research department where a task cannot be clearly defined, but it must be left to staff how best to use their skills.

The systems approach is increasingly being adopted in merchant banking activities.

ORGANISATIONAL CULTURE

Some of the items just mentioned e.g. vertical and horizontal communications, are closely related to organisational culture.

"Structure" is the organisational framework within which people work e.g. the formal channels of communication.

"Culture" refers to the deep set beliefs, norms and attitudes of the people in an organisation e.g. the extent to which it is customary for executives to consult each other before making decisions, or whether it is normal for staff to inform their managers of any matters of interest which may affect their department, as opposed to assuming they know. Spheres where there is considerable difference in culture between different firms include:
>   How people should be rewarded
>   How far ahead one should plan
>   Whether dress or hours or punctuality matter
>   Whether committees are favoured or abhorred
>   How secure jobs should be
>   The basis on which people are promoted
>   How smart offices should be etc.

Handy identified four varieties of organisational culture

In the *power culture* found in small entrepreneurial businesses such as property and finance companies, there are few rules and procedure and control is exercised by key individuals whose quality is of paramount importance. These cultures put a lot of faith in individuals, who are judged by results.

The *role culture* is found in bureaucracies which were fully described in Chap.1.

The *task culture* is found in Matrix organisations and its emphasis is on expert power, rewards for results, groups and group objectives.

The *person culture* is rarely found in commercial operations as the organisation only exists to foster the objectives of the individuals in it – as for instance in a small consultancy partnership.

Organisational "climate" refers to relatively short time changes in attitudes e.g. the tension that may occur when people are working under pressure, or the enthusiasm created by improved equipment.

Organisational culture and structure must be compatible and it is important to remember that changing a structure, which can be done more easily and quickly, does not change the culture – which is usually a longer and more difficult process. The objective of a change will not be achieved unless appropriate changes are made in both the structure and culture.

Culture is also related to the personalities of people and it may not be possible to change the culture without replacing staff.

Many of the mergers taking place between Building Societies cause cultural clashes and the same is liable to occur when one company is taken over by another e.g. clearing banks taking over stockbrokers.

COMMITTEES

The classical theory has as one of its principles that each person should only be responsible to one superior. From this it follows that a manager should have sole authority over the activities he directs, and that he should have personal and exclusive responsibility for the decisions which he makes. This has the added advantage that blame – or credit – can be given where it is due. Research and practice have found that unless such a manager has very wide ranging powers, it may be very difficult to get both subordinates and colleagues to carry out the decision. A further difficulty is that many decisions require extensive knowledge of many technologies which one manager is unable to possess or even to evaluate. The solution is decision-making by committee.

A committee may be defined as a group of people *committed* to reach a joint decision and to support and implement that conclusion. It should be noted that a member of a committee, unless he resigns, is expected to support the committee conclusions even if he opposed them during the committee work.

Committees have gained a very bad reputation because of ineffectiveness, time-wasting, delays, indecisiveness and almost every other management malpractice. It is indeed very frustrating to serve on a badly run committee, or wait for its deliberations. The circumstances in which group decision making is preferable to individual decision making are analysed in Chapter 7 of this book. Assuming this choice has been correctly made, the effectiveness of a committee depends in the first place on its proper organisation. This requires:

(1) A constitution.
(2) Proper procedures.
(3) Effective officials.

(1) THE CONSTITUTION

The constitution of a committee *may* be a formal and elaborate document, but it is not essential for it to be elaborate or even written. What *is* important is that it is known, understood and accepted by all the members, and that the committee has a formal and recognised place within the management structure. The constitution should cover:

The objectives of the committee
The authority it possesses
The membership
The decision making i.e. voting procedure.

In addition to the above essentials, it may lay down details of the officials, the frequency of meeting, and other procedural matters. These can, alternatively, be left to the chairman.

Little needs to be written about objectives beyond reiterating that no management activity is likely to be successful unless its purpose is clear.

The Authority of Committees

Lack of authority, or misunderstanding of the extent of the authority, in committees is a major source of frustration. It should be made clear whether a committee is "consultative" i.e. its purpose is to gather information and opinions from a larger body of people, or "advisory" – i.e. that it fills an investigating and evaluating role and makes recommendations without having final "decision making" duties, or whether it is responsible for making decisions and implementing them. The first group includes consultative committees in industrial relations, and for consultation with consumers and other sections of society by Nationalised Industries. Advisory committees are used for project evaluation, problem solving, market exploration and many other management activities. Decision making committees may replace any individual manager. It is essential for their effectiveness that they must also be responsible for implementing their decisions. To make this possible, at least some members must have the necessary authority.

Membership

The number of members and from where they are to be picked should be defined, as well as the method of selection if there is any risk of the committee's deliberations being intentionally distorted. In practice more than twelve members tend to make a committee too unwieldy to be efficient. Members should be recruited for their knowledge, skill, experience or authority, rather than for their personality, but the ability to communicate well is a necessity. Variety of members is, of course, the whole point of the arrangement. A development committee determining the future layout of a public space should include, perhaps, a cashier, a senior clerk, experts on machinery, systems, security and architecture, as well as an accountant to monitor costs and a senior manager with the authority to have the decisions implemented.

Decision Making

The quorum – i.e. the minimum number that must be present for a vote – should be specified. Voting rules must be such that stalemates cannot occur.

(2) COMMITTEE PROCEDURES

The aims of the procedures are:

(a) to ensure that a proper contribution is made by all members;

(b) that the committee is not misused to further sectional or vested interests;

(c) to eliminate errors and misunderstandings;

(d) to ensure continuity – because many committees meet at relatively long intervals;

(e) to maximise efficiency.

The main tools to achieve these aims are the agenda and minutes.

Agenda

This is a programme for the meeting, which is sent to all members in advance of the meeting, giving them sufficient time to prepare their views. It should be accompanied by any documents, such as reports or reviews, which need to be considered at the meeting. Time spent at meetings reading new documents is not only wasteful, but means members cannot check such documents against their own records.

The items on the agenda usually include an opportunity for members to comment on the "minutes of the previous meeting", any matters arising from those minutes, and arrangements for the next meeting.

Minutes

These are the records of the meeting. They should include:

(a) Conclusions or decisions reached;

(b) the basis on which these have been arrived at;

(c) action delegated to members and the date by which this is to be concluded.

Minutes should be circulated to members shortly after the meeting. They act as an *aide-mémoire* in the short term as well as a long term record and should be constructed to fulfil both functions.

(3) EFFECTIVE OFFICIALS

The Chairman

The chairman is the key to successful committees. His functions are to ensure that the constitution is upheld and that the actual meetings are run to reach their goals efficiently. He should ensure that meetings are timed to enable all members to attend, that members are given the opportunity to place matters on the agenda, that only matters on the agenda are discussed, that the discussion is free, open and balanced, and limited to a reasonable time. It is his skill which encourages the less eloquent members of the committee to make their contributions and perhaps enables a consensus to be reached after initial dissent.

The Secretary

The most difficult task of the secretary is to prepare minutes which contain all necessary records whilst avoiding irrelevancies. The timeliness with which minutes and agendas are sent out also contributes to the success of the committee.

It should be noted that the approaches to organisation which have been described in this chapter are in effect design methods. Using, for example, either the classical or systems approach, may in a particular case, result in the same organisation structure. An analogy would be using two different methods of transport to reach the same destination. The proponents of each specialised approach will argue that their method is most likely to achieve a successful organisation structure. Those who favour the contingency approach say that the various variables identified must be considered before making a choice of method.

Writers on the Scientific Approach

1947 M. Weber   *The Theory of Social and Economic Organisation*
1916 H. Fayol   *Administration Industrielle et Générale*
1911 J. W. Taylor *Principles of Scientific Management.*

Writers on the Behaviour Science Approach

1963 Eric Trist   *Organisational Choice*
1933 Elton Mayo *Human problems of an Industrial Civilization*

Writers on the Systems Approach

1966 Katz and Kahn *The Social Psychology of Organisation*

Writers on JIT

1983 (Spring) R.J. Schonberger   *Operations Management Review*

Writers on the Contingency Approach

1965 Joan Woodward   *Industrial Organisation. Theory and Practice*
1967 Lawrence and Lorsch *Organisation and the Environment*
1961 Burns and Stalker   *The Management of Innovation*
1975 H. Norman in J. W. Newton *Contingency Approach to Management*

Practice Exercises

(1) Look around for organisational units – e.g. (departments at work, offices, shops, transport, entertainment) where
    (a) communications are vertical ⎫
    (b) jobs are clearly defined   ⎬ classical
    (c) jobs are specialised   ⎭

    (d) employees themselves decide what they should do ⎫
    (e) hours of work are not fixed   ⎬ human relations
    (f) employees help each other out when busy ⎭

    (g) there is team working with permanent teams
    (h) there are employees who move to-and-fro between teams.

(2) Identify some roles concentrating on one specialist skill either at work, or at businesses you visit.

(3) Find an example where economies of scale have been obtained by grouping activities together.

(4) How many people report to your immediate superior?

(5) Is your office divided functionally? or by product (service)?

(6) List some examples of "informal organisation" which you have met.

(7) Identify one of each of the following sub-systems of your company:

Productive
Supportive
Maintenance

From Chapter 3 you should have learnt:

The features of the four approaches to management.

The steps in establishing an organisation according to each theory.

Fayol's "General Principles of Management".

The meaning of "span of control" and the factors which influence it.

The difference between "process" and "functional" lay-out of work, and their respective advantages.

The difference between formal and informal organisation and the issues related to these concepts.

The meaning of the "man-machine" system.

The concepts underlying systems theory.

Five types of organisational sub-systems.

The difference between the four technologies of production.

The purpose and advantages of committees.

The factors contributing to successful committee work.

Proper committee procedures.

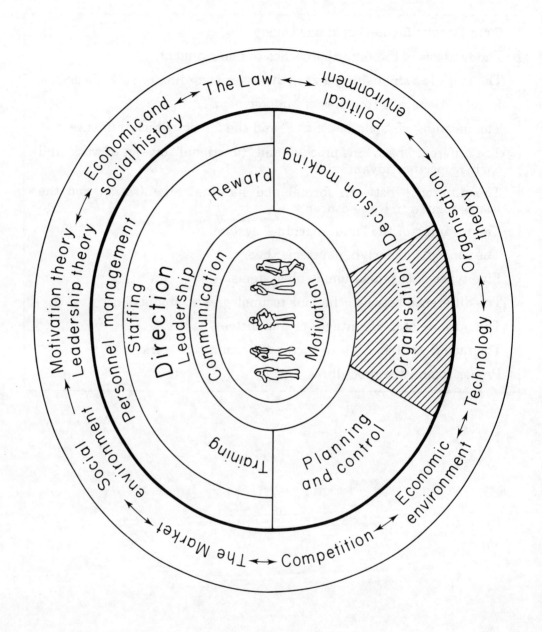

Chapter 4

Organisation Structure

FUNCTIONAL ORGANISATION

When a small enterprise is formed it usually consists of a number of experts who join to complement each other's expertise. A valuer and an accountant might become partners in a Pawnbroking – i.e. money lending business. Initially they might be supplemented on a part-time basis by property and security specialists. If the business expanded to the size of a Public company, these part-time specialists might head their own "functions". Thus a "functional organisation structure" is created.

The "functional organisation structure" is also the most frequent result of the "classical approach" to organisation. The classical emphasis on grouping for specialisation brings all the similar activities – e.g. all data storage activities, under the direction of one "functional manager". Because the majority of managers in the past have graduated to management through some functional role, the functional organisation structure has become accepted as the "natural" form of organisation. It is certainly true that in small companies it is the only practical form of organisation, and in small isolated units of large companies it is probably the most practical form. Typical of such a unit is a branch of a clearing bank. Figure 4.1 shows the functional division on an organisation chart. It must be remembered that in large companies with functional organisation specialised functions such as data processing and training are provided from the centre.

ADVANTAGES

Apart from developing naturally and being easily accepted by managers and operatives because it is the traditional structure, a functional departmentation has several specific advantages.

79

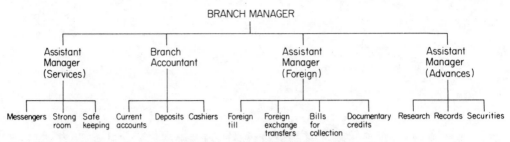

Fig. 4.1 Functional organisation in a branch

(a) it encourages the development of specialised skills;

(b) it facilitates training in such skills;

(c) it has potential for high productivity in specialised areas, and pride in achievement may give satisfaction to employees at the same time;

(d) it focuses attention on activities in which a company may have superior expertise. This may help to identify new services and new customers;

(e) the preoccupation of departmental managers with specialised activities limits their awareness of other aspects of a business. Thus they are unlikely to make commitment which would embarrass the company or divert it from its objectives. Control remains firmly in the hands of top management.

Unfortunately some of these advantages may, in other circumstances, prove to be disadvantages.

DISADVANTAGES

(a) *Overspecialisation* results in repetitive boring jobs, low morale, high labour turnover and finally in industrial unrest. All these are liable to dissipate any gains in productivity.

In the financial sector this problem is partly overcome by training operatives in a number of skills, and rotating their roles.

(b) managers do not get any experience in general management, creating problems of management succession;

(c) *emphasis is on functional efficiency*, as opposed to marketing orientation.

Managers of functional departments are normally given targets for output and costs. To achieve these targets, operations, purchasing etc. have to be carried out in economic batch sizes. For instance a security transport section would route its vehicle to cover, say, twenty branches in a day with a minimum mileage. This might well mean that the time at which some branches might receive fresh funds is not satisfactory from a customer's point of view. Any special arrangements for customers might also be difficult to accommodate.

(d) *lack of cost control*, of each service because of the difficulties of measuring departmental input and output. Many functional operations do not supply a chargeable service, even if they have a measurable cost.

This applies, for instance, to a branch machine room, a typing pool, money transmission and data processing functions. It therefore becomes very difficult to measure, and consequently to control costs.

(e) *conflict between interdependent departments*. In practice this is the most serious drawback of functional organisation. Conflict arises because the output requirement of a department is greatly influenced by the demands of the client department. Any functional manager who has difficulty in meeting his targets is thus tempted to put the blame on unreasonable demands which he is expected to meet. On the other hand he himself will expect perfect service from supplying departments, because delayed or inaccurate documents, or service, will again make it difficult for him to meet his targets. Similar problems arise due to functional managers trying to avoid taking responsibility for excessive costs incurred on output. Considerable management time can be expended in tracing costs to a department. Errors in functional target setting will generate so much friction that the essential co-ordination and co-operation between departments may be permanently adversely affected.

Functional organisation or departmentalisation are larger scale equivalents of "functional lay-outs" described on p. 51 earlier in this book.

PRODUCT ORGANISATION STRUCTURE

Product organisation is the corporate equivalent of product lay-out of operations, and the same criteria apply to its choice. Product organisation is indicated where a company has a service or group of services for which the demand is reasonably stable and predictable, and where the demand is

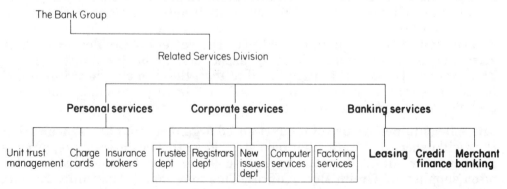

Fig. 4.2 Typical product organisation structure of the related services division of a banking group

sufficiently large to justify setting up resources, such as buildings, equipment and specialised staff, which are specifically designed to produce these services efficiently. If the services themselves, or the process by which they are produced differ considerably, the case for product organisation is reinforced. Depending on the size of the particular service in relation to the whole, they may be set up as departments or divisions within the company, or as separate businesses within a group of companies. These criteria apply to many of the non-banking services of the clearing banks which tend to be separately organised on a product basis, and may be grouped together in a separate division as shown in Fig. 4.2.

ADVANTAGES OF PRODUCT ORGANISATION

(a) The attention and effort of all staff is concentrated on the service.

(b) The organisational unit can be a profit centre. Because it is a separate autonomous unit all the costs incurred in providing the service have to be recovered. On the other hand, except for a (usually insignificant) contribution to Head Office costs, no charges not attributable to the service have to be borne. Thus the profitability of the unit can be monitored very easily.

(c) Because they are profit centres the performance of top management is measurable. Smaller units are therefore excellent training grounds for general managers expected to progress to larger units.

(d) Co-ordination of functional activities within the unit is improved.

(e) It makes it easier to channel funds to particular services to take advantage of growth opportunities. Conversely services which are in decline can be phased out or reorganised without affecting other units.

DISADVANTAGES OF PRODUCT ORGANISATION

Because the whole concept of product organisation is to make each organisational unit completely responsible for all its inputs and outputs, the managers in charge of these units must have the ability and training to maintain an overview of the whole unit, deal with the variety of problems that may arise, and make decisions taking all aspects of the business into account. This requires persons of a higher calibre than those in charge of functional units. To obtain such people higher salaries have to be paid. More comprehensive training is also needed. This again adds to the cost.

The self-contained nature of product based organisational units means that they will expect to recruit their own staff, keep their own accounts, provide their own O & M; i.e. they will have little demand for the specialist services often supplied by Group Head Offices. This may make the maintenance of central services uneconomical. Some authorities regard this as a disadvantage. In view of the conflict often generated between specialist and operating departments, and in view of the problem of controlling the costs of specialist departments, the difficulty of maintaining such departments might be considered a positive benefit.

A similar query may be raised about control in general, which is often cited as an argument against product organisation. Managers of self contained units have much greater authority than functional managers. Functional managers normally have to ask permission for a course of action which affects other functions. This is very restrictive and senior management therefore is constantly aware of any innovation functional managers propose. The only limitation on managers of product units is normally that capital expenditure above a certain amount requires approval. This leaves these managers free to run their business in a way which does not always meet with the approval of the head office. This is a penalty which has to be paid for allowing them the freedom to grasp opportunities from which head office is, of course, quite happy to profit!

TERRITORIAL ORGANISATION STRUCTURE

There are four sets of circumstances in which neither the functional nor product structure are appropriate. These are when:

(a) *the market is geographically extensive* and the product or service is difficult or expensive to transport;

(b) *there are substantial differences in the demand* or buying habits between different types of customers;

(c) the life of the product or services is unpredictable;

(d) *demand fluctuates rapidly* or unpredictably for seasonal or other reasons.

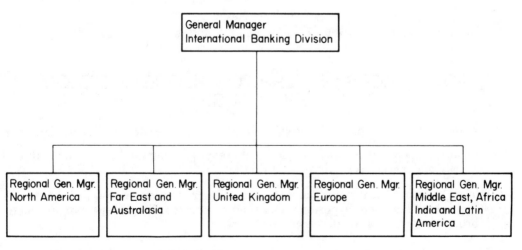

Fig. 4.3 Example of territorial organisation structure

The first of these circumstances arises when a large proportion of the product is represented by the cost of transport (the cost may be incurred by the producer or the customer, but in either case it is part of the cost). It also arises when the product or service is "perishable", either because it has a short life or because it cannot be transported. Financial services fall under both these headings.

Illustrations

● A market trader or shopkeeper who has large cash takings wants to bank these several times per day – any delay, or distance to travel, increases the risk and is unacceptable. The service is "perishable", in the sense that it is no use unless it is available immediately and in close proximity.

● A person wishing to draw cash for shopping purposes would expect to draw it on his journey to, or at, the shopping centre. Any longer or extra trip to a bank would incur additional travelling expenses and cost of time, and would make the service that much less attractive. The same would apply to a business man seeking advice, who would be reluctant to travel farther than the nearest town centre to meet, say, a tax or investment advice specialist.

● Building Societies are organised on a territorial basis because the cash deposit and withdrawal services are perishable as described above, and because mortgage applications require a personal interview. The travelling time and cost are part of the cost of the service. So is the cost of surveyors visiting properties.

● The domestic banking divisions of most of the clearing banks are organised on a territorial basis because:

  (a) banking services are perishable, and costly or impossible to transport. In many cases they require face to face contact between the customer and the manager providing the service;

  (b) there is substantial variation in the needs and attitudes of customers, between different regions of the country. Territorial Organisation enables managers to concentrate on developing those skills most appropriate to their area e.g. to deal with farmers, small shopkeepers or holiday landladies. It also enables them to keep in touch with local economic and social conditions;

  (c) it is possible to co-ordinate, within an area, all the services provided for a customer e.g. deposit taking, lending, securities, travel facilities.

ADVANTAGES OF TERRITORIAL ORGANISATION STRUCTURE

A territorial structure shares the advantages of a product structure. In addition:

(1) it places responsibility at a lower level, thereby speeding up the decision making process, and increases job interest at that level.

(2) Small branches furnish a measurable training ground for general management. General management experience can then be developed by a career progression through branches of steadily increasing size.

DISADVANTAGES OF TERRITORIAL STRUCTURE

Autonomously operating branches pose similar problems of control and maintaining central services as were described for product based organisation units. The control problem can be reduced if a bureaucratic approach to management is adopted. This also enforces the use of central services. It has in the past been the approach to branch organisation in the financial sector. The bureaucratic approach is still adopted by the National Giro and to an extent by the larger Building Societies. In the banks two different approaches are developing under the pressure of competition:

(a) Standard routine services such as cash transactions and small personal lending are carried out in largely mechanised "money shop" branches. These have very little independent authority.

(b) Specialised services and larger customers are dealt with from a smaller network of "town-centre" or "corporate" branches. These in some cases are independent profit centres with a high level of decentralised authority.

Another disadvantage of the branch structure is its high cost in terms of premises, equipment and staffing, particularly in areas of low demand, – e.g. those not highly populated or where a company's market share is low.

AGENCIES

By appointing agents either purely to sell, or to provide a full service, costs are substantially reduced. The agent is paid a commission only on the business which has been introduced or the work done. The agent's own cost is spread over other business. It is therefore essential to have sufficient control over agents to ensure that they make the desired effort and provide a service up to required standard.

Illustration

Insurance Consultants are the most common examples of selling agents.

Solicitors are suitable agents for Building Societies because of their involvement in house transfers, but Estate agents are even better because their offices can be used for cash transactions.

Correspondent Banks act as overseas agents for banks.

MARKET BASED ORGANISATION STRUCTURE

It is quite common for whole groups of customers i.e. segments of the market, to have particular requirements, or a particular attitude. This, in turn, means that a special organisation structure is needed which is not suitable for other groups. More often the firm's staff who provide the service need to have knowledge and experience of the market segment and may have to have special skills to deal with their problems.

Illustrations

Farmers have high credit requirements for seed and fertilisers at the beginning of the season. They have little regular income or expenditure. There is a large inflow of money at harvest time.

The energy industry requires high risk capital, and investment capital from which there is no return for a long time.

The property sector is able to offer very safe security for development capital.

Industries such as the above are regarded as separate market segments. Special departments may be organised to serve these segments.

ACCOUNT EXECUTIVES

A particular example akin to a market based structure is the arrangement now common in the financial sector of having account executives who are responsible for all the work related to one large national customer. The account executive usually has a team working for him and may be purely responsible for marketing. Alternatively he may be responsible for overseeing all the work done for the client by all the departments in the company. This then becomes akin to a Matrix structure.

This type of customer based structure is facilitated by Distributed Integrated Networks as they are being installed by clearing banks because information about activities throughout the country can be accessed from one point.

ADVANTAGES OF MARKET BASED ORGANISATION STRUCTURES

(a) Attention and effort of all staff is directed towards one sector.

(b) Staff are able to acquire specialised knowledge and experience, and develop appropriate skills for the sector.

(c) The organisational unit can be a profit centre.

(d) Co-ordination of functional activities is good.

(e) Good training ground for general management.

DISADVANTAGES OF MARKET-BASED ORGANISATION STRUCTURES

(a) They require high quality staff.

(b) They make maintenance of central services uneconomic.

(c) They create problems of top management control.

CENTRALISATION

The idea that firms should centralise was one of Fayol's original fourteen principles of management. Fundamentally it is based on economies of scale.

Economies of scale arise from a number of causes:

(a) Discounts or lower prices are usually available for bulk purchase.

(b) A large machine or piece of equipment having the same output as several smaller ones usually costs much less than the combined cost of the small ones.

(c) The number of operators required for a large machine is often no more than for a small one. Therefore the cost per unit of output is much less.

(d) Ancillary costs – i.e. the costs of space, maintenance, and providing services such as lighting, electricity and compressed air – are proportionately much smaller per unit of output on a large piece of equipment than on a small one.

(e) In a branch there is often a need for a specialist function which does not require a person to work full-time. If such a specialist is put on the staff he will either be underemployed, or create work to fill his time. In either case a more economic solution is to have the specialist at a central office to service several branches.

Examples

(a) Contracts for central heating oil negotiated centrally show a large saving although deliveries are made to local branches;

(b), (c) and (d) data processing equipment is the prime current example.

(e) A single telephonist at a town centre branch can handle all incoming and outgoing calls for a number of satellite branches.

Solicitors and surveyors in Building Societies act for all the branches in an area.

STANDARDISATION

Standardisation fulfils several purposes:

(a) *It provides customers with a standard product or service.* Standardisation has become so much part of our culture that it is often forgotten how valuable it is. New high technology products tend not to be standardised so they illustrate the difficulties which can arise when, say, disks from one word processor cannot be used on the replacement machine. Large companies with nationwide outlets gain considerable benefit from supplying a standard service at all branches. Customers know what to expect, and the service is "interchangeable" i.e. a process started at one branch can be completed at another.

Example

Travellers cheques can be ordered at one branch for collection at another.

(b) *A standard product* can establish a reputation for quality and reliability which makes it attractive to customers.

Example

Travellers cheques from most of the Building Societies are accepted throughout Europe.

(c) All companies carry stocks of materials or components as part of their processes. For each item there is a minimum safety level. If several items, e.g. envelopes, can be standardised to one size – only one safety stock is needed. Moreover all the ancillary costs – space, insurance, purchasing and wastage are only a fraction of what they were before standardisation.

(d) *Economies of scale* can be obtained.

(e) If processes and procedures are standardised, training becomes quicker, easier and cheaper, and less mistakes are made.

(f) Interchangeability. Standardised procedures make staff interchangeable.

Standardisation requires centralisation. It means that if a service is to be standardised the operating system must be standardised – an organisation and methods department will design the system, a head office department will order and arrange for the installation and servicing of equipment, the property department will design the layout of branch, and stationery and forms will also be centrally supplied. Decisions at local level will either have to be made according to centrally determined decision rules, or referred upwards to ensure that a customer putting the same problem to two branches will get the same answer. Centralisation ensures that high standards are maintained throughout the structure.

SPECIALISATION

Specialisation is fundamental to the classical approach to management. At manager level a role can be split into two groups of activities – those which must be done by the manager himself, and those which can be done on his behalf by someone else. Specialisation means that all the work which can be done by someone else is passed to specialist departments. This allows the operating manager much more time to concentrate on the work he has to do himself, and to improve his expertise in this type of work.

Some of the activities within the operating manager's role may require skills which he does not possess. This is a further reason for centralising these skills.

Similarly, if some decisions only have to be made infrequently, a specialised department will have much more experience in such matters.

Centralisation may also take place if mistakes in a decision have a major impact either on the company or on branches other than those at which the decision is made.

Centralisation facilitates the maintainance of a clear strategy for the business.

DISADVANTAGES OF STANDARDISATION

Standardisation and Specialisation have been shown to give rise to centralisation. They do, however, create problems which may in many cases outweigh the benefits derived from them. Standardisation is very useful to customers provided that there are large numbers of customers with the same wants, or who will be satisfied with the standard service. Large firms organised to provide such a standard service often find it very difficult to satisfy unusual requirements.

If processes and equipment are standardised it becomes very difficult to change. Not only does it require a high expenditure for wholesale change of equipment, but retraining of staff is costly and time consuming, particularly as staff who have become used to standard routines with which they can cope easily, may resist the change. Standardisation breeds rigidity.

Another aspect of standardisation is in managing employees. The concept of fairness which is one of Fayol's fourteen principles, is interpreted by some as a need for consistency – i.e the standardisation of salaries, conditions of work, and ways of dealing with staff. While the broad principle may be all right, it overlooks that in reality employees are individuals who differ greatly. The need for consistency may become an excuse for avoiding the sometimes difficult decisions needed for good personnel management methods.

Illustration

Fig. 4.4 is an organisation chart showing the trend in the clearing banks. The shaded blocks show the operating departments. The bracketed headings the centralised specialist departments. Only a selection of special departments is shown on the chart for clarity. For a similar reason only one Operating Manager is shown at each of Regional, Area and Branch level. The personal and counter services are provided by several thousand branches spread throughout the country. Area or town offices are responsible for a number of such branches. The marketing, personnel management and control of advances for the area are centralised in this office. These specialists are responsible to the area manager for their day-to-day actions and to the functional regional managers for the quality of their work. The corporate accounts are also centralised at the area office and expert staff are available for non-banking services such as insurance, taxation and investment advice. The trend to centralise area offices has been reinforced by the cost and physical problems of introducing machines and complex equipment into small branches.

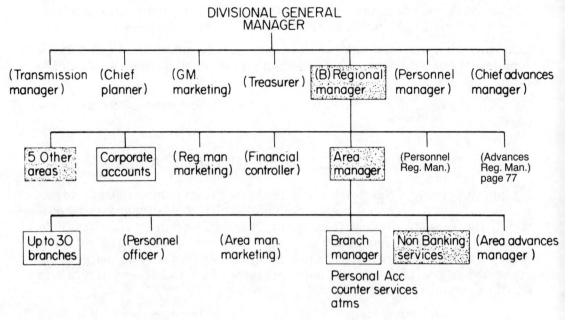

Fig. 4.4 Organisation structure: domestic banking division

A number of areas are supervised by a regional manager who has on his staff a regional functional manager responsible for the specialist work at the area offices. The Regional Personnel Manager will be responsible for training, briefing and supervising the personnel officers in the area offices. All the financial control for the region is centralised in the regional offices.

Additional central functions such as planning and money transmission are provided at divisional level. At this level dividend policy on personnel, marketing, advances and the other specialities is made.

DISADVANTAGES OF SPECIALISATION

When applied to staff, specialisation allows them to develop their personal skills and abilities to develop expertise in a relatively narrow field. This is certainly cost effective for the company. For the specialist advisers and managers it provides challenging and varied work, because they are often dealing with problems referred to them because they are out of the ordinary. However, it leaves the operating manager with only the routine work, and he may well become jaded and uninterested. At operator level the problem becomes even more serious as has already been described.

Loss of Power

Operating managers theoretically have the final say in making local decisions, but they go against the advice of the specialists at their peril. When they get conflicting advice from several specialists e.g. personnel and security, the position is made even more difficult. The profit responsibility of operating managers must be reduced each time decisions are taken out of their hands.

Illustration

The manager of a branch has to accept terminals and other equipment, the lay-out and rent of his branch is decided by property departments, personnel recruitment and training are the responsibility of personnel, base and mortgage rates are set by the finance department, and publicity arranged by marketing!!!

«Services Departments, Ch. 12, pp. 243–252»

Conflict

Some specialist departments are only justified because they prevent mistakes in operating departments – management accountants and inspection departments are of this type. Thus the more mistakes they can find, the greater their success. If the operating departments are successful in meeting all requirements the need for the departments declines. Here are the seeds of a battle for power and survival which often use up a lot of management time and energy.

«Conflict, Ch. 11, p. 230»

Waste

Centralisation requires massive information flows. Instructions from Head Office departments and senior management; advice from specialist departments, requisitions, proposals and reports from operating managers to their superiors and specialists. Inevitably much of this becomes routine, and much routine is continued after its usefulness has ceased. Hence centralised organisations tend to be swamped with paperwork but information technology may well change this.

Delay

The guidance given to operating management ensures that routine decisions are made quickly and efficiently. As soon as anything unusual occurs, the lack of power of the operating managers leads to delays while the request for instructions is transmitted, processed, considered and in due course complied with.

DECENTRALISATION

As companies have grown and technology and knowledge have developed over this century, the opportunities for centralisation have grown and the advantages have, in many cases, been overtaken by the disadvantages. Decentralisation is concerned with bringing facilities and decision making as close to the point of action as possible. Decentralisation:

(a) allows services to be adapted to the varied requirements of customers;

(b) encourages innovation;

(c) enables the company to react quickly to change and competition;

(d) makes jobs more interesting and improves motivation for operators and operating managers;

(e) creates a more "human" atmosphere for staff;

(f) speeds up decision making;

(g) gives an opportunity for managers to use their local knowledge to improve decision making;

(h) reduces conflict with service departments;

(i) reduces frictional overheads.

> The need for more centralisation in the finance sector has developed in recent years because of the entry into the industry of overseas companies with new ideas. Competitive pressures demand quicker and more customer-oriented decision making.

«Policymaking, Ch. 1, pp. 10–14»
«Delegation, Ch. 10, pp. 204–206»
«The Personnel Department, Ch. 12, p. 244»

In practice the real management problem is to maintain the best balance between Centralisation and Decentralisation.

PROJECT ORGANISATION

When the life of a product or service is unpredictable or where it has a very short life, the time and cost involved in setting up a permanent organisation structure may not be justified. Project Organisation is a solution where the structure is specifically designed for one or more projects being undertaken by a company. If there are several projects these may vary in size, and in the length of time they take to complete, and in the skills required in them. Thus the number of employees of various skills and levels will also vary. Employees are engaged on a contract basis, so that at the end of the project their employment ceases. In large companies the redundant employees are returned to the "pool" of their particular speciality, and are available for the next project. In smaller companies they would leave the company altogether and apply for new jobs with other employers in the industry.

The only permanent employees are the head office staff concerned with marketing and planning new projects.

ADVANTAGES OF PROJECT ORGANISATION

(a) The organisation is custom-made to suit the project.

(b) As new staff are engaged each time, the most suitable person for each job can be chosen. There is no need to make do with whatever is available within the company.

(c) There is no problem of what to do with barely adequate staff, or those without further promotion prospects, because they will all go at the end of the project anyway.

(d) There is no problem of surplus staff due to work fluctuations, because as soon as a project finishes everyone leaves.

(e) If projects are widely separated geographically, staff can be recruited locally, avoiding the heavy costs associated with either transferring staff or paying them for living away from home.

DISADVANTAGES OF PROJECT ORGANISATION

(a) The company may not benefit from the experience gained by employees on each project. How important this is depends on how similar each project is to the previous one.

(b) Each new project has a costly learning phase during which the new staff have to be trained to understand the organisation and its systems, and to work together as a team.

(c) There is no career structure or promotion potential to provide an incentive for a person to excel.

(d) The quicker the project is finished, the sooner they have to look for a new job, therefore it may be to the benefit of employees to work slowly or make little effort to overcome problems delaying completion.

(e) Employees may not develop any loyalty towards the company or their colleagues. This leads to strife, industrial relations problems and poor quality of work.

(f) At the point in time when a new project is to be started good quality staff may be difficult to obtain. If certain skills are in great demand at the time there may be no potential recruits available at all. There may also be nobody possessing specialist skills in the district in which the project is to take place.

Fig. 4.5 Project organisation

Project organisation was at one time very common, but the disadvantages far outweigh the advantages if there is a tight labour market, or if specialised skills are required which are not readily and widely available.

In banking projects are used for problem solving, investigations, and research.

MATRIX ORGANISATION STRUCTURES

Matrix organisation structures were evolved in response to the problems posed when a company provides a number of services, the demand for each of which fluctuates independently and widely. These structures also overcome the disadvantages of the project structure and have replaced these in progressive industries.

▒ Major Involvement
X Some Involvement
☐ No Involvement

OPERATING DEPARTMENTS \ FUNCTIONAL DEPARTMENTS		Money Market Operations	Management Accountancy	Management Consultants	Auditors	Taxation	Investment Analysts	Economists	Country Specialists
	Corporate Investment Advice	▒	X	X	X		▒	X	X
Investment Services	Charitable Fund Management	▒			X		▒	X	X
Investment Services	Pension Fund Management	▒			X		▒	X	X
Investment Services	Unit Trust Management					X	▒	X	
	Corporate Loans		▒	▒	X		X	X	X
Corporate Advice	Taxation Strategy					▒	X		
Corporate Advice	Dividend Strategy		X			X	X		
Corporate Advice	Capital Reconstruction		X	X		▒			
Corporate Advice	Amalgamations	X	▒	▒	▒	X	X		X
Corporate Advice	Stock Exchange Listings		X		▒		X		
Corporate Advice	New Issues	X	X		▒		X		

Fig. 4.6 Matrix organisation

Illustration

Figure 4.6 shows a matrix of operating departments providing services on the vertical axis and "functional specialists" on the horizontal axis.

In the Corporate Advice Division, the manager of the New Issues Department is responsible for marketing the service and dealing with any matters connected with providing it. This will involve a heavy demand on auditing capacity (to fulfil the obligations of the issuing house). For the same reason management accountants may have to be employed to investigate companies not very well known to the issuers. Money market operators and Investment Analysts are required to advise on pricing and timing.

Unfortunately the demand for new issues is not a steady one, and depends upon market conditions. An Issue House may have no business for six months, and whether it obtains business depends on whether it can provide the service required promptly when market conditions are right.

The New Issue department in a company with a matrix organisation structure will have its own permanent marketing staff, as well as some staff on research and records. When it has secured its "order" for a new issue, it may need large audit and management accountancy teams which will be drawn from the appropriate functional staffs. The advice from Money Market and Investment experts is important, but may only require the services of these experts for, say, two half days per week. The costs to the operating department are limited to the time for which the functional specialists are used.

The aspect of matrix organisation which is quite different from the structures previously discussed is that people are responsible to several "masters". The masters may be individual supervisors or committees. A functional expert is responsible both to the manager of his function, and to the manager of the operating department to which he is assigned. In such circumstances the operating manager has the authority to plan, organise, and direct the work of the expert and to control these aspects of his work. The method of working and the control of quality fall under the auspices of the specialist functional superior.

An even more complicated situation exists if a functional specialist is working on a number of projects for different operating managers. In addition to satisfying his functional superior regarding the quality of his work, he must satisfy all the operating managers that the work of each of them is being carried out in accordance with their plans. This puts severe stress on the specialist.

Management by committee represents a way of reducing the stress on the employee. Each service is run by a management committee. The members of this committee are representatives of each of the functions which supply a major input, as well as the marketing and general manager of the service. This means that responsibility for the success of the service is *shared by all the functional managers* involved. Minor specialist functions may be represented by part-time members of the committee.

In parallel with this the Functional Management committee, in addition to specialist experts, is made up of the managers of the operating departments which the functions serve. This committee determines the total resources – particularly in manpower – which the functions need, how the manpower is to be allocated to the operating departments and any priorities. The operating managers are present to make the case for their own departments, but they *share the responsibility for the success and profitability of the function*. This involves the ability to consider other peoples' problems as well as one's own, presenting one's own case forcibly, and seeking solutions which satisfy all requirements.

Illustration

The General Manager of the New Issue department will present the audit requirements for his Project to the Audit Manager together with a deadline. The Audit Manager will select a suitable team from his staff and assign it to the project. They will have been fully trained in company procedures and standards, in addition to their professional qualifications. Once attached to the project they will be under the direction of the New Issue department manager until their task is complete.

Similarly requirements will be presented to the Investment Analysis and other functions, and staff assigned from these functions to the project will be expected to supply their services as required by the project manager.

If a committee structure is used in conjunction with the matrix structure the Audit Manager will be on the New Issues Management Committee, together with the General Manager (New Issues) and the New Issues Marketing Manager. Other functional managers may be included according to the scale of the demands likely to be made from them. This committee will be responsible for the success of the New Issue business.

The Audit Function Management Team will comprise the General Audit Manager and the General Managers of the New Issues Department, Investment Services Stock Exchange, and Amalgamations (see Fig. 4.1).

«Uncertainty, Ch. 3, p. 69»

ADVANTAGES OF THE MATRIX STRUCTURE

(a) The main advantage is that it can cope efficiently with situations for which conventional structures are not suitable – especially large fluctuations in demand for a variety of services.

(b) It can cope with short-life projects without the disadvantages attached to short-contract employment.

(c) The varied work attracts high quality, highly motivated staff.

(d) It is cost efficient.

DISADVANTAGES OF THE MATRIX STRUCTURE

(a) The stress on staff and the high ability and motivation required from them means that high rewards must be offered to attract suitable staff.

(b) There is a high risk of losing staff because of breakdown under stress.

(c) Staff may be lost because it may not be possible to offer advancement to all those who have the potential for it.

REVIEW OF ORGANISATION STRUCTURES

It is evident that there is a wide choice of possible structures open to managers. In small companies it may be possible to create a single homogeneous structure which promotes the operations of the enterprise successfully. In large companies producing a range of services for numerous markets different structures will be needed for different parts of the enterprise.

Illustration

In Fig. 4.7 the Group is divided into three divisions – firstly on a "Market" basis into "Banking" and "Non-Banking".

Banking is then divided territorially into Domestic and Overseas.

Overseas Division is organised territorially into countries and through several lower territorial groupings into branches.

Domestic Banking is divided on a "functional" basis into Money Transmission and Branch Banking. The Branch Banking system itself being organised territorially as illustrated in 4.4, which also shows the varying extent of centralisation applied at different levels in the Domestic Banking Division.

The individual branches in both Domestic and Overseas Divisions are organised "functionally" as shown in Fig. 4.1.

The Non-Banking division is organised on a "Product" basis.

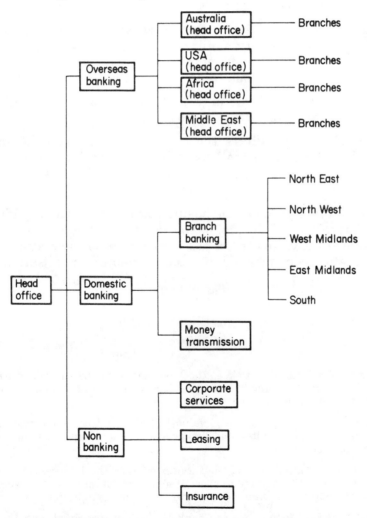

Fig. 4.7 Organisation of an international bank

What are the factors which have to be considered in choosing the structure appropriate to these various parts of a business. *The market and the products* have already been noted.

The market may be "homogeneous" – i.e. large numbers of one type of customer, or "differentiated", with many different types. It may be geographically concentrated, e.g. the government securities market in the City of London, or widespread – as the consumer market. Again as in the consumer market, it may consist of millions of customers – requiring standardised products and mass marketing techniques, or it may have a small number of customers each requiring a specially designed package – as in aircraft leasing.

The Size of the business is important as "product organisation" is only economically feasible if the demand for the product is large enough to justify a self-contained operation.

The width and diversity of the product range have a major impact on the structure. If products are very similar and there are sufficient of them a "product structure" for a group of products may be practical, whereas diverse products may oblige one to use a "functional" or matrix structure.

Grouping for economies of scale may apply to purchasing or marketing as well as to the operation aspects of the business.

The stability of demand affects the choice between the different structure, the product structure being least able to cope with short-term fluctuations. Centralisation also requires stable conditions for its benefits to be reaped.

The variety of resources used in the business affect the structure. If expertise is an important resource is it local or specialist expertise? Money as a major resource requires the close control associated with bureaucratic structures; machinery creates economies of scale and therefore centralisation.

Illustration

In the financial sector the main resources used are:

Money	People
Property	Technical know-how.

Money, its control and the need to keep check on the risks of bad debts and fraud has been a major factor in causing the clearing banks to centralise their organisation structure and standardise their operations.

Property requires specialised skills (e.g. valuation) and services which create centralised departments. It also inhibits rapid change and therefore contributes to maintaining a bureaucratic structure.

People are at the "point of sale" of the services offered. The inter-personal skills of branch managers and the attitude of his staff are essential ingredients to success. To utilise these skills and maintain morale, decentralisation is indicated.

The technical expertise in the clearing banks is mainly associated with the money transmission system. This requires centralisation.

The number of skills required in the business and the diversity of these skills has an impact on the structure. Where only a limited number of skills are used, wide spans of control are possible and roles can be clearly defined. If many skills are needed team working may be essential. It is also important to note that different skills may require a different managerial environment to flourish. Selling, research and development, and advertising skills only flourish in an atmosphere free from restrictions – so as to permit creativity. The balancing of accounts requires strict discipline which is best maintained in a rigid structure.

The degree of interface with the public, government unions and other outside groups may dictate the organisation structure. Close working with government may require centralisation, whereas contact with nationally distributed customers requires a territorial structure.

The Technology of Operations – i.e. whether "one-off", batch, mass or process production, affects the choice of structure. Where different technologies are used functional separation is almost inevitable and where the difference in technology applies to different services it may require product divisions.

Illustrations

The difference between branch operations, which are effectively batch production, and real-time terminals, requires that the latter are directed from the centre whilst the branches are more and more decentralised.

The substantial difference between both these methods of operation and the one of work handled by merchant banks, means that where a clearing bank wants to provide "one-off" services these are usually handled by a separate subsidiary business.

ASSESSMENT OF ORGANISATIONAL DESIGN

Management must from time to time assess the suitability and effectiveness of the organisation under its authority. This applies to the Chief Executive of a large group, to all the managers in the hierarchy, and down to the first level manager who is responsible for organising his departmental work. A number of "indicators" of organisational effectiveness can be used. Some of these are direct measures of how well the organisation is designed, some of them are more general in the sense that they highlight a fault, but further investigation is needed to find whether the fault is a symptom of bad organisation, or of some other problem.

Non-organisation problems in companies may be due to:

Faulty market orientation
Bad or outdated services
Unrealistic company objectives
Lack of resources, including undercapitalisation
Lack of planning
Lack of control

Bad industrial relations history

These problems, as well as organisational problems, will produce symptoms of:

Failure to achieve objectives
Low or declining profitability
High cost of operations and production
Low or declining sales and market share
High labour turnover
Customer complaints
Delays in implementing agreed changes
Missing marketing opportunities
Failure to match the standards and progress of competitors
Lack of awareness by managers of who is responsible for making decisions and taking action within the company

More direct indicators of organisational problems are:

Overmanning: people not having sufficient to do, or officiously interfering in other peoples' work.

Undermanning, often shown up by high illness and accident rates due to stress on employees. Many mistakes and omissions may occur.

Delays in making decisions: this may be the reason for business being lost to competitors, or for industrial relations disputes.

Managerial disputes: not disagreements about the best tactics or strategy but fruitless arguments about allocating blame and costs, or division of authority. Shift working, functional departmentalisation, centralised control, and conflicts between operating branches and specialist departments often cause such disputes. All these causes are organisational in nature.

Blocks in communication may be due to faulty organisation of the communication system, to gaps in the organisation structure, or to an excessively formal organisation.

Delays in producing or completing services.

The *attitude* of employees to *change*, to unusual requests, to co-operation and to performance is often based on the design of their jobs.

(*Absenteeism* is a good indicator of employee attitudes.)

CHARTING THE ORGANISATION

The descriptions of the various organisation structures in this chapter have been supplemented by a number of "organisation charts", including vertical, horizontal and matrix specimens. They have been used as an educational or training tool. This is probably their most useful function. Specific company and departmental organisation charts may also be used:

(1) to provide information to outsiders, to new entrants to the company and to those taking up a new post within the company;

(2) to record formal relationships within the company;

(3) to record channels of communications within the company;

(4) to form a starting point for organisational change.

The mere activity of constructing a chart forces the manager involved to think about his organisation.

The main problems of charts are that they rapidly become outdated, that they may give a wrong impression and that they may create status problems. Complicated charts are time-consuming to agree, construct and produce, and there is a danger that the organisation will not be changed because of the bother of recharting it. Human relations, which may be more important than the formal structure, cannot be shown on a chart.

«Wilfred Brown, *Explorations in Management,* Heinemann, 1960»

Practice Exercises

(1) Look around for units organised:

   (a) territorially;   (d) on a market basis;

   (b) on a functional basis;   (e) on a project basis.

   (c) on a product basis;

(2) Identify a centralised function in your company:

    Does it create standards?

    Does it provide economies of scale?

    Does it cause conflict or disagreement? – if so why?

(3) Identify a service-giving function and also an advisory function.

(4) Watch the indicators of organisational health in your firm. What do you conclude from them?

From Chapter 4 you should have learnt:

To distinguish between functional, product, territorial, market and project or matrix structures

The advantages and disadvantages of each.

The reason why firms centralise or decentralise.

The advantages and disadvantages of centralisation/decentralisation.

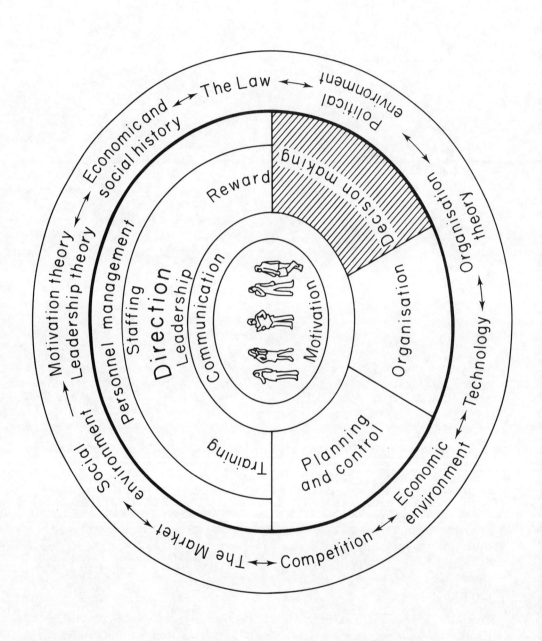

Chapter 5

Management Techniques

DECISION MAKING

A decision is a choice between a number of possible courses of action and is thus one of the most important components of a manager's job. Decisions range across the whole spectrum from routine to emergency and from critical importance for the business as a whole, to insignificant; from those whose results are achieved in minutes, to plans covering several years. Even operatives without management responsibilities have to "decide" on the pace and quality of their work, and on how to react to management initiatives.

«Job Evaluation, Ch. 15, p. 291»

The following are a few examples of decisions which have to be made by management:

The growth rate of the company –   a "corporate" decision

Raising new capital
Switching from cashiers to ATM's
Acquiring an overseas bank   "strategic" decision
a Building Society offering
unmeasured lending
Salary policy

The first of the above is a strategic decision because new resources are being acquired, the second because there is a major switch from one resource (skilled staff) to another (machinery). The latter two decisions are strategic because they affect the market/product orientation of the company.

All the above decisions are made by top management.

The make of computer to replace the existing one ⎫
The firm's salary structure
Closing and opening new branches   ⎬ "Management"
Personnel selection   decision
Lending decisions
Advertising   ⎭

The management decisions do not require "new" recourses, but they all require a degree of subjective judgement. They take place at all management levels – e.g. some judgement will be required by a junior personnel manager selecting school leavers, as will the appointment of a General Manager by the Personnel Director.

Rejecting a cheque   ⎫
Allocating work
Branch cash requirements   ⎬ "Operating" decision
Purchasing stationery
Appointments to see prospects
Arranging one's work   ⎭

Strictly speaking an operating decision is one in which the best choice can be determined quantitatively, e.g. by calculating the lowest cost, or by means of decisions rules – e.g. an unsigned cheque is rejected. There is, however, no clear dividing line between operating and management decisions on such a basis. It can therefore be assumed that most decisions of junior management are operating decisions.

It should also be noted that many operating decisions, because they can be based on calculation and decision rules, can be automated. An ATM can be made to "decide" whether to pay out cash by referring to the drawer's balance. Orders for new supplies can be automatically issued by monitoring demand and stock levels. These types of decision can also be described as "programmed".

COMPUTERS IN DECISION MAKING

Where there are a large number of similar decisions, computers, apart from any economic considerations, have certain advantages:

(a) *Speed* – in terms of the number of decisions which can be made, or of the time taken for a very complex calculation.

(b) Reliability.

(c) Accuracy.

(d) *A large memory* with instant recall and the ability for items to be deleted from the memory.

(e) Absence of bias.

The above advantages cause computers to be used for credit scoring for limits on credit cards and for personal loan applications.

Human beings have the advantage of:

(a) Flexibility.

(b) Access to non-programmed information.

(c) *The ability to judge* the quality of information provided.

From the economic point of view the cost of programming mainframe computers is very high. Costs there favour people, unless the number of decisions to be made is great, and the decision process will remain unchanged. This disadvantage is being reduced by the adoption of micro and personal computers.

THE PROCESS OF DECISION MAKING

Decision making can be informal or formal.

Informal or "traditional" decision making, as it is often called, is based on either experience or copying.

Experience

Many routine decisions are based on "repeating past successes". A personnel selector, for instance, may prefer candidates from a particular school, because they have proved more loyal and efficient than those from other schools. Cashiers may exceed their discretionary limits for cash payments because particular customers have proved honest in the past.

Experience can also be based on modifying failure. A manager may withhold certain types of work from a person just taking up a new position, because experience has shown him newcomers find this type of work difficult.

It is clear that many minor decisions are rightly made on the basis of experience. Experience may also be taken into account in more important decisions.

Copying

Fashion plays a large part in decision making in practice. Smaller banks send their young employees on AIB courses – because the clearing banks do so. Minor American banks open offices in the City of London because the majors do so. It may be that these decisions are reached on a rational basis. There is nothing wrong with doing the same as others, provided the decision has been sensibly arrived at.

The danger of simply copying, is that the reasoning behind the original decision may be valid for the originator, but it may be quite wrong for another firm with different objectives and resources. Building Societies tend to offer a similar range of products to their competitors e.g. a National Building Society may need a full range of savings account options, whereas a local Society in a town with a large retired population may only need selected schemes. Copying does of course involve a minimum of cost, but it is only acceptable where the consequences of a wrong decision are insignificant.

DECISION MAKING AS A MANAGEMENT TECHNIQUE

A "formal decision making" process is needed in the many situations where the traditional method is inadequate.

This process consists of six steps:

(1) IDENTIFY THE ISSUE

(2) ANALYSE THE ISSUE

(3) DEVELOP ALTERNATIVE SOLUTIONS

(4) CHOOSE THE BEST SOLUTION

(5) ORGANISE IMPLEMENTATION

(6) SET UP CONTROL SYSTEM

The relative importance of these steps varies greatly according to the issue to be decided, but only very rarely can one of the steps be left out completely.

(1) Issue Identification

This step is perhaps the most important one at senior level. Most *corporate* and *strategic* decisions require anticipation. ATM's have become a major feature of banking services in the 1980s, but the first experimental models were ordered in 1967.

At *operating* level this step is seldom required because the issues are quite clear and present themselves.

A cheque is presented for payment – can it be met?

A queue is forming at a branch – should another position be opened?

Stocks of forms have reached minimum level – how many should be ordered?

A machine has broken down – can the operator deal with it or is a service engineer required?

At *management* level some issues may present themselves clearly – e.g. normal lending propositions. However in many situations it is far from clear what the real issue is. A high labour turnover in a department could be due to a dozen or more causes. If a quick assumption is made that the cause is, say the attitude of the departmental head, it may be decided to re-train or transfer the manager concerned. Neither of the decisions will reduce the labour turnover if it is due to a local competitor for staff paying higher wages. It is, therefore, extremely important that a decision is made on the "real" issue, and not on a symptom arising from the issue. Where there are a number of possible causes, each one must be separately subjected to the following stages of the decision making process, until they are eliminated.

Once the issue has been correctly identified the objective for solution should be determined – i.e. what should the solution achieve? In the example of the previous paragraph the objective could be to "build up a staff, in this location, with unrivalled experience". The best way of achieving this might be to raise salaries to outbid the competition for the best staff, disregarding the company salary structure.

If, however, the objective is to "provide an economical service to branches", a better solution might be to relocate the department to an area where there is less intense competition for staff.

(2) Issue Analysis

This comprises: Fact finding
Separating subsidiary issues
Identifying constraints and obstacles

Perhaps the first point managers should consider at this stage is whether they should make the decision themselves, or whether it should be referred elsewhere.

Reference to superiors is indicated if the decision is outside the authority of the manager, if it commits the company for a period beyond the time for which the manager normally plans, and if it involves other parts of the business.

Reference to subordinates is indicated if it is an issue normally dealt with by subordinates, or if it arises so frequently that it ought to be delegated. This is an example of a revised objective – i.e. training a subordinate to deal with the type of decision needed.

Fact Finding

The quality of decision making depends on whether all the necessary information has been obtained.

Sources of information include:

Internal records – now often available quickly from VDUs or computer terminals.

Published information.

Personal contacts both inside the firm and outside and Service departments.

Chapter 6 of this book deals more fully with how such information can be obtained.

Subsidiary Issues

This point is mainly relevant to major issues which may have to be broken down into their component parts. In such cases the subsidiary issues may be investigated by different people, and even by whole project teams.

Limitations to Solutions

The difference between an obstacle and a constraint is that the latter is accepted as unavoidable, whereas obstacles can be overcome. Time is often an unavoidable constraint. A customer may have to meet a deadline, or higher management may require a planning schedule to be met. Staff reaction may, however, only be an "obstacle" to a solution, which may be overcome with appropriate leadership or compensation.

Other constraints arise from:

Lack of knowledge
Staff abilities
Government Rules and Laws
Image and reputation of the enterprise
Lack of Capital, space, equipment and other resources.

«*Ch. 1, pp. 13–14*»

(3) Developing Solutions

A decision is not a decision unless a choice has been made between different solutions.

Sources of solutions are:

Past experience
Advice from specialist and service departments
Colleagues
Subordinates
Clients
Competitors
Suppliers
Literature and exhibitions
Consultants
Creativity

In many situations there are a number of standard solutions. In a manning decision, for instance, the selector normally has a short list of several candidates, plus the possibility of re-advertising. Sometimes, however, alternative solutions may not be readily available. Before proceeding with what is only one possible course of action one should always consider the alternative of *no* action – which may often be preferable in such a situation.

Innovation

In a competitive and changing environment "creativity" may gain one a considerable advantage. Creativity does not necessarily mean dramatic new inventions. It is the regular adoption of novel procedures, methods, equipment etc., where they are an improvement on the old, which keeps an enterprise in the vanguard of progress.

Creativity requires an open mind, adequate time to think, a variety of interests, a willingness to accept the rejection of one's ideas and occasional failures, and an organic organisational environment. Thus creativity cannot be expected from people in a mechanistically or bureaucratically organised enterprise.

Forecasting Consequences

When a number of solutions have been promulgated it is necessary

(i) to forecast the outcome of the solution, including likely deviations and the probability of success;

(ii) to assess any adverse or positive impact on other activities.

(4) Choice Between Alternatives

Evaluation of solutions should be based on how likely they are to achieve the objective and at what cost, not only in financial terms but also in the use of other resources such as space and managerial effort. Risk is an important criterion for bankers and "timing" may be decisive in many cases. It should be noted that in choosing between different solutions, as the choice is based on comparison, the overall value of the forecasts is not important. Only the difference needs to be reasonably accurate. The choice may sometimes be influenced by a manager's inability to determine which of several possibilities is the real cause of a problem. In such cases a solution has to cover all the possibilities.

In the forecasting of consequences and choosing between alternatives in complex decisions, managers in larger enterprises can usually avail themselves of:

(a) specialist departments – e.g. management accountants, management services, legal and property;

(b) the many operational research techniques which are available to provide mathematical solutions:

    Decision Trees
    Statistical Sampling
    Regression Analysis
    Network Planning (PERT)
    Queuing Theory
    Modelling

Operational research techniques can be used through the medium of specialist departments, or by operating managers themselves, provided they have the necessary skills. Nowadays many of these techniques are available as standard computer programs so that mathematical knowledge is not essential. What is important if such techniques are to be used, is that:

(a) the techniques which are made available are selected on the basis of demand, i.e. that they are relevant to the needs of the managers who might use them;

(b) they have been tested and found satisfactory by specialists before being offered for use;

(c) their availability is fully publicised;

(d) top management supports the use of such techniques and gives credit to those who successfully apply them;

(e) initial training is provided when a manager first uses a technique. This must include following up the use of the techniques throughout implementation and control of a project, to ensure that unexpected difficulties can be dealt with properly. During training temporary assistance must be provided to ensure that the manager's routine does not suffer. This help must be repeated until the manager is comfortable with using the technique.

The initial cost of training must be balanced against the benefit of improved quality and speed of decision making.

Some operational research methods are briefly described later in this chapter.

(5) Organising Implementation

A decision is not finalised until it has been decided how it should be carried out. In some cases, e.g. a decision to introduce retail banking terminals, this may require a full five year plan with a detailed one year action plan. In other cases it may be desired to allow as much freedom of action as possible. In all except routine decisions to be carried out by the manager himself, it should be determined.

 (i) WHO is responsible for implementing the decision?

 (ii) What is the DEADLINE for completion?

(iii) What RESOURCES are necessary to implement the decision. Time, money, personnel, space and equipment must be reserved or made available.

(6) Control

It has been explained that Control is the element of management concerned with ensuring that objectives are met. In the formal decision process control has exactly this function. It is particularly important when implementation is divided among several members of a team, when it is delegated to sub ordinates e.g. mortgage lending decisions made by branch managers, and when it is implemented over a period. Controls must be considered for three purposes:

(a) *progress* towards and achievement of the end result;

(b) *evaluation* of the process used;

(c) *validation* of the end result.

Methods of control will be described in the next chapter.

GROUP DECISION MAKING

Emphasis was placed in previous paragraphs on the importance of making sure that decisions which have been made are actually carried out. If persons decide on courses of action for themselves they have to discipline *themselves* to keep to that course of action. A manager is, however, often in the position of making decisions which have to be implemented by *others*, usually direct or indirect subordinates. Regional managers may decide to compete with Building Societies by a more friendly service – but how do these managers ensure that cashiers actually behave in a more friendly manner? They may also decide on certain priorities in lending, but as it is normal to honour commitments made by a branch manager, how can the regional managers make sure that the priorities are kept to?

One solution is total supervision – where the managers watch their subordinates continually and make all decisions themselves. This overloads managers and is very unpopular with staff, and therefore not practical.

The answer to this problem is to convince subordinates of the need or value of the course of action chosen. However, subordinates tend to suspect any arguments put forward by management. The best way of convincing them is to let a group of them reach the same conclusion themselves – group decision making.

Group decision making has the additional advantage of enabling a wider range of experience, knowledge and attitudes to be brought to bear on a problem. The discussion on alternatives and elimination of obstacles may give rise to new ideas. It is also less likely that adverse consequences for other departments will be overlooked, if people who work in or with such departments are included in the discussion.

Group decision making is a very widely used technique. Examples are:

Corporate decisions at the Board of Directors
Investment decisions at senior management level
Marketing decisions at divisional level

Organisational decisions at area level
Training decisions in personnel departments
Work allocation at branch level
Disciplinary decisions by staff consultative committees.

Any decision *can* be made on a group basis. It is not desirable, or necessary, to make all decisions on a group basis because decisions made in such a way usually take longer and are more costly since more people are involved. There is also the risk of no agreement being reached, and of bitterness being created in the course of heated discussions.

INDICATIONS FOR GROUP DECISION MAKING

Group decision making should therefore be used selectively. The indications for group decision making are one or more of the following:

The decision will affect the work of others.
The decision has to be put into effect by others.
Information is required from a range of people.
Different viewpoints are required.
The manager cannot think of a satisfactory solution.

GROUP DECISION MAKING AND COMMITTEES

A committee is an organisational structure which is designed to formalise group decision making. The conditions for improving group decision making are the same as those described in Chapter 3. However it must be stressed that while all decision making committees are a form of group decision making, group decision making does not require a committee. Committees have a formal constitution, agendas and records. None of these are necessary for group decision making.

A common example of group decision making is a daily or weekly meeting of a manager and his or her subordinates to discuss the programme for the day or week. On the other hand group decisions may be on occasional subjects – e.g. to decide who goes on holiday when, or on special problems, e.g. how to deal with disruption due to building work.

According to Chester Barnard (1886–1961), decision making is an art which comprises

Not making decisions on irrelevant issues.
Not making decisions prematurely.
Not making decisions that cannot be effective.
Not making decisions that others should make.

»Meeting«

«Participative Leadership, Ch. 11, p. 223»
«Contingency Approach to Leadership, Ch. 11, p. 227»
«Action Centred Leadership, Ch. 11, p. 228»

MANAGEMENT BY OBJECTIVES (MbO)

This is a management technique designed to improve the performance of individuals. It is mainly applicable to middle managers. It combines a number of commonly recognised management activities into a formal process. This formal process is as useful in obliging the head of a department to "manage" as it is in improving the performance of his subordinates:

The process comprises

(1) Target setting
(3) Reviewing performance   } (2) Identifying and meeting resources
(4) Rewarding success   }   and training needs

Each of these steps requires the involvement and agreement of the manager and his superior. This co-operation at each stage is a feature of MbO. If a state of trust is absent MbO will fail. The process may be described by analysing the role of both manager and superior.

Superior	Manager
(1) Target Setting	
Defines objectives and demonstrates their relationship with departmental and company objectives. Defines duties and limits of authority.	Asks about anything he does not understand. Makes sure he is clear about purpose and relationship of objectives. Checks on doubtful areas of authority. Asks for extra authority if considered advisable.
Defines key results areas.	Confirms key results areas and priorities or suggests alternative ones based on his experiences.
Sets correct performance standards.	Considers performance standards and agrees these, or justifies proposed changes.
Makes allowance for possible difficulties identified by manager or contingency plans to help manager overcome them.	Anticipates difficulties or obstacles to achieving standards, particularly those which may be beyond his control – e.g. interference by higher management, or accidents and illness of staff, and explains what effect these would have on targets.
Transfers incorrectly allocated work to other section.	Draws attention to any unnecessary or irrelevent work with which the section is burdened.

(2) Resource Provision

Provides additional resources as required	Asks for any addition or changed "resources" – e.g. alternative staff, replacement equipment, additional space, increased expenditure allowance, access to information.
Makes changes to organisation, communication systems and control systems required.	Points out any deficiencies in organisation, communication systems or control systems.
Provides immediate advice, training or counselling to improve performance.	Identifies weakness in own performance and performance of subordinates and training needed to overcome such weakness. Requests such training.
If it is not possible to provide for these needs, targets must be lowered: Alternatively the superior must be able to demonstrate and convince the manager that the target can be reached without them.	Does not accept target unless he is convinced he has the necessary resources and ability to achieve them.

(3) Performance Review

Arranges for regular flow of control information to keep the manager informed how he is getting on.	Raises with superior any unexpected events interfering with progress. Raises any difficulties being experienced, either personally, or by his staff, or with any of the resources or systems. or systems.
Monitors this information and discusses deviation with the manager. (Note that discussion of deviations should be between manager/superior rather than manager/specialist.)	
Arranges periodic review of performance (e.g. monthly for a quarterly target, or quarterly for an annual target) to identify any obstacles in the way of achieving the target.	

(2) Provides assistance

Does so to ensure objectives are met.

Requests help if required. Requests further training if required by himself or his staff. Requests additional resources if thought necessary, or changes to organisation and systems.

(4) Reward

One of the features of MbO is that the reward is tied to the achievement of targets. This is very simple if there is a salary scale with annual increment, which is also annually adjusted for inflation. The "reward" for achieving the target is then the award of the increment. Missing the target by a small amount would result in only the inflation adjustment being awarded. In the case of a serious failure no salary increase would take place. In inflationary conditions this is effectively a salary reduction. If a reduced reward, or even no reward is given because of failure to achieve targets, this is not intended as a punishment, but is intended to concentrate the mind of the manager on anticipating problems and difficulties, so that a realistic plan can be made in the first place.

To compensate for the possible loss of increments under adverse conditions, there should be a bonus award available if performance is exceeded.

Note that stage 2 – the provision of resources – may be repeated after each performance review. Provision of "resources", in this context includes "knowledge" and ability which may be provided through training.

AIDS TO DECISION MAKING

GAP ANALYSIS AS A MANAGEMENT TECHNIQUE

It will have been noted that in MbO the need for targets and objectives to be *agreed* has been emphasised. The reason for initial disagreement often occurring is that the target visualised by the superior is derived from higher level objectives which are based on what higher managers think the firm ought to achieve.

The lower level manager is actually producing a forecast, rather than a target. It is therefore no more than a coincidence if forecast and target agree at the first attempt. It is quite pointless simply to replace a forecast by a target which is higher; the better the manager's forecasting skill the more likely it is that the original forecast, rather than the target will be achieved. Gap analysis may be used to eliminate the difference between target and forecast.

Illustration

An objective has been proposed which requires an additional 7500 Automated Teller Machines in 5 years. This has been broken down into annual objectives as shown in Fig. 5.1. It is known that for the next two years suppliers are only able to supply 1000 units per annum. They are increasing their capacity to meet the demand and this new capacity will be on stream in two years' time.

The computer services department, aware of the general objective to speed up automation of personal account transactions has produced a forecast of prospective installations as per the dotted line in Fig. 5.1.

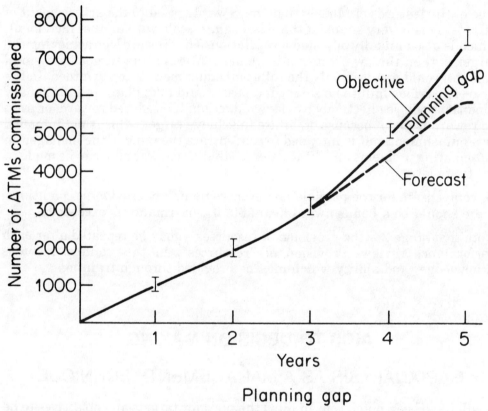

Planning gap

Fig. 5.1 Gap analysis

The difference between the objective and the target is the *planning gap*. The General Manager has called for an analysis of the gap to decide the optimum plan.

Gap analysis requires an analysis of how both objective and forecast were reached.

Factors considered in this forecast were:

Available delivery schedule of ATMs

Annual capital budget available

Cost of ATMs allowing for inflation and increased output/competition

Available central computer capacity

Training time of internal computer staff to service computer centre and communication links

Wastage rate of cashiers who would be replaced.

Availability of branches with growing demand and structures suitable for through-the-wall machines

Demand for machines in non-branch locations

Cost of installation – particularly in inconvenient structures.

Factors considered in setting objectives were:

Need to compete with services provided by competitors

Customer demand for quick standard services

Importance of convenient location

Capital required

Capital available.

On analysing the forecast in detail it was found that the gap in year four was due to all easily converted sites having been used, and high conversion costs limiting the number of sites which could be converted in years four and five within the proposed capital budget – in year five the capacity of the central computer would also be exhausted.

Pending a decision on additional computer capacity it was decided to reduce the objective to 5800 installations, but to allocate part of the capital saved to year four. This would allow branches to be converted more quickly so that the 5800 installations could be operative early in the fifth year, as originally envisaged.

Gaps may also be identified during the planning process, and when actual performance is found to vary from planned performance at the control stage. The same method of analysis is applicable in both cases.

OPERATIONS RESEARCH

This term covers a whole range of mathematical techniques designed to predict the outcome of decisions managers are considering, and compares them with alternative decisions. Some of the more important ones are listed here with the situations in which they may be applied.

Regression Analysis

It is useful to record the values of a continuing series of events, usually in the form of graphs. Regression analysis is concerned with identifying the mathematical equations of these graphs. If this can be done, the future values of the events can be predicted, provided the underlying behaviour pattern is not changed.

Economic Order Size

This is a relatively simple technique. In any purchasing situation there are three major costs per unit:

(i) The managerial and administrative costs of placing the order, following it up and paying for it.

(ii) The extra price paid for small quantities.

Both the above costs suggest that the largest feasible quantity should be ordered at one time.

(iii) The cost of holding a large quantity in stock. Apart from storage and insurance, this must include the risk of pilferage and obsolescence, but above all the cost of capital tied up.

It will be noted that as the order size increases the first two costs decrease, but the third increases. EOQ techniques try to find the size of order which will be most economic. They are effective as long as the underlying costs are readily available, realistic and up to date.

Linear Programming

This is an algebraic technique which can be used graphically on simple problems; more complex problems can easily be dealt with on a computer. It is useful where there are a number of resources, with limited availability, each of which can be employed for a number of income producing activities. Linear programming seeks to find the best "mix" of both resources and uses.

Queuing Theory

The basic problem of avoiding queues is to minimise the sum of two classes of costs:

(1) The cost of waiting for service;
(2) the cost of providing service facilities.

The length of a queue depends on the rate and regularity of arrival of customers. This is often determined by statistical sampling. It also depends on how long each service takes. If the arrival rate is faster than the service rate a queue will first form and then lengthen. Queuing theory aims to keep waiting time to an acceptable level without excessive idle time at the service points.

There is an obvious application for this theory in the counter service of branches. There are also many examples *within* the organisation where the waiting time of one department and the capacity of another have to be balanced.

Statistical Sampling

There are two aspects of statistical theory which are useful for managers. Statistical sampling is useful because it has been found that the behaviour of very large numbers of events can be predicted within accepted limits of accuracy by sampling quite a small proportion of the whole. This obviously represents an enormous saving in time and money. The correct size of sample depends on the behaviour patterns and the accuracy needed. The mathematics are quite reliable, but the key to successful prediction lies in correctly selecting the sample.

An application of sampling techniques is predicting the numbers and arrival patterns of customers in branches. The danger is of picking a test branch which does not conform to the standard behaviour pattern, e.g. one near a station − where train departures affect the demand; or a branch near a large employer with unusual lunch breaks.

Statistical Decision Theory

Many decisions have to be made on the basis of uncertainty. Statistical decision theory tries to inform managers of:

(a) the range of possible outcomes;

(b) the most likely one of these outcomes actually to occur;

(c) the possible environmental events which might distort the outcome;

(d) the likelihood of these events occurring;

(e) taking all the above into account, which is the decision most likely to meet the objectives?

The mathematical predictions are very useful, particularly in marketing and at strategic level, but they depend very much on subjective managerial input. There is therefore a danger of over-relying on the mathematics rather than ensuring that the quality of input is right.

Decision Trees

Are used to aid decision making when decisions have to be taken sequentially depending on the outcome of previous decisions.

E.g. Opening a branch network in a foreign country,

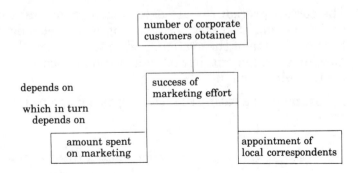

by assigning probabilities as to the outcome of various events, the course of action most likely to be successful can be identified.

Grading Systems

Statistical Theory has identified a number of characteristic ways in which events or attributes can be distributed in a large population.

Exceptionally high	2.3%	
High	13.6%	
Average	68.2%	NORMAL DISTRIBUTION
Low	13.6%	
Exceptionally low	2.3%	

A normal distribution can be divided into five grades. The percentages in each grade can be predicted and are as shown. This system obviously lends itself to judging many qualitative characteristics.

Where finer judgements can be made and are desirable seven grades can be used, or three where rougher assessments are adequate.

One of the features of this grading system is the idea of the majority of events, or people, being "normal" or "average". On the one hand this is a sound basis on which to make a judgement. On the other hand it offers an easy way out for managers who are reluctant to make any judgement at all. This is a common fault with managers who are afraid of being proved wrong and therefore prefer to sit on the fence.

Similar problems occur when managers with unrealistically high standards value everybody as "below average", or those, trying to make themselves popular, rate everyone above average.

The problem can be avoided by choosing a system with an even number of grades and therefore force managers to make a choice – e.g. between "good" and "bad". A forced distribution system is a slightly more sophisticated form of coercion, where the proportion of judgements in each grade must be according to predetermined ratios. Both the "forced choice" and "forced distribution" systems are unsatisfactory because they may not conform to reality.

The correct procedure is to define each grade sufficiently to give managers the confidence that they are making a correct judgement, to train them in the application of the system, and to teach them the importance, not only of making a judgement, but of making one which is informative and meaningful to their colleagues.

An example of a rating scale for appraisal can be found on p. 213 later in this book.

«Selection, Ch. 13, p. 269»
«Personality Characteristics, Ch. 7, pp. 149–153»

Practice Exercises

(1) When you make minor decisions do you make them by "copying" or on the basis of "past experience"?

(2) When you make a more important decision, go through the steps in the decision making model. Which step have you found most valuable?

(3) What constraints are there on your travel-to-work decision?

(4) If you buy a new camera/television or other durable item, where do you seek information?

(5) Think of an issue to which you could make a useful contribution if asked. Would you be willing to join in making a decision on this issue? Why do you think you were/were not asked?

From Chapter 5 you should have learnt:

The difference between corporate, strategic, management and operating decision.

The formal decision making model.

The difference between symptoms and issues and how to proceed to identify causes rather than symptoms of problems.

The sources of information.

The requirements for satisfactory implementation of decision.

The necessity of setting up controls for progress, validation and evaluation.

The purpose of group decision making and when it should be used.

The applications for which EOQ, Linear programming, gap analysis, network analysis and queuing theory are useful.

The necessary steps to encourage use of operational research techniques.

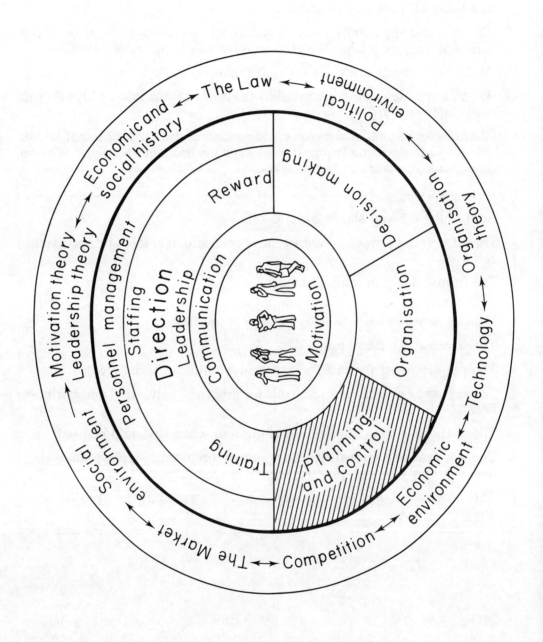

Chapter 6

Planning and Control

PLANNING

The structure of planning in an enterprise is closely related to the structure of decision making:

Corporate Plans embrace the whole of the enterprise. The long term planning horizon is *5-25 years*.

Strategic Plans concerned with introducing change – usually confined to specific areas of the business, e.g. establishing a presence in the USA, or capturing the unbanked. The medium term planning horizon is *2-5 years*.

Management Plans concerned with:
    (a) implementing stages of the strategic plan;
    (b) performance improvement;
    (c) correcting weaknesses and making up shortfalls
    (d) up-dating resources;
    (e) adapting to changes in the current environment.
       The time horizon is usually *one year*.

Operating Plans concerned with implementing shorter stages of management plans, and with the normal activities of departments. Time horizon – *up to one year*.

Budgets concerned with predicting the cash requirements of operations. Time horizon *up to one year*.

It will be noted that plans cover a range of time horizons and that the longer term plans are made up of a series of short-term plans. Longer term plans lay down a strategy within which only those decisions, which have to be made immediately, are taken, while others are left until later.

«Manpower Planning, Ch. 12, p. 239»

Example: A new computer centre requires a building, a set of "programs", managers and operating staff. For a completion date of 1990, the whole project would be included in the 1985–1990 Strategic Plan. The 1985–7 Management Plan would include placing the contract for the building, but the order for the computer itself would be in the 1986–8 management plan. This would be followed in 1988 by the appointment of managers to establish computer software and the 1989–90 management plan would involve engaging operating staff. Operating plans would not be made until 1990, when the project is established.

It will be noticed that the management plans can be modified from year to year to take account of delays or changed circumstances – e.g. if delivery times shorten, placing an order can be postponed. At the same time the long-term plans provide a steady objective.

THE PLANNING PROCESS

Objectives

The starting point of any plan is determining the departmental objective and identifying how this fits into the hierarchy of objectives of the enterprise and how it relates to other departments. In particular the contribution of the objective to higher level objectives should be established. Next the planning "premises" must be obtained from higher management, or, when these exist, from central planning departments. These are the fixed assumptions around which a plan is constructed, e.g. the staff and salary levels, or that there will be no new services introduced during the planning period. If assumptions cannot be firm, several plans may be prepared. For example if there is a steep jump or drop in interest rates, a revised plan will come into operation.

Defining Activities

This requires a listing of all the activities involved in achieving the objectives, and the type of decisions which have to be taken. This is the organisation aspect of setting up a new department, but it should be noted that in an existing department the organisation is established. When a plan is set up to reach a new objective, all that is required is a review of the activities to see whether any new ones have to be added, or older ones become unnecessary. The work load on different jobs may also change. It is useful at this stage to consider the relative importance of all activities and identify key results areas.

Key Results Areas

Key results areas are those activities which, if they are carried out well, will make a considerable contribution to achieving the objectives or areas where sub-standard performance will almost certainly lead to failure. It is neither practicable nor desirable to plan in too much detail. It is much more satisfactory for the manager to plan the Key Results areas, leaving it to his sub-ordinates to prepare their own shorter term plans for less important activities. There may even be other optional tasks, which will only be undertaken if time becomes available.

Target Setting

This is the process of determining what is to be achieved by the important sub-sections of the department. These will be mainly those which have been identified as key results areas, but all other activities should also have targets to promote efficiency and maintain motivation. In most cases targets take the form of a performance level to be attained – i.e. a standard.

Standards must be:

- relevant
- measurable
- specific
- attainable

Standards must be *relevant* to the key results areas and the departmental objectives to be achieved. It is necessary that they should be *measurable* – not only because otherwise one cannot tell whether they have been reached – but also to avoid misunderstandings about what was intended. It is for this same reason that very generalised standards – e.g. "promptness of service", should be defined more *specifically* as, say, "all enquiries to be answered within 24 hours".

Finally the importance of having *attainable* targets and standards cannot be overstressed. It was at one time thought that very high targets improved performance. In practice unattainable targets either lead to frustration – resulting in employees leaving – or to the standards being ignored completely and replaced by lower "group norms". This is just as if no standard had ever been set.

Experience has shown that the best results are achieved if standards and targets are set by discussion between a manager and his subordinates. It is best if the manager defines his expectations. This can be based on O & M work, on his own experience, or on standards previously achieved by his subordinates or other departments. Having told subordinates his opinion, the manager should then let them decide for themselves what standard is attainable (in the light of their own capabilities and prevailing circumstances). This standard should be accepted by the manager unless he can demonstrate how an improvement can be achieved, or unless he can provide additional training or resources to create better performance. Using this procedure it is found that overenthusiastic subordinates' ideas are kept to a realistic level, while reluctant subordinates will be committed to achieving the standard which they themselves have set (although it was influenced by the manager's expectation).

«MbO, Ch. 5, p. 115»
«Setting Objectives, Ch. 1, p. 9»
«Group Decision Making, Ch. 5, p. 113»
«Participation, Ch. 11, p. 224»

Resource Provision

Once the plan has been agreed, the necessary resources must be made available. This includes sufficient staff, space and equipment, but also resources of skills and knowledge, i.e. by providing training and specialist back up, and of information, by setting up appropriate communication systems.

«Ch. 4, p. 88»
«Ch. 12»
«Ch. 7»

Budget

Invariably money is one of the resources required. The "budget" represents the financial requirements for the plan.

Control

No plan is complete unless a system has been incorporated which enables the manager to monitor progress. Control systems are described in detail in the next section.

Illustration: Planning Deposit Taking Activities

Deposit Taking Targets

The Divisional General Manager has been set an objective of increasing the total deposits in the year by 10%. He will discuss these with area managers and suggest the amount by which each one should increase their deposits. He will take into account existing deposit levels, the strength of the competition in each area, and the new potential.

The area managers will carry out the same exercise with each branch manager. After due consideration each manager will confirm the target he expects to achieve. His report will include an action-plan – i.e. how he is going to do it. This action plan will include the proposed sources of new deposits, new contacts to be made, and any requirements of resources. Such extra resources might include the services of consultants from specialist departments to work out proposals for corporate service.

The area manager will check that the proposals are acceptable. By combining all the proposals from his branches he can present a summary proposal to his Divisional General Manager which will be within acceptable tolerance of the original suggestion.

Illustration: Planning for a Branch

A typical set of branch *objectives* is:

Maximise profitability
Increase deposits by 6% within 12 months
Attract mortgage lending of £600,000.

Branch activities are not significantly altered by these objectives. The plan is for expansion, therefore consideration must be given to possible extra clerical assistance during the year.

Key results areas: For maximum profitability the main areas are

(a) Increasing turnover

(b) Balancing deposits and lending volume (to avoid charges for using central funds, and low profit on lending to H.O.)

(c) Bad debts

(d) Minimising costs – optimum cash level

                               staffing level

                               overtime

For increased deposits the key areas are:

Development of business relations

Quality of service – because 90% of new business comes from recommendation by satisfied customers

Development of business relations is usually the province of the branch manager himself. He therefore has to decide how much time to devote to this activity and to prepare an action plan which will enable him to extend his contacts with local prospects. Usually the action plan is a combination of individual meetings with potential clients, meetings with those able to introduce clients – solicitors for example, and joining in group activities such as Rotary Clubs. Help may be sought from Marketing departments for promotions to students and other special market segments.

Quality of Service requires action by most of the staff. Taking counter staff as an example, a target for maximum waiting time may be agreed between the Chief Cashier and the manager. The Chief Cashier then is responsible for involving the tellers and associated staff in reaching this target. This is an instance where group decision making is probably essential to gain the co-operation of staff. There could be a weekly meeting to agree manning of counter positions at lunch- or other peak-times, as well as early and late rosters. It should be noted that because flexible working is essential – e.g. switching of staff to cover unexpected demand, or illness, it is not practical to set targets for individuals. For individual targets to be effective, the person must be able to concentrate on their job without interference.

Length of waiting time can be controlled visually. This requires that the Chief Cashier should be located where he can *see* queues building up.

Similar quality of service targets need to be agreed with other junior managers in the branch.

The balancing of deposits and avoidance of bad debts require partly good decision making by the branch manager and partly good research and accurate information. The supervision of this will probably be delegated to an assistant manager.

To minimise cost, targets should again be set for each section – e.g. the machine room, by agreement with the manager in charge of that section, say the machine room supervisor. In a large branch several such sections will be responsible to an assistant manager who will summarise the individual targets into a target for his area of responsibility. This combined target is then subject to approval by the branch manager.

Planning is an activity which many people, including many managers avoid. In order to ensure that it is properly carried out in a firm, it is necessary to identify why people avoid planning, so that they can be helped to overcome their reluctance.

Among the common reasons are:

- fear of being committed, and being assessed against predicted perform-ance.
- difficulty of making decisions under conditions of uncertainty
- planning being considered a waste of time
- preference for action rather than planning

All the above are attributable to the person concerned. It is, of course, essential that people appointed to managerial positions do have the confidence, willingness to think ahead, and analytical and decision making abilities required for the planning element in the job. Often fears are due to inadequate training, and newly appointed managers must be properly coached in planning as described earlier in this chapter.

- lack of resources, particularly time and information
- unrealistic targets set from above
- no feed back on progress
- lack of commitment by higher management
- unrealistic planning parameters
- key areas wrongly identified. This is usually because higher management identifies universal key areas which are not relevant to a particular department
- an excessively unstable environment

These are all problems which are outside the control of the manager. It is up to the company to ensure that these problems do not arise.

CONTROL

Control may be defined as "The comparison of actual results with expecta-tion and the taking of corrective action". This may be illustrated diagram-matically as in Fig. 6.1.

It immediately becomes apparent that control is impossible unless there is an initial "expectation" or standard. When a result has been achieved this is compared with the standard. Any difference is known as a "variance". If there is no variance, no action is necessary. If a variance is found during the comparison it has to be reported back to the "originator" of the standard. This is known as "feed-back". The "originator" then has to decide what action to take.

The closed loop feed-back system applies equally to single activities, to a series of similar activities or to continuous processes.

In the case of a single activity the originator has to decide whether any corrective action is to be taken at all, or whether the feed-back information will simply be retained for future reference.

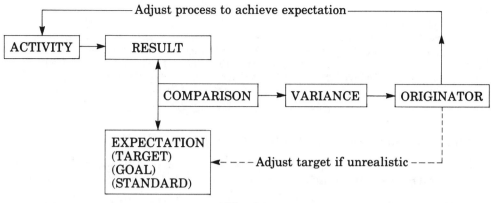

Fig. 6.1

Illustration

The management services department is required to print 60,600 copies of the House Magazine (Target). It assumes print wastage of 1%. Enough paper for 60,000 copies is ordered and the print run is executed. *Actual* wastage is 3%, resulting in a shortage of 1200 copies (Variance). In view of the high cost of printing only 1200 copies, it is decided that no further *action* is taken. If the shortage had been 10% a further run might have been ordered.

A series of events which are similar to each other occur in a plan. The plan involves an activity which for control purposes is divided into a number of stages or subsidiary goals. These are usually divisions of time – e.g. an annual plan has twelve monthly control periods. Whilst time divisions are traditional and by far the most popular, they are often very arbitrary and sub-divisions based on a fraction of the ultimate objective may make more sense.

If one of the branch objectives was to "increase deposits by 6% within 12 months". The action plan with the control information for a period may look like this:

Period	Target Deposit £ '000	Actual	Variance
0	1,000	1,011	11
1	1,006		
2	1,012		
3	1,035		
4	1,045		
5	1,050		
6	1,060		

In period one the performance has exceeded expectation. The branch manager then has to decide whether to maintain the target for periods 1 and 2 combined, which is very easy to achieve, or whether to maintain the original target for period 2 alone, which was an increase of (1012–1006) = £6000, making the target for the end of period 2 £1,017,000.

In continuous processes the "expectation" is that the output should be within a range of values. If the output falls below the minimum or rises above the maximum, the process is adjusted to rectify the position.

Illustration

Space heating is controlled as described above. A thermostat is set to a nominal temperature, say 20°C. The thermostat contains a thermo-couple which measures the temperature at a key position. If the temperature drops below 18°C the heat input will be increased, if it rises above 22°C it will be reduced. 18° – 22° is the target range.

Evaluation and Validation

In many situations there are three aspects to control:

(a) *Progress* towards the goal and achievement of performance levels. The two control examples just described deal with this aspect of control.

(b) *Evaluation* of the activity. If trends show that there is a possibility that the target will not be achieved, the question must be asked whether the most suitable plan was chosen, or whether an alternative plan is more likely to achieve the target. Similarly if a target performance is rarely met, the operating process should be evaluated.

(c) *Validation* of the target itself is also necessary. It is not unusual for mistakes to be made in the target, or for tolerance to be too narrow. Such factors may be the sole reason for apparent underperformance. Even if the targets or performance-levels are regularly met, they should be regularly validated to assess whether their contribution to higher level objectives is appropriate.

REQUIREMENTS OF A GOOD CONTROL SYSTEM

(1) SATISFACTORY STANDARDS

The importance of setting satisfactory standards has already been stressed in Chapter 5 in respect of planning and target setting. For control purposes standards must be:

(a) relevant
(b) measurable
(c) realistic

Relevance

As has previously been emphasised, the purpose of all management activities is ultimately to improve the economic performance of an enterprise, or to help in achieving corporate objectives. Control activities are no exception. It must also be borne in mind that the control processes – measuring performance, comparing performance with expectation, recording and reporting variances, and taking corrective action – all cost money – i.e.

there is a cost involved in control. The cost of unnecessary or badly designed controls may well exceed any benefits or savings. Moreover they may actually inhibit the company from optimising its performance.

> Controls to avoid bad debts on personal accounts could easily be tightened to reduce bad debts, but the loss of profit on the creditworthy customers who would be lost by such procedures would outweigh the saving in bad debts.

80/20 Rule

It has been found that in general 80% of the costs of any operation is caused by 20% of the activities. Conversely this means that 80% of the activities only involve 20% of the cost, and most of these activities do not justify individual controls.

Illustration

> Branch cleaning materials, or the heating oil requirements, are insignificant in relation to total branch running costs. Controls on these are therefore irrelevant to the objectives of the branch. Those costs will be included in the branch operating budget.

It is necessary to emphasise relevance of controls, because often irrelevant controls, such as control of electricity for lighting and heating, are much easier to apply, than important controls such as bad debts. They therefore offer an apparently easy way for centralised management information departments to enhance their prestige and power, while in reality they misdirect scarce management resources to the wrong areas.

Controls should thus be focused on the Key Results areas described in Chapter 5.

Measurement

The activities which are easiest to control are those which can be expressed in terms of money costs or other numerical variables. Much effort has been expended in developing quantitative measures of productivity, organisational health, managerial performance, quality of service, and other qualitative activities. This makes control much more effective. It is however not possible to quantify everything. Both grading and direct comparison, which are described in Chapter 5 are acceptable ways of measuring, provided the standards and grades are unambiguously defined, and proper training is given both for measuring and understanding of variances.

Spurious accuracy is a common error which results in excessive control costs.

Realism

«Target Setting, Ch. 5, p. 115»

It was seen in the description of target setting that standards must be attainable from a motivational point of view. It is equally important from the point of view of minimising the cost of control.

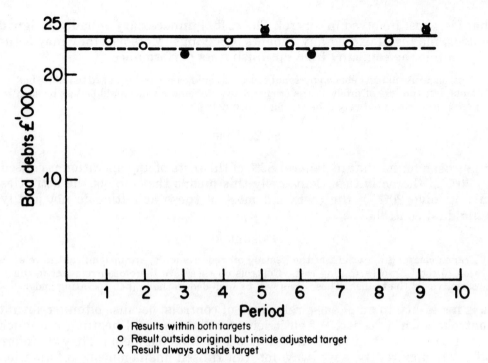

Fig. 6.2 Effect of target adjustment on variance frequency

Illustration

In Fig. 6.2, if the maximum for bad debts is set at £23,000 the results are unsatisfactory in all except two months. In each of the unsatisfactory months a variance has to be reported, an investigation carried out, and recommendations for improvements made. It may well be that the bad debt target is unrealistic in the prevailing circumstances. By altering the target to £24,000 there is no change in the actual bad debts, but not only is the cost of reporting and investigation reduced, but the manager has much more incentive to keep within the limit because he can see that it is possible.

Tolerances

The tolerance attached to any standard should always be clearly indicated, unless the standard is an upper or lower limit. Tolerances can be positive or negative, or each way.

Illustration

The percentage of funds lent to small business by a bank is set at 12% of the total. The actual percentages are shown in Fig. 6.3 by means of dots. The two solid lines represent a tolerance of ± 0.5%. About half the results are outside the limits set. If a more realistic tolerance of ± 1.0%, as represented by the broken lines, is adopted, there would have been no variances at all.

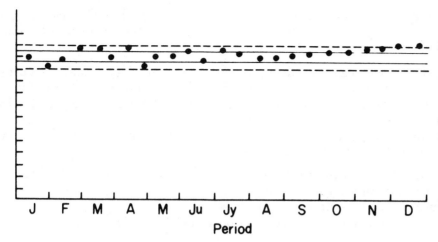

Fig. 6.3 Effect of wider tolerance on variance frequency

(2) TIMELINESS

Finding out why results were unsatisfactory and where to attribute blame is very secondary to the prime purpose of controls, which is to make quite sure that objectives, plans and performance standards *are* reached in the first place. To this end variances must be reported early in the process so that corrective action can be taken before a process is completed. The review stages of MbO are an example of the application of timeliness. It is incorrect to sacrifice timeliness for excessive accuracy, which may not be relevant to the control process.

The best way of preventing failures is to monitor "trends". By doing so it is often possible to predict that tolerances will be exceeded at some time in the future. Corrective action can then be taken before the unsatisfactory position is reached. Figure 6.3 is a clear example of how a trend could be identified. Corrective action should be taken in the third quarter to avoid lending to small businesses rising above 13%.

(3) RELIABILITY

Control information must be reliable. Investigations of variances are time consuming and often cause considerable worry and stress to those concerned. If the variances turn out to be merely mistakes or miscalculations in the control process, resentment is created towards the control departments. Perhaps worse, future reports may be disbelieved, and investigation and corrective action held back until much more damage has been done.

(4) FEED-BACK PRESENTATION

Ideal control information is specific and concentrates on variances. It goes only to the manager directly concerned and to his superior. A limited amount of background information, e.g. comparative figures for other departments or previous periods, may enhance the value of the information provided.

One of the draw-backs of modern information technology is that data processing equipment is capable of churning out large quantities of standardised information cheaply and quickly. It is actually cheaper and easier to circulate this computer output widely to all those who *might* have an interest, rather than provide more selective control information. It must however be remembered that excessive data will:

- distract attention from essentials;
- absorb valuable management time;
- reduce attention paid to control reports;
- cause errors when managers try to extract key information.

METHODS OF CONTROL
VISUAL CONTROL

While there are many sophisticated methods, it must not be forgotten that simple methods may be extremely effective. Visual Control is particularly useful for monitoring the behaviour, attitude and appearance of personnel, but standards of tidiness and cleanliness of offices, and quality of service are probably better controlled in this way than in any other. The requirement of having a proper standard must however not be neglected.

Illustration

Continuous Visual Control
A manager in an open plan office can monitor work load continuously.

Periodic Visual Control
The property department sends a representative twice-yearly to each branch to check decorative standards and cleanliness of areas to which the public have access.

CONTROL BY EXCEPTION

The idea behind control by exception is that managers should assume that activities are going to plan unless there is evidence to the contrary. It is part of the concept of "Management by Exception". Management by Exception is probably the most universally accepted management concept, and one of the least practised. In control terms it requires:

(a) *confidence* in the reliability and responsibility of their subordinates which few managers have;

(b) thorough *training* of subordinates, including making them aware of the importance of reporting trends and deviations, and of the key results areas;

(c) a *prompt and reliable reporting system* from associated departments.

Illustration

Attendance records are a common example of control which is conventionally exercised by some form of "signing in" of staff. Effectively this means that the attendance of each staff member is recorded daily. Control by exception *assumes* that each member of staff is in attendance. It is only *absence* which is recorded. This requires the immediate supervisor to record absences daily and send a weekly report to the personnel department. This method has the added advantage of directing the attention of the supervisor to the absence.

AUTOMATIC CONTROL

In automatic control a predetermined corrective action is immediately triggered if the completion of a process falls outside the accepted tolerances. There may be a number of alternative corrective actions, which will be automatically selected according to the type or size or variance. Automatic Control can be effected by humans, or mechanised. Due to advances in technology mechanised automatic control is more and more common, but it should be remembered that the automation lies in the inevitability of the corrective action, not in the means of achieving the correction. Mechanised controls are more reliable, but human ones more flexible.

Illustration

"Manual" automatic control
A wrongly made out cash cheque is automatically rejected by the cashier. He has the choice of a refusal to pay, or accepting an amendment.

Mechanised automatic control
If a Cashcard is presented to an Automated Teller machine, the balance on the customer's account is checked. If it is insufficient the card and the cash request are automatically rejected.

CONTROL BY MOTIVATION

Control is always necessary because managers are responsible for the actions of their subordinates and cannot rely on the subordinates to make absolutely certain that objectives are achieved and plans kept to. If it were possible for the objective of the department or firm to mirror the personal objectives of staff exactly, the need for imposed controls would be greatly reduced. This can be achieved in some instance by involving the staff in the decision making and objective-setting process. The staff is then committed to the shared objectives. The control system only needs to supply information which is otherwise not available to the people controlling their own progress.

Another method is to relate a person's reward to how well he performs. MbO may use this idea, as does payment by commission. One of the problems of MbO or other payments by results methods, is that they only apply to performance which is independent of the actions of others. This situation is not

138   THE NATURE OF MANAGEMENT

often found in modern businesses. It is more likely to apply to team working.
A second problem is that unless the reward is clearly tied to well defined
Key Results areas the efforts of the person concerned may be misdirected.

Illustration

In some banks the branch managers get commission on any insurance business they
bring in. The idea is that it encourages them to sell a service which many would not
regard as part of their job. There is an immediate danger that the income this might
generate might cause some manager to over-concentrate on selling insurance at the
expense of the bank's mainstream business.

«Ch. 5, pp. 113, 114»
«Ch. 7»
«Ch. 15»

BUDGETARY CONTROL

In the last chapter the importance of planning as a management technique
was investigated. Planning is particularly useful and necessary where
changes are involved. In the many cases where there is no significant
change from one year to the next, the preparation of a new plan each period
may be unjustified. When there is a plan it provides the standard against
which performance can be measured. In the absence of a plan control can be
maintained by establishing a budget instead. A budget is defined as the
monetary implication of management activity. An operating budget is the
money required for the operation of the department concerned. The
activities have to be analysed and the cost of each activity assessed. In the
type of stable department being considered, this information is normally
available from current and recent records. They are usually divided into
significant cost areas. A budget for a forthcoming period is prepared by
modifying past expenditure in the light of increases (or decreases) in
expected costs. This is a much simpler, quicker and cheaper way of establishing standards than a detailed plan. If each cost area is sufficiently wide,
there should be sufficient flexibility to compensate for minor demand or cost
fluctuations during the period.

If the budgeting process is not properly managed there is a risk that managers will claim for increases in demand and costs, and suppress possible
drops in demand. There is also no incentive to reduce costs. Budgets can
easily become inflated over a period of years.

Zero budgeting is an alternative in which each activity is costed from
scratch at the beginning of a period, completely ignoring the expenditure in
previous periods. While it is more time consuming to determine a zero based
budget, the risk of steadily rising costs is reduced.

Because budgets are measured in financial terms, the information which
has to be gathered for budgetary control purposes can be handled by the
normal accounting facilities. Budgetary control is therefore relatively
simple and cheap. Deviations can be detected quickly, permitting rapid
feedback for the responsible manager to take corrective action.

Secondary benefits of the budgetary control process are that the discussions in which managers are involved when budgets are set, improve general co-ordination. The information gleaned during the process is also useful for future planning, and can form the basis of performance related reward systems.

It also provides a common yardstick for comparing the effectiveness of control in departments with widely differing activities, and for controlling waste.

«Decision Making, Ch. 5, pp. 108–113»

DIARY CARDS

This simple planning and control method consists of cards filed in date order, each card carrying a reminder of an event which should occur at that date. When the date arrives, the clerk responsible takes out all the cards for the date. Either he takes action himself, or issues a reminder to the person due to take action. For routine repetitive events, diary cards have largely been superseded by data processing equipment. They are still a very useful technique for non-routine events. As a control technique a diary card system is only as reliable as the clerk in charge of it.

GANTT CHARTS

These planning and control charts are named after H. L. Gantt (1861–1919). They are graphical recording systems which show the relationship of events against each other and against the relevant time or planning period. These large scale charts are normally wall mounted and are nowadays available in a variety of constructions, using cardboard strips, or plastic or magnetic markers. By erasing or removing planned activities from the chart, those which are outstanding are highlighted. Date cursors are often used to indicate imminent events.

NETWORK ANALYSIS

Network analysis is the generic term which applies to a number of well known planning and control techniques. CPM (Critical Path Method) and PERT (Programme Evaluation Review Technique) were both developed in the late 1950s in the USA and have been succeeded by a number of variations. They are all designed to manage "once and for all" projects. They all depend on identifying these interdependent activities within the project, which are critical in determining the minimum cost or time for the project. Small projects can be handled manually, while computer programs are available for large projects. For control purposes the programs draw attention to activities which are falling behind and which may result in the completion of the project being delayed or the budgeted cost exceeded.

COMPUTERS IN CONTROL

The use of computers in place of diary cards and to monitor the progress of major projects has already been mentioned. In general the combination of data-storage and computing ability make computers very powerful tools for controlling large numbers of repetitive events.

Standards are programmed into the computer. If sufficiently large computers are available, these standards may be complete operating plans.

Actual performance figures are keyed in, either from management information supplied or by on-line connection with the process itself.

The computer is able to make virtually instantaneous comparisons between actual performance and the standard.

Action necessary as a result of the performance may be programmed into the machine, or control information can be supplied to management.

Illustration

As a loan is made, all relevant details including repayment terms can be input into the computer's data store. As each interest payment becomes due, the computer compares the actual payment with that required. If the payment is not made a print-out is produced in the form of a reminder to the customer. A copy of the print-out is despatched to the manager responsible for the loan as control information.

«Personnel Control, Ch. 12, p. 250»

PROBLEMS OF CONTROL

Common defects in control systems can be summarised as follows:

Lateness of control reports (whether verbal, written or printout).

Inclusion of *irrelevant* information in reports.

Inclusion of *too much* information in reports.

Suppression of information, usually by subordinates fearful of the consequences of mistakes.

Hidden judgements occur when a set of information is missing. In order to avoid delays the compiler may estimate what the missing figures are likely to be. This is acceptable (if speed is more important than accuracy) provided the recipient of the report is made aware of the estimate and the possible error it may cause. Badly written or defaced vouchers may cause similar problems.

Misinterpretation of the system by people supplying, evaluating, or receiving information.

Misdirection of management effort due to controls on non-essential areas.

Excessive frequency of control reports is likely to cause people to disregard them.

Excessive cost of the control system.

Budgets which are used to put pressure on staff to reduce costs cause resistance, lack of co-operation and possible alienation.

There is also a danger that budgets focus on activities which are easy to measure rather than those essential to the business. This will irritate and demotivate the staff.

Feedback information may be confusing and overload the recipients with unimportant detail.

If budgets are based on past expenditure instead of planned needs, there is a risk of overspending.

Practice Exercises

(1) Make a plan for your activities at work, or at home, using all the steps in the planning process.

(2) Identify the key results areas in your work.

(3) Do you know what level of performance is expected of you in your key results areas?

(4) Formulate an appropriate target or performance standard in one of your activities, paying particular regard to making it specific and measurable.

(5) How frequently should the performance be checked or how much time should you have to reach your target?

(6) Select activities at work, at home, or elsewhere which would lend themselves to visual or automatic control.

From Chapter 6 you should have learnt:

The difference between corporate, management and operating plans.

The meaning and use of budgets.

The meaning of key results areas.

The steps in the planning process.

The essential characteristics of a good target and performance standard.

How to draw a diagram of a closed-loop feed-back system.

The requirements for good controls.

Common faults in control systems.

The meaning of budgetary control
            control by exception
            control by motivation.

Section B

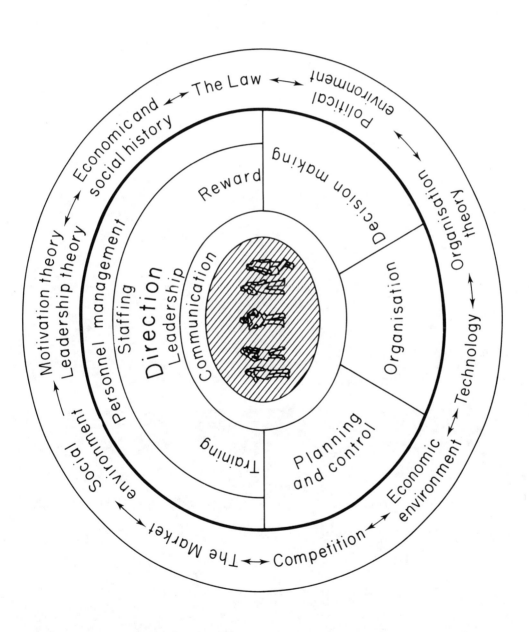

Chapter 7

The Nature of People

"Personnel" are people, personnel management is people management, and people are first and foremost individuals. The study of how individuals behave is therefore central to a study of personnel management. We shall first consider the individual on his own and in twos and then people in "groups".

SIMILARITY OF PEOPLE

Common factors in human behaviour which may be identified may include concepts such as selfishness, consideration for others, laziness, and creativeness which appear to be contradictory. Researches into the common factors have produced three major ideas: Causality, directedness and motivation.

(1) *Causality*. This is the idea that human behaviour is caused, just as physical objects only move or change due to outside forces. The main forces acting on people are hereditary and environmental.

(2) *Directedness* is the idea that in addition to being "caused" activity is also pointed towards something, i.e. that it is "goal directed".

(3) *Motivation* indicates that underlying behaviour one finds a "want", "need", or "drive".

This situation may be illustrated by the model in Fig. 7.1.

In considering this type of model it must be borne in mind that psychological goals, such as "status", or "security" are ephemeral and not easily defined, so that achieving a goal may itself stimulate an enlargement or variation of the goal, e.g. once a person has satisfied an ambition to visit Paris, a desire to visit Rome may take its place – or a promotion to grade 3 may stimulate the ambition to get to grade 4.

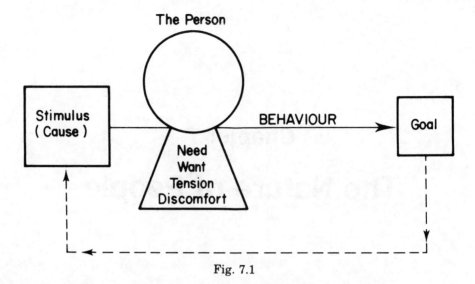

Fig. 7.1

DIFFERENCES BETWEEN PEOPLE

People are born with simple physical needs – e.g. for warmth and liquid food. These become more complex and wide ranging and are soon followed by "social" and "egotistical" needs both of which are psychological as opposed to physical. The psychological needs may be thought of as largely the results of:

(a) physical needs
(b) the nervous system of the physical body
(c) dependency on other people.

The dependency on other people causes differences in future behaviour in addition to those inherent in the physical makeup of the person. If a parent's behaviour satisfies a child it will become secure and more socially inclined, whereas if a parent's behaviour or other factor frustrates a child it becomes insecure, hostile and its egotistic needs are accentuated.

Even in later life people depend on others, and how this dependence is rewarded affects the person's behaviour.

A new recruit to a company will feel strange and nervous when he first starts work in a department. If he is ignored by the existing staff and expected to find his own way around; if, when he requests guidance, he is referred to the supervisor or told "I don't know", or "that is not my responsibility", he will (assuming he does not leave) also adopt a self centred attitude to his work. If, however, he is welcomed into the department, introduced to everybody and helped at all stages in his work until he settles down, he will become an equally helpful and co-operative team member. In effect the recruit's future behaviour pattern has been shaped by his environment, i.e. *the attitude of others towards him.*

«*Induction Training, Ch. 14, p. 281*»

PERCEPTION

There is a difference in the way different persons see things. This applies even to physical objects and much more so to "facts" or other events. People will most quickly and clearly perceive things which appear to be aids to satisfying one's needs. Things which look like obstacles, even if seen, may be suppressed mentally so that they appear not to have been seen at all. By denying obstacles people hope they will vanish. They will probably only be faced if they become a danger to satisfying one's need.

Among things perceived are other people and the person itself. The person tries to manipulate his or her own image to show other people what he or she would like to be. The skill with which a person can put across how he wants to be seen depends on his ability to judge audience reaction. The difficulty in this is that the audience is acting too.

«Motivation, Ch. 8, pp. 170–172»
«Management of Change, Ch. 8, p. 181»
«Communication, Ch. 9, p. 188»
«Delegation, Ch. 10, p. 204»

FRUSTRATION

Frustration is important even if it is a feeling rather than a fact. It may arise out of an inability to achieve a goal, or out of "conflict", either between two equally attractive goals, or between two equally unattractive decisions or courses of action.

The inability to achieve a goal leads to frustration primarily in those instances where it affects the person's well being – i.e. when the goal affects oneself.

The normal reaction to frustration is *aggression*. This will be directed against the self if the person has a history of failure and is unsure of himself, and against others if the person is confident of his own ability. A person is more likely to avoid this type of frustration if their assessment of their own abilities is realistic.

Other reactions to frustration are:

(a) *resignation* – the person loses interest in the activity or goal which he is pursuing and his performance suffers as a result;

(b) *regression* – this is an extreme reaction which involves the person reverting to a previous stage in their development, lowering their sights and probably becoming difficult to deal with;

(c) *sublimation* – re-direction of energies to alternative goals. This is the most constructive way of dealing with goal conflicts, which are inevitable in any real-life situation.

The degree of frustration experienced by individuals will differ according to their present circumstances, their heredity, and their environmental experience. Their reaction to frustration, which will again vary according to the same factors, will differentiate them further from other individuals.

Illustration

A situation which inevitably causes frustration and which occurs at some stage in almost everyone's lives is when one is unable to achieve a desired promotion. This may be simply due to inaccurate manpower planning if too many people of equal calibre are competing for a small number of senior posts. Not all of them *can* achieve their goals.

Outwardly Turned Agression

Some of those frustrated will have had fast moving careers and success at every stage. They will be confident of their own ability and they will not accept this barrier to their progress. They will actively pursue their goal of increased seniority by applying for posts outside the company, and leaving at the earliest opportunity.

Inwardly Turned Agression

For others the same situation, the "failure" to gain promotion, may be only one incident in a succession of failures to achieve goals. The other incidents may be in totally different fields, e.g. in marital relations, politics, sport or other leisure pursuits. These persons will blame themselves for mistakes and inadequacies, they will become unsure of themselves, double-check all their work and as a result become bogged down and neglect duties which can be postponed. They will fail to make decisions which are not clear cut, and resist change because they are doubtful of being able to handle new situations successfully.

Regression

Inwardly turned agression may turn into depression and in extreme cases to regression. In this condition the person is no longer capable of coping with his previously successful job. He "regresses" to an earlier stage in his career. In his relations with colleagues and subordinates he becomes "childish" – refusing to pass on communications or even to talk to some people, misusing his authority by making petty rules, or making arbitrary decisions. This condition is pathological and may require medical intervention.

Resignation and Sublimation

In practice a proportion of the staff in large organisations have reached a point in their careers where they no longer expect promotion. They "resign themselves" to this and often do no more than the minimum required to prevent them losing their jobs. The well balanced individual uses any extra energy for pursuing other interests. This activity is what is known as sublimation.

Good management tries to harness some of this surplus energy for the firm by increasing job interest or offering opportunities in areas such as training, project work or research.

PERSONALITY CHARACTERISTICS

What are individuals really like? This has been a fascinating problem for ordinary people as well as for psychiatrists and those concerned with occupational guidance and personnel selections. As a result of their heredity and environment people become very complex and the need for a systematic approach to assessing their personalities becomes essential.

FRASER'S ANALYSIS OF PERSONALITY CHARACTERISTICS

One of the approaches most useful from the personnel manager's point of view was developed by A. Munro Fraser, who based his analysis on the aspect of each characteristic which is statistically most common in a population and can therefore be regarded as "normal". Deviations from this "norm", in whatever direction, are by definition abnormal. Despite this, an "abnormal" characteristic may be relevant, and often essential, to particular working, and life, situations.

RODGERS' SEVEN-POINT PLAN

Another approach to the assessment of personality characteristics was developed by Professor A. Rodgers. He made a plan adopted by the National Institute of Industrial Psychology, as suitable for assessing the employment potential of individuals. This is more specifically directed to the purpose of personnel selection than Fraser's investigation into personality characteristics. The points were chosen to conform to four criteria:

(a) *To be relevant* in that they pin-point influences connected with occupational success or failure.

(b) *To be independent* so that they avoid overlapping assessments that would be wasteful.

(c) *To be assessable* in the circumstances in which the assessments usually have to be made.

(d) They should be few enough to keep the risks of hasty judgement to a minimum, but numerous enough to cover the ground adequately.

The seven points assessed under Rodgers' plan are:

(1) Physical Make-up

(a) *Has the person any defect of health or physique that may be of occupational importance.* The sooner this question is answered the better, because the answer to it may make further investigation a waste of time. However, a poor health record or apparent physical disability should not be judged without expert medical advice. There are also moral, and in some cases legal, obligations not to exclude people from employment for handicaps which may be irrelevant to a job or which can be overcome with some help from the employer.

(b) *How agreeable are the person's appearance, bearing and speech.* These are particularly relevant for occupations involving frequent direct contact with people – for example customers – on whose favourable attitude the future of the enterprise largely depends. Attention should be primarily given to enduring characteristics rather than remediable or temporary defects. In order to separate the above physical characteristics from concepts such as aptitude or disposition, assessment of them can be based on the impression which would be gained by looking at the person's photograph, passing them on the street, and hearing them on a telephone respectively.

(2) Attainments

(a) *Education* – Type and standard reached. Points which may be relevant include:

The type of school
Number of subjects studied
Number of examination subjects taken, failed and passed and what grade
The subjects in which the person is better or worse than other people
The best and worst subjects
Scholarship and prizes won
Nature of and attainment in further education
Extra-curricular activities and attainments in teams, clubs, etc.
Responsibilities undertaken

Supportive evidence of above from parents, teachers or others is very important.

(b) *Occupational training, experience and success.* The purpose of this section is to assess the person's current knowledge compared to what he can be expected to know, and his range and depth of experience in relation to what can be expected. All types of training – low or high grade, theoretical or practical, full or part time – are therefore relevant.

It is most important also to examine in detail the tasks, decisions, scope, and authority contained in the roles the person has filled, and the ease or difficulty which he found in dealing with them.

(3) General Intelligence

It is important, though difficult, to distinguish between a person's attainments and his "innate" intelligence. The same level of attainment may well be reached by persons of different intelligence level, by the expenditure of different amounts of time and effort.

This characteristic is most satisfactorily assessed by means of tests which attempt to eliminate previous knowledge and experience. They are very effective, but normally need to be administered by qualified assessors.

These intelligence tests give no indication as to the level of his intelligence at which a person normally operates. This can be assessed by comparing the person's achievements in real life compared to what could be expected from him on the basis of the tests.

The question arises of the relevance of "intelligence" in roles which a person is to occupy. It is a characteristic which indicates the person's learning ability and therefore is most relevant in situations subject to frequent innovation.

(4) Special Aptitudes

This does not mean "unusual competence" which may be a combination of intelligence and attainment. Special aptitudes may be regarded as supplementary talents, e.g. manual dexterity, musical, artistic, whose usefulness depends on the scope, level and effectiveness of the attainments and intelligence. The greater a person's attainments and intelligence the less important his special aptitudes. The special aptitudes become most important where the other basic abilities are low, and they are required in the role the person is expected to occupy.

There are a range of tests available for special aptitudes.

(5) Interests

The purpose of investigating this characteristic is to establish the type of activity in which a person's abilities may be most successfully employed.

It is important to find the real interests and eliminate:

(a) Declared interests which do not tally with actual behaviour.

(b) Genuine enthusiasms of short standing which may be based on false or inadequate ideas.

(c) Short-lived interests.

(d) Compensatory interest which may indicate a refusal to admit lack of competence.

The seven-point plan postulates a list of processes and proposes that a person's interests should be analysed to decide to which group he can be most suitably allocated. The processes are:

(a) Intellectual (mental)
(b) Practical – Constructional
(c) Physically active
(d) Social – i.e. involving some sort of relationship with other people.
(e) Artistic.

(6) Disposition

(a) *Acceptability to others*
This involves assessing how other people take to the person, how well he "fits in" and whether he will make a good member of a group.

(b) *The ability to influence others*
This is characterised by the weight which his opinions carry, whether other people take notice of what he says or does, and by how good he is at getting people to do what he wants.

(c) *Steadiness and Reliability*
The person's career record should indicate whether he pursues long range objectives in a determined way. It is also relevant to establish whether his future actions can be reliably anticipated.

(d) *Self-reliance*
This establishes the person's tendency to work things out for himself and manage with little supervision, as opposed to having to be watched, and helped, to decide on goals and to achieve them.

(7) Circumstances

The previous six points have dealt with a person's personal characteristics. These are to a large extent determined by his past environment and up-bringing. Similarly a person's future behaviour will be determined by the circumstances in which he finds himself. The opportunities and restraints imposed by family and economic factors must not be underestimated.

The circumstances to be considered include:

(a) *Financial circumstances*
(b) *Numbers and relationships within his family*
(c) *Occupation and income of relatives*

All these tend to be inter-related and affect, for instance, an individual's mobility, his ability to invest or to take risks, his attitude to salaries, bonuses, security of employment, and to various social, economic and political issues, and his interests and relationships with other people.

Rodgers' 7 points plan is a *guide* on which personalities assessments can be based. Managers assess personality for a specific purpose and only those characteristics relevant to this purpose need to be examined.

Illustration

Personality requirements for school leavers entering a clearing bank:

Physical Make-up

Pleasant appearance; articulate; speech free from impediment.

Attainments

Academic success at the General Certificate of Education. (Minimum four at O-level.)

Special Aptitudes

Neatness
Speed and accuracy at clerical work
Concentration

Interests

Practical
Social

Disposition

Helpful manner
Honest
Integrity

«Selection, Ch. 13, p. 269»

PEOPLE TWO AT A TIME

There are many situations where a person has to deal with another. These situations involve:

interdependence
relationships
communication.

INTERDEPENDENCE AND RELATIONSHIPS

These normally involve influencing the partner in the transaction. Influence can be exerted in the form of:

(a) *Authority* – this may be managerial, or based on expertise or experience.

(b) *Manipulation* – by the use of the other person's needs or desires to achieve the goals of the originator.

(c) *Collaboration* – the use of the fact that a number of individuals acting in unison may be able to achieve better results for each one of them separately than they would on their own.

(d) *Money incentives* – Money or its equivalent can be used to influence another individual.

All the above will be dealt with more extensively later in this book.

GROUP PSYCHOLOGY

Arising out of the Hawthorne Experiments and other work, it has been discovered that the behavior of groups of people differs from that of people individually and in twos.

THE HAWTHORNE EXPERIMENTS

The Hawthorne experiments were carried out under the auspices of Elton Mayo at the Western Electric Company near Chicago from 1924 to 1932.

The initial experiment was a study to determine the effect of lighting levels on output. Two groups were studied. In one the level of lighting was gradually built up over a period. An increase of output was noted for each improvement in lighting. The other group was used as a control, with the lighting being kept at the same level. The investigators were astonished to find that despite this the output of the control group rose at about the same rate.

As a result the effect of reduced lighting and random variations was tested. In each test further improvements in output were recorded.

Relay Assembly Room

The company engaged consultants to investigate these phenomena further. The relay assembly room was organised so that five girls worked with a supervisor who was a trained psychologist. Based on the girls' previous output various techniques for increasing the output were assessed. These were:

 (i) Group piece-work. This resulted in an increase of output.

(ii) Increases in and variations of rest periods. These resulted in an increase of output.

(iii) Shortening the working hours. This resulted in an increased rate of output.

(iv) Returning to the original conditions. This resulted in a further increase in output!

Additional Experiments

Experiments were carried out on other test groups to determine the effect of physical separation of the girls from each other and of individual as opposed to group bonuses. In each case output increases were also achieved.

It was concluded from these experiments that the output increases were the result of the formation of primary work groups, rather than of the alternative working conditions.

Bank Wiring Operations Room

This room consisted of nine wiremen, three solder men, two inspectors reporting to specialist managers and one part-time supervisor.

In analysing the work of this room initially it was found that output was low, the records kept were meaningless, untrue bonus claims were being made, and the quality of the work varied.

Experiments similar to those in the relay assembly rooms resulted in no output increases. It was found that the output was kept down by organised work limitation controlled by unofficial leaders.

Interview Programme

Over a period of three years 20,000 employees were interviewed for half-an-hour each to assess their motivation. The conclusions emphasised the importance of:

(a) the social role of the supervisor;
(b) intangible factors in motivation;
(c) attitudes rather than facts.

PRIMARY GROUPS

Apart from being the most extensive investigations ever carried out, the main effect of the Hawthorne experiments was the birth of the Social Man Theory, and the Human Relations School of Management. These drew attention to primary groups, on which much work has been done since.

A primary group is defined as a "well integrated group working towards a common goal". Groups are called segmented if the members have differing goals, incompatible attitudes, or are in conflict with each other for any reason.

TYPES OF PRIMARY GROUPS

Primary groups can exist at several different levels:

(1) small social groups;
(2) common job groups;
(3) large common interest groups;
(4) the total organisation comprising a number of interlocking groups.

They may be classified as:

social	(1)
technological	(2)
socio-technological	(3) and (4)

BASIS OF PRIMARY GROUPS

The reason for the existence of primary groups is firstly the nature of human beings as a society based on social rather than individual attitudes, and secondly in the assistance a group provides to the individual in achieving his desires, which include Status, Prestige and Power.

Dependence

The social basis for society is rooted in the concept of "dependence". The human being's potential is such that its full achievement can only be obtained with the help of others. A person is dependent on others not only for training and help with tasks which are outside his ability, but also for advice, the opportunity to share worries and pleasure, the opportunity to play games, sexual satisfaction and companionship.

Power

Power may be regarded as the opposite of helplessness. Many individuals are frustrated by their real or imagined helplessness in dealing with the many problems facing them in the working environment. Grouping themselves with others facing the same problems will not only share the burden, but actually reduce the helplessness and often enable the group to overcome the problems.

Status

Prestige and "Standing" are important human desires. They are associated with success. The less successful an individual is the more he gains from being associated with a successful group. Yet even very successful people like to improve their standing even further by belonging to high status groups, such as the peerage.

Loyalty

Another intangible human desire is loyalty to a person or cause. Loyalty must have a readily identifiable target which is within the comprehension of the individual. It used to have its outlet towards simple causes such as patriotism or the owner of an employee's business. The combination of a higher level of education and a much more complex social system has redirected loyalty towards a wide range of possible groups with which an individual may be associated. The problem of conflicting loyalties imposes a severe strain on many people's emotional balance.

«Trade Unions, Ch. 16, p. 306»

CHARACTERISTICS OF PRIMARY GROUPS

For a primary group to be well integrated it should ideally possess the following characteristics:

Cohesiveness   i.e. the members should have the same personal objectives.

Common objective i.e. the group objective must be clear.

Hedonic tone   i.e. the individuals must like each other.

Attitudes   to the objectives, tasks and decisions should be alike.

Flexibility   i.e. the organisation of the group and its attitudes must be able to adjust to changing situations.

Loyalty   members must be prepared to subordinate their own to the group's objectives.

Openness   members must be able to express their views and be prepared to accept criticism.

In practice it is unlikely that there will be many groups possessing all these characteristics, but even without several of them groups may still be well integrated.

GROUP MANIFESTATION

There are a number of ways in which the existence of informal or formal groups can be recognised:

(a) *Occupational language*
    This is particularly strong in technological groups, i.e. those which have a science, skill or even job in common. It is however also applicable to much wider groups, examples being dialects, and also terminology characteristic of public school education.

(b) *Ceremonies and Rituals*

These are common to all types of group. Initiation rites are common in religious and professional groups and apprenticeships. Many types of ceremonial are used to intensify the loyalty of members of religious, national, military and other groups. Rituals are the most common manifestation ranging from formal orders of precedence, national occasions, through the various procedures prevalent among the managers of a business to the ritual of making coffee or having birthday celebrations in small social primary groups.

(c) *Myths and Beliefs*

Are again very prevalent. At international level characteristics are attributed to certain peoples. People from different parts of a country are often credited with special abilities or disabilities. Specialist groups in particular have strong views on methods and premises which are frequently based on tradition rather than fact. The more isolated a group is, e.g. sailors and actors, the more important their "lore".

(d) *The Majority Effect*

Particularly among people of average or below average motivation and balance there is a strong desire not to be differentiated from the group. Thus a "follow my leader" attitude arises which is most evident in voting by a show of hands. S. E. Asch has carried out experiments showing that individuals were prepared to reverse logical and correct judgements to avoid being in a minority.

It is this majority effect which results in the creation of *group-norms*. In the first place a group exerts, probably without individual members being aware of it, psychological pressure on a member to conform to accepted standards of behaviour or levels of performance. Most members are only too anxious to conform. If they do not, the remaining members, first informally as individuals and later formally as a group, will try to persuade the dissident to change his ways. If necessary more positive action will be taken to force him to toe the line.

THE IMPORTANCE OF PRIMARY GROUPS

In modern society the disciplinary power of a well integrated group is much more effective than that of managers, and is probably the most potent force for maintaining high standards of behaviour, quality and output.

The importance of managing groups well is primarily based on this benefit, but one must also be aware of the damage caused by antagonising groups. If management behaves unfairly or irresponsibly, makes unreasonable demands on employees – e.g. by unattainable objectives, or tries to introduce change without consultation, an existing loyal group may become an adversary. A common cause or "enemy" may also create a new group from people not yet organised.

Once an antagonistic group have agreed among themselves a low performance norm, or a refusal to adapt to change, management becomes virtually powerless. It is unfortunately much easier and quicker to antagonise a group, than to change a hostile group to a loyal one.

The group effect is just as applicable to people who are not members of formal Trade Unions, as to those who are.

SOCIOMETRY

This scientific approach analyses the structure and development of groups. it is based on the premise that individuals can have three types of personal attitudes to other individuals:

Attraction
Repulsion
Indifference.

This results in five possible types of small primary groups:

(i) *Mutual Choice Groups*
Here the group is made up of a number of smaller nuclei, usually of two or three people, who are mutual "friends".

(ii) *Non-Mutual Chains*
In these the person to whom an individual is attracted is indifferent to that individual, and this situation is repeated a number of times, thus:

Fig. 7.2 Interpersonal relations in a "non-mutual" chain group.

NB In the two first types informal leadership may be assigned to different people in different situations.

(iii) *Star Formation*
When one individual is popular with all the rest, he becomes known as a star, and is likely to become the informal leader of the group.

(iv) *Powerful Star Formation*
In large groups having several "stars", a person popular with all the stars, becomes a powerful star.

(v) Any of the above groupings may have within them isolated individuals to whom the attitude of the group is repulsion or indifference. These individuals often become the cause of conflict or create a variety of problems.

MANAGEMENT OF GROUPS

In the management of human resources it is vital to recognise the existence and effect of groups. While it may be critical to avoid the problems of groups when they become antagonistic, the existence of groups is in fact of immense help to a manager in organising and directing an enterprise. This occurs mainly in motivation and direction.

DIRECTION

Particularly in a large organisation, the task of directing great numbers of individuals becomes very onerous. If this direction can be applied to groups the task becomes correspondingly smaller – e.g. *1200* individuals become 100 groups. The way this works in practice is that the task is delegated to the group. Where it may be necessary to ask 12 people to work overtime, eight of which want to, and four do not, the task of persuading the minority is left to the group, which is able to get the desired result not by pressure, but by the need of the individual to conform.

MOTIVATION

One of the problems of modern technology is that specialisation makes it very difficult for the individual, particularly at operator level, to obtain satisfaction from producing an identifiable product or service. By combining the effort of a number of operators it is often possible to create a group with an identifiable end product.

Loyalty to the group, the desire to improve its status and its power, all help it to perform more effectively provided it is set realistic objectives.

ORGANISING GROUPS

To achieve better direction and motivation it is necessary for the manager to create and/or maintain well integrated groups. To do this he must:

Assess individuals and their relationships to each other.

Identify existing groups.

Identify "popular" individuals.

Identify "isolated" or unpopular individuals.

Develop organisational groupings which are suitable for the creation of primary groups, particularly in the design and layout of machinery, plant and facilities.

and facilities but also by grouping people with similar work. There is no "social" effect between people separated by more than about 40 metres.

«Fig. 3.3 p. 60»

It is common practice already to allow members of a group at least to have a say in choosing additional members.

Isolated or difficult individuals can either be allocated to particularly well integrated groups where they will be overruled, or grouped together and accepted as a problem group.

An important factor in establishing well integrated groups is a common background. If this does not already exist, it can be provided by training courses or a job transfer system.

Differing time schedules e.g. people on different shifts, or part-timers among full timers, make it difficult to integrate groups.

One very effective way of integrating people is to pressurise them or make unreasonable demands. This is obviously very undesirable because an antagonistic group will be created, whose power to obstruct may be very great.

TEAMS

It will be apparent from the above that a "group" is held together by psychological factors. A "team" on the other hand, is created by management to perform a task which is too large for one person. Teams do not necessarily become well integrated groups – e.g. when the task is a temporary one such as a fraud investigation. Research, design and construction projects are typically run by teams, and in many modern companies the role of the chief executive is filled by a management team.

In each case the team members are chosen for their different skills. A team does not necessarily have to have a leader, but if a team leader is required at any time the most suitable member will be chosen.

Leadership may pass from one team member to another if the experience or skill of the other person is more relevant at that time.

The most successful teams do not only have people with different skills and experience, but also with different personalities. Researches by Dr. M. Belbin based on work done at the Henley Staff College suggest that seven "roles" should be in a team. These are:

Chairman –	to co-ordinate the activities
Shaper –	to act as unofficial chairman
Ideas man –	to be creative and help solve problems
Critic –	to draw attention to draw-backs in ideas and to monitor progress.

Team worker –   to develop the team
Resource provider – to be the contact with the environment
Co-worker –   to implement the ideas etc.

Several of these roles can be performed by one person, but it is unsatisfactory to have several people attempting to fulfil roles such as that of the Chairman.

Illustration

(1) In international banking multinational companies are often serviced by "Account executives" who have total responsibility for an account. They have a back up team of researchers, analysts and clerical staff who accumulate, record and analyse the information required by the account executives.

(2) In Building Societies small branches work as a team. Most of the team members have skills and experience appropriate to several of the jobs in the branch. Some of them will do several jobs, others have a principal job but help out where needed.

«Induction, Ch. 14, p. 281»

TEAM CHARACTERISTICS

A team must have *defined objectives* which are accepted by all members.

The attitude of all members to the job should be the same.

It should be adaptable to a changing environmment.

It should be timely in its decision-making.

It should use communications intelligently.

It should use meetings constructively.

It should use constructive dissatisfaction by encouraging criticism and innovation.

New Members

In introducing new members to a team, apart from encouraging existing team members to take part in the selection, it is essential to explain to a new recruit the background, history, motivation and attitude of the team and its present members.

GROUP DEVELOPMENT

Group development is the process of integrating a number of differentiated people, more or less unknown to each other, into a cohesive team which has established customs and norms, and which operates successfully.

An understanding of Group Theory will help a manager to identify the condition of a group, to promote the group development, as well as ensuring that he does not impede its development. These requirements are most likely to arise either when the manager is setting up a new department, or when he is taking over an established team.

A simple model of group development contains four discrete phases:

(a) Forming   (c) Norming
(b) Storming   (d) Performing

(a) Forming

In this phase the members are anxious and uncertain. They are uncertain of their roles and their relationships to each other and the manager. Symptoms of this phase are that some members withdraw psychologically from the situation while others try to impress with their particular skills and talents.

It is very important for a manager to recognise this phase and be aware that many of the members will be relying on him to sort out problems of task allocation, procedure and internal relationships.

(b) Storming

In the second phase the individuals will show preference for various group or individual activities and will try aggressively to gain for themselves the roles they wish to play. This may show in open conflict between members, or in open or covert resentment towards each other and the leader; he may be blamed for non-intervention, yet have his ideas rejected.

It is particularly important for the leader to understand that this is an inevitable phase, but a passing one. He should monitor conflict and ensure that it is brought into the open and resolved, while at the same time emphasising firmly what the objectives and strategies of the group *should* be to meet company needs.

(c) Norming

When the members begin to realise that their behaviour does not make for a satisfactory working environment, they will start the third phase which involves agreeing, perhaps implicitly, how to allocate the work between members, what is expected of each one and how much the group can achieve. They will also establish group procedure and customs to which all will commit themselves. At this stage the manager should try to ensure that group norms and behaviour are, or become, compatible with other groups and functions of the enterprise.

(d) Performing

This is the final stage to which the group settles down to execute its task. The normal group "task" and "maintenance" functions begin and continue to operate, with members contributing to each according to their wishes and abilities, as accepted by the group in earlier phases. The manager's role in these two functions should also have been established, and must not be neglected, even if the group operates successfully without him for short periods.

It will be seen that an awareness of each development stage, how it will affect him, and what response is needed, will be of benefit to a manager.

Practice Exercises

(1) Ask a group of friends or colleagues to make a list of the five most interesting things in the room, or out of the window.

(2) When you come across a person behaving in an unusual manner, consider whether the person is showing signs of frustration.

(3) Assess yourself or a friend against the criteria in Rodgers' 7 point plan.

(4) When you use persuasion (for a colleague to join you for lunch or a friend for a disco) what form of influence/s are you using?

(5) List the things which make you put more effort into your work. (Or, those which *might* make you put in more effort.) Put them in order of importance.

(6) In a group of which you are a member (a team at work or sport, your family, church or club, your department or company), identify examples of:

    (a) common language, "in" words, jargon (anything outsiders will not understand);

    (b) ceremonies or rituals;

    (c) myths or beliefs;

    (d) the type of group formation;

    (e) whether there is a leader and if so, what is his function;

    (f) whether there is an isolated individual.

From Chapter 7 you should have learnt:

The importance of both heredity and the environment on the character of people.

The meaning of perception.

The meaning and causes of: frustration
                          aggression
                          resignation.

The seven points in Rodgers' Plan, their content and relevance to the type of business in which you are interested.

How one person can influence another.

The findings of the Hawthorne Experiments, including:
          the social role of managers
          intangibles in motivation
          attitudes as opposed to facts.

The types of primary groups and the bases on which they are founded.

The characteristics of well integrated primary groups.

The common types of group manifestations.

The types of group formations.

The steps in identifying and managing groups.

Team characteristics.

Tuckman's model for group development.

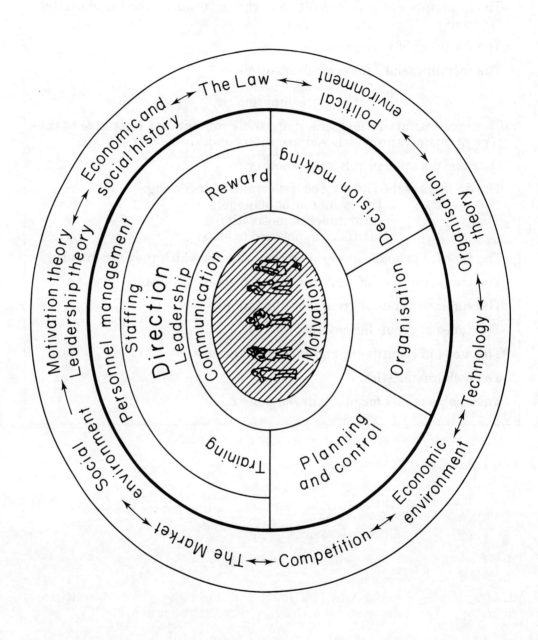

Chapter 8

Motivation Theories

Motivation can be interpreted as "why people do or do not do things". Some of the reasons why are too obvious to warrant investigation, e.g. response to a specific instruction or event, such as eating when hungry. Often the underlying reason for a given response is not obvious, such as eating when one is not hungry. The importance of "motivation" in management is the value of employees carrying out a range of tasks without constant instruction and supervision. This relieves the load on managers and reduces the number of managers required, and thus their cost.

McGREGOR'S THEORIES X & Y

One of the first examinations of motivation among operators found that managers made the following assumptions about their workforce:

(1) They are by nature indolent and work as little as possible.

(2) They lack ambition, dislike responsibility, prefer to be led.

(3) They are by nature "self-centred" and indifferent to group needs.

(4) They are by nature resistant to change.

(5) They are gullible, easily led by demagogues or activitists, and generally not very bright.

This was called Theory X by McGregor and this theory led to motivation by monetary reward (wages) backed up by threat of unemployment.

THEORY Y

Based on his own investigations and the findings of psychologists such as Fraser, McGregor argued that the following was more in line with reality:

(1) People are by *nature* motivated and it is only society and the working environment which frustrate their potential.

(2) People would like to contribute positively to the organisation of which they are members, if only they were given the opportunity.

(3) People will only follow leaders antagonistic to management when there are genuine, unrequited grievances or a lack of more positive leadership.
«D. McGregor, *Leadership Motivation*, MIT Press, 1966»

MASLOW'S HIERARCHY

Maslow tried to determine and classify the main "needs" of people and developed the hierarchy shown in Fig. 8.1 in a simple form. This provides a basis for understanding motivation.

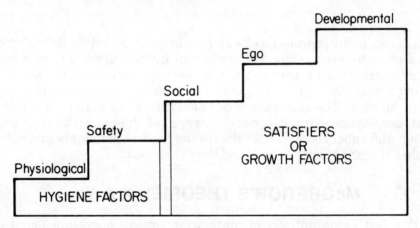

Fig. 8.1 Maslow's "Hierarchy of Needs"

PHYSIOLOGICAL NEEDS

These comprise the needs for food, clothing and shelter – satisfied by wages. Other needs are not generally regarded as important until at least the essentials at this level are satisfied.

SAFETY NEEDS

These include the desire for safety itself as well as being able to *rely* on food etc. In western industrial society these needs concern job security and reliability of income while working, sick, or retired.

SOCIAL NEEDS

This is the need for a person to belong, be loved by and accepted by others; first by their families and later by other primary groups.

EGO NEEDS

People need to have a firm, stable and high valuation of themselves and this must be confirmed by the esteem in which they are held by members of the group to which they belong. They must also be able to get confirmation of their status by being able to achieve the status symbols generally accepted by their peer groups.

SELF-ACTUALISATION

At this fifth level people are concerned with the development of their full potential. They are concerned with improving their knowledge, skills and activities both in and out of the working environment. Many people never reach this stage, although the number is increasing as extra leisure time is becoming available.

«A. H. Maslow, *Motivation and Personality*, Harper, 1954»

COMPARISON WITH McGREGOR

It will be noted that Maslow presupposed that individuals and society develop themselves. This agrees with Theory Y. According to Maslow:

(1) Motives of adults are highly complex and no single motive causes behaviour.

(2) Lower level needs must be at least partially satisfied before a higher level need is satisfied.

(3) A satisfied need no longer motivates. Another need or want will take its place.

(4) The higher level needs can be satisfied in many more ways than the lower ones.

THE TEXAS STUDIES

Myers identified two types of person, which he called "Maintenance" and "Motivation" Seekers.

The former give a conservative impression, are socially motivated and react sharply to outside influences. Their motivation, therefore, depends heavily on their managers and on group norms.

The Motivation Seekers look for personal responsibility. They are classified by McClelland as having high Achievement Needs.

ACHIEVEMENT MOTIVATION

McClelland identified three motives which compares with Maslow's higher ranking motives, *viz.*

- affiliation   = social
- power   = esteem
- achievement = self-actualisation

While Maslow postulates a progressive hierarchy, McClelland found that any of these three motives could be present without the others. He regards the last of these – called Achievement – as the most critical to economic success. People with high "achievement needs" respond best to moderate targets, and positive feed back confirming that the targets have been met.

«D. C. McClelland, *The Achieving Society*, Van Nostrand, 1961»

HERZBERG'S TWO FACTOR THEORY

Herzberg and his associates used semi-structured interviews to elicit from a large number of accountants and engineers the factors which:

a) made them like their work most – these were called SATISFIERS.

b) gave them cause for dissatisfaction – these were called HYGIENE FACTORS.

- achievement
- recognition
- nature of the work
- responsibility
- advancement

DISSATISFIERS

The factors listed most frequently as giving rise to dissatisfaction were:

salary   ineffective management policy
poor working conditions   unfair management policy

This list is called "hygiene" factors because meeting people's needs of this type leads to removal of dissatisfaction rather than to positive effort on their part. Later work suggests that in western industrialised countries these hygiene factors are similar to the two first levels of Maslow's Hierarchy. The important implication, which is born out by experience, is that increasing wages, and at a later stage, security of employment beyond what is *necessary* for physical and to some extent social and status needs, has no motivating value.

«Herzberg, Mauser and Snydeman, *The Motivation to Work*, Wiley, 1954»

EXPECTANCY THEORY

Expectancy Theory postulates that:

Level of Motivation = Valency $\times$ Expectancy

Valency is the extent to which the outcome of the activity and its success *matters* to the individual.

Expectancy is the individual's *expectation* of whether or not his efforts will succeed.

Vroom points out that for high motivation both parts of the formula must be high. If the individual is indifferent to the success of his efforts even the expectation of success will not create motivation. If he is hostile to the objective, motivation may even be negative – i.e. he may, probably unobtrusively, ensure failure. Similarly, motivation may be very low despite high valency, if the individual feels that the task is hopeless. The connection with "Identification" as described by Galbraith, and with "Achievement" as a motivator, may be noted.   «V. H. Vroom and E. I. Deci, *Management and Motivation*, Penguin, 1970»

Porter and Lawler felt that in addition to Valency and Expectancy the amount of *"Effort"* required to achieve the objective affects motivation – i.e. given that Valency and Expectancy are high motivation could be further improved by making the job easier – through better organisation, information or equipment.

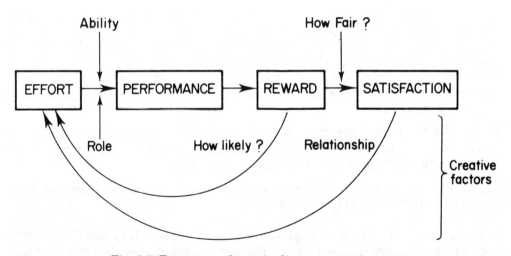

Fig. 8.2 Expectancy theory in diagrammatic form

A further important point, according to Porter and Lawler, is the *"role perception"* of the individual. This means:

(a) that the linkage between *Valency*, *Expectancy* and *Effort* must be reasonable; and

(b) that individuals must perceive the task and associated decisions to fit their "self image", i.e. as being appropriate to what *they* consider their position in the business to be.

«L. W. Porter and E. E. Lawler, *Managerial Attitude and Performance*, R. D. Irwin, 1968»

EQUITY THEORY

This theory is based on the finding that people have a concept of *Equity* or fairness which makes them attempt to match their performance to the reward received. If people sense "inequity" they will react accordingly. In the case of staff paid on a salaried, i.e. time basis, the reactions will be as follows:

Underpayment Reduced quality or quantity of output.
Overpayment Increased quality or quantity of output.

Practical experience indicates that these results do indeed follow. Underpayment typically occurs when salary increases do not keep pace with inflation, and staff often become less helpful and co-operative as a result.

On the other hand, unexpectedly large wage increases cause people to put more into their work than normal.

«J. S. Adams, *Journal of Abnormal and Social Psychology*, 1964»

INSTRUMENTAL THEORY

In a study in the 1960s of Luton car workers of above average affluence, J. H. Goldthorpe found that they stayed in their jobs principally because of high pay. They did not expect any "satisfaction" from their work. Their status needs were met by using their earnings to buy substantial houses, luxury cars and other status symbols such as boats. Their self-actualising needs were satisfied by holidays and leisure activities often also only possible on high earnings.

It was also found that their social needs were met outside rather than inside work. "Workmates" were seldom the same as "friends", and group needs were satisfied by the family and leisure activities.

These findings suggest that a section of people in modern society have accepted that there will not in future be enough interesting, creative, satisfying jobs for everyone. These people have taken advantage of the shorter working hours and decided to aim in that relatively small proportion of their lives to earn enough money to enjoy themselves the rest of the time. For this section of the population Taylor's classical reward system would again become appropriate.

PSYCHOLOGICAL CONSIDERATIONS AND THE ENVIRONMENT

LEVEL OF MOTIVATION

It has been established that the degree of motivation of individuals varies through the whole range of possibilities and is "normally distributed" in the statistical sense. It follows that the need for managers to provide stimuli will similarly vary. Some people will have so little "drive" that full external direction of their effort is essential to obtain any output. This can be provided by a production line, which moves at a steady pace and thus controls the operators' output.

HIGH MOTIVATION

At the other end of the scale people who have reached senior management positions are often so highly motivated that external stimuli are not required at all. These are the people identified by McClelland as having high achievement motivation. The "wants" of individuals also vary according to their environmental background and history, the influences to which they are exposed, and their family circumstances. The external level of incentive which has to be provided is also influenced by the basic needs of people and the extent to which these are met by society. Basic needs are, for instance, much more easily filled where climatic conditions are warm and equable, than where they are harsh and unreliable.

THE "WELFARE STATE"

When society provides a satisfactory minimum standard of living without the need to work, a percentage of the population will find this level satisfies its needs. This situation also reduces the effort the "normal" majority have to make to satisfy their needs. It is with this section of the population that management's greatest effort to increase motivation must be made.

DIRECTION OF MOTIVATION

It has been established that there are wide differences in the direction of motivation of individuals, i.e that they have much more interest in certain types of activity, in which they therefore need much less external stimulus. This also applies to groups of people, the variation being due to their social, political and economic history, as well as current influences such as advertising and social fashions.

PERFORMANCE

There is a very wide assumption in this country, not only among students, that performance – whether it is in a profession, an industry, a company or a department, – depends primarily on the effort and, by implication, the motivation of the people at the operating level. Quite apart from the role of managers in providing incentives for effort, it must be emphasised that there are *three* groups of factors which determine performance – Ability of staff, Resources at their disposal, and Motivation.

ABILITY

Ability is a function of the innate characteristics of persons, of their experience, and of training. An adequate supply of staff with the right ability requires careful manpower planning and selection. This and training are normally carried out effectively in the financial sector. In the rapidly changing current environment the right experience may require a much higher recruitment of mature staff than has been the practice hitherto, and re-training will become a regular necessity.

Ability may be seriously impaired by fatigue. It is fortunate that technology is making a shorter working week both possible and desirable, because the increased stress of "enriched" jobs will make shorter hours more desirable. Overtime should only be permitted to deal with short-term peaks in the work load.

Alcohol in the quantities drunk at lunch time quite commonly, lowers effective ability substantially, as does, in the longer term, smoking. In some countries drug abuse is becoming a serious problem.

RESOURCES

Training provides knowledge and skills. It has already been mentioned under the previous heading, but the availability of training, for new equipment for instance, can also be regarded as an essential resource. Up-to-date, efficient and well maintained machinery, equipment and tools – such as calculators – improve performance dramatically and adequate space and efficient lay-outs are equally important.

Working conditions are only relevant in so far as they actually affect the work e.g. excessive cold, or inadequate lighting. Less obviously, excessive or constant noise has an adverse effect on performance.

Under this heading, because they are often due to inadequate resources, overload and stress should be listed. Both of these result initially in mistakes and omission and then set off a cycle of deteriorating performance.

The amount of support available from a person's own manager and from specialists, in terms of advice, information, reassurance and actual help, has a major impact on performance. The speed and ease with which such support is available also makes a difference.

It is only if people have the right ability and resources that their motivation comes into play. The manager's role includes applying incentives either to individuals or to groups, to improve their performance.

THE MANAGER'S ROLE

BASE PERFORMANCE

By selecting the correct motivational stimulus managers reduce the need for direction. The greatest saving is provided by forming cohesive integrated primary groups which respond to a common stimulus. The hygiene or "maintenance" factors are the essential basis which will produce basic performance. They include wages and all its equivalents, including such items as company cars, which are effectively wages paid in a form which reduces tax liability. Hours of work, avoiding red tape, and other organisational frustration come into this field. Security of the job, of the firm, of the working environment are important. Apart from the security provided by contracts of employment and profitable operation, employees' security is greatly enhanced by keeping them informed of future plans.

SUPERIOR PERFORMANCE

To obtain average, or even superior performance more positive stimulants must be provided. Among these group motivation, loyalty, desire for companionship and power are some of the most important. People will make great efforts, for instance, to maintain the reputation and performance of an enterprise of which they are proud and with which they identify. Many stimuli are applicable both to groups and individuals.

STATUS

The desire to be "esteemed" can be stimulated by the provision of status symbols. For groups, cups and prizes, or simply ranking charts can be used, although status can also be based on simple recognition of excellence in a particular field. External status symbols such as the quality of accommodation, various privileges such as reserved parking, or freedom from restrictions such as fixed tea breaks, are equally applicable to groups and individuals. The motivation of status may be totally out of proportion to its costs to management.

People's status within an organisation depends not only on their role, but also on their "latent status characteristics". These comprise age, sex, colour and social background.

ACHIEVEMENT

On an individual level achievement in the field of particular interest is probably the best motivator. The craftsman takes pride in his finished product, the designer and scientist in innovation, the manager in meeting goals or deadlines, the specialist in anticipating enquiries, and even among unskilled operators the opportunity to improve on output or quality is very stimulating. Unfortunately, modern operating techniques do not lend themselves to providing many opportunities for achievement at operative level. MbO is based on achievement as a stimulus.

JOB ENRICHMENT

Job enrichment attempts to reverse the de-motivating effect of routine, repetitive jobs by redesigning or re-structuring them to provide greater job satisfaction. The most effective way of enriching jobs is to allow people to plan their own work, and vary the method of carrying out the work. Thus the manager replaces detailed instructions and supervision, by targets and performance standards and exercises his control by ensuring that these are met.

One of the dangers of enriching a particular job, whether as described above or later, is that other roles may be affected and may become more difficult or less interesting. It is obviously necessary for managers to balance all the roles under their direction, unless they are deliberately catering for different types of staff.

«J.I.T.»

RECOGNITION

While achievement is an end in itself, its value in stimulating effort is multiplied if it is recognised by those in authority. This includes senior management, specialists and outsiders as much as immediate superiors and colleagues. The effect of achievement is dissipated if it is subjected to carping criticism or even ignored. Because most people find it easier to criticise than to compliment, this is a common fault of untrained managers.

JOB INTEREST

Although it may often not be possible to design working systems which afford the opportunity to "achieve" satisfying results, jobs can often be made interesting in their content by job enrichment, by variety, by creating a physically or socially interesting environment, by background information, and in many other ways depending on the ingenuity of managers. The selection of staff whose interests match the job content is obviously important.

MISDIRECTION

Determining the correct stimulus is not easy, it will depend upon factors concerned with the job, individuals, groups and their environment, and it is important to monitor the effectiveness of any action taken. This can be done by setting specific goals, or by the use of control groups. Examples of techniques which have been found not to improve overall motivation are:

(a) Competition
(b) Job rotation
(c) Horizontal loading of roles
(d) Reducing supervision
(e) Change of job name

It must also be remembered that any form of bad management acts as a disincentive to subordinates. Misdirection, i.e. the giving of wrong, unnecessary, or contradictory instructions is most disheartening.

(A) COMPETITION

"Open" competition is competition where success by an individual or a group does not adversely affect others. It results in friendly rivalry, so that performance is judged by that reached by the best competitors. Others may be spurred to improve their own performance. There are few opportunities for such competition in a modern working environment. "Closed" competition occurs both when there is a "race" for supremacy, and when there is a limited benefit available to be shared by the participants. In a race there are several losers for every winner, and it is important to be aware of the effects of this type of competition on both individuals and groups.

Individuals

The competing individuals are much too busy ensuring their own success to worry about co-operating with each other for the benefit of the department. If competition is fierce they may even undermine the work of others to the detriment of the department. In distributed benefits, for any one who gets more than an equal share, someone else gets less. The combination of these side effects of competition almost invariably means that, while it may motivate some people, the net result for the department in which they work is counter productive. Closed competition can therefore not be regarded as a motivator.

Groups

The effect of inter-group competition has been described by Schein as follows:

1. Each group becomes more closely knit and elicits greater loyalty from its members; members close ranks and bury some of their internal differences.
2. The group climate changes from informal, casual, playful to work and task oriented; concern for members' psychological needs declines while

concern for task accomplishment increases.

3. Leadership patterns tend to change from more democratic towards more autocratic; the group becomes more willing to tolerate autocratic leadership.

4. Each group becomes more highly structured and organized.

5. Each group demands more loyalty and conformity from its members in order to be able to present a "solid front".

The above developments occur *within* the group. Between the groups the following changes occur:—

1. Each group begins to see the other group as the enemy, rather than merely a neutral object.

2. Each group begins to experience distortions of perception – it tends to perceive only the best parts of itself and tends to perceive only the worst parts of the other group.

3. Hostility toward the other group increases while interaction and communication with the other group decreases.

4. If the groups are forced into interaction – for example if they are forced to listen to representatives plead their own and the others' cause in reference to some task – each group is likely to listen more closely to their own representative and not to listen to the representative of the other group, except to find fault with his or her presentation.

In group competition the effect of one group winning is rather different to what happens among individuals. The group spirit of the winning group tends to improve and it becomes more concerned with the welfare of its members but its performance tends to deteriorate because it becomes complacent. The danger with the losing group (e.g. some British firms in relation to foreign competition) is that they blame everyone but themselves and there may be no improvement for some time. However once they come to terms with reality they are likely to re-evaluate their ideas, become tougher with their members, re-organise and improve their performance.

(B) JOB ROTATION

Job rotation in its simplest form is *not* a motivator.

Among the repetitive routine jobs which occur in banking are inputing details from credit card vouchers, and filing those vouchers. To a person who finds both these jobs boring and unsatisfying, having to spend mornings on one and afternoons in another is not a real improvement.

Job rotation can be used to improve motivation if it is part of team working and job enrichment, i.e. if there are a number of routine jobs which have to be dealt with by a group of people who have the authority to rotate the work among themselves. It may even be effective if certain people have prime responsibility for certain tasks provided that they can be aided and relieved by others. The significant difference is the freedom to decide when to rotate and the responsibility that goes with it. This situation is typical of small to medium sized branches.

(C) HORIZONTAL LOADING OF ROLES

When people complain that their work is boring, it is also often found that they can comfortably do it in the time available. This is probably because they have developed a fast routine for completing the work to the minimum acceptable standard of quality and are not interested in any improvements or side issues which are not compulsory. "Horizontal loading" or "job enlargement" is said to occur when managers give these people more work, different but equally repetitive, with a view to making them happier. Horizontal loading is not an effective motivator because these people will still be bored, but probably become harassed as well. What they want is not more *work*, but more *responsibility*.

(D) REDUCING SUPERVISION

Giving people greater responsibility is not the same as reducing supervision. If employees are not supervised they feel neglected, and that their work is unimportant. They will also be unsure of whether their performance is acceptable. Both these factors are de-motivating. Control must be maintained to an extent that employees will know that their performance will be checked before a mistake causes serious harm. If the employee is adequately trained, the intervals between performance checks can be increased. This is an effective form of enrichment.

(E) CHANGE OF JOB NAME

Attempts have been made to enhance the status of certain roles by renaming them. Many salesmen have become "business development executives". This is totally ineffective unless the change of name genuinely reflects a difference in the level of work or authority. If a role for which it has been difficult to find recruits has been genuinely modified to make it more attractive, it may be useful to publicise this change by a new name.

ABSENTEEISM

Absenteeism is said to occur when staff are not available for the work for which they have been employed, due to unauthorised absence. Absence as part of their holiday is not regarded as absenteeism, but absence due to sickness is. Some firms exclude from absenteeism figures major illnesses and accidents – e.g. those requiring hospitalisation. In the case of short and mild illnesses it is recognised that even though the original illness may be genuine, the number of days spent away from work depends very much on the attitude of the individual and how attractive he finds his job.

Security during the first four weeks of illness has meant that firms have had to establish reporting and recording systems for absence due to sickness, even though absenteeism as such has not been a problem. The information thus available can be used to identify individuals or groups with low morale. The data processing capabilities of computers make it easy to draw attention to sickness patterns which might otherwise not be noticed, e.g. five short absences within two months. This enables managers to assess the cause of the absenteeism. If found necessary disciplinary action may take the form of a deduction from leave entitlements.

Absenteeism in Banking is likely to be as low as 5%, but it should be noted that even this means that for every twenty persons an additional one must be employed to cover absence. Like other indicators of motivation absenteeism is a symptom – it does not give the cause. The cause can only be found by carefully examining all the Hygiene factors and Motivators.

MORALE

Morale is an indicator of the discipline and confidence of a group of employees. High morale usually improves productivity but is mainly reflected in the attitude of the group to problems and change. If morale is high problems are regarded as a challenge. They are tackled with enthusiasm but in a disciplined and systematic way, with each person in the group applying themselves to their own sphere of responsibility, whilst helping and advising others. Similarly change is welcomed because of the opportunity it provides to acquire new skills and knowledge.

If morale is low, minor differences are magnified into major problems. All non-routine queries are referred to superiors, people tend to blame others for their own failures, and co-operation suffers because everyone puts their own interest first. Any change in established practices is resisted because people are afraid that they will not be able to cope.

Attitude surveys are sometimes used to identify low morale groups in situations where the state of morale is not evident because of the routine nature of the work.

PRODUCTIVITY

Productivity is a much misused term. As far as labour productivity is concerned it means the output per person *under given conditions*. Productivity is normally used as an indicator of efficiency, but as output depends to a certain extent on motivation, productivity can be said to be an indicator of motivation. The importance of identical conditions must however be emphasised. These obviously include the resources available to the people being measured – i.e. machinery and space, but it also includes less obvious support such as:

- the initial educational level of staff
- the level of training provided
- back up of information, control reports, maintenance and management services
- the availability of managers for problem solving
- the authority people have to modify their working methods to cope with the unexpected.

Other factors which may adversely affect productivity are variations in:

- Demand from customers and client departments
- Quality and reliability of supplies
- Pressure from other departments.

All these factors affect productivity and it is only if all of these have been eliminated, that the level of motivation can be credited with high productivity, or blamed for low productivity.

CHANGE

Fundamentally, people resist change if they expect, with or without justification, that the change will cause them a "loss". Where details of future change are not known people make assumptions about what they may lose. To reduce resistance to change, management must either demonstrate that there is no loss, or compensate in an appropriate way for the loss. The provision of information about future plans will, of course, reduce unwarranted worries about the future.

One of the major problems of implementing change, which management usually intends as a benefit, is to identify how the change threatens individuals. The Hierarchy of Needs described by Maslow can be used to list such threats.

(1) *Physical needs* in modern society are met by wages, including bonuses, pensions and non-discretionary fringe benefits. The extreme threat here of course is the risk of redundancy, but generous redundancy payments often bring forth more volunteers than are required. Appropriate introductory schemes should be used to encourage adoption of new processes and work methods, recognising that otherwise earnings would inevitably be low during a learning period. In the case of mergers and take-overs, integration will be speeded up if salaries and other benefits are compared, to ensure that any change is for the better.

(2) *Security*. Redundancy is also the major threat to security, the other physiological need. Those people not threatened with redundancy must, therefore, be reassured. Actual redundancy or early retirement plans should be clarified and dealt with promptly. But security also means "preferring the devil you know, to the devil you don't know". People are particularly frightened that they may not be as good at a new job as their existing one, and that new methods and environments will be less satisfying. Proper preliminary training will help in the first case, and full information, assuming new conditions are satisfactory, in the second.

(3) *Social needs*. Change may disrupt a person's relationship with individual colleagues and friends, or may cause informal "groups" and formal teams to disintegrate. These are considerable losses. If managers know if such losses may occur they can often avoid them when making changes. Social needs must be satisfied in a new situation. Similarly, loss indirectly incurred by an employee's family, when he is asked to move, may be even more important.

(4) *Ego needs*. A person's status in an existing situation may be determined in a variety of ways. He may be the oldest, most popular, most knowledgeable, most skilled person, or simply have a recognised ranking. Any of these may be changed in a new situation. The resultant loss cannot normally be avoided, but must be compensated in some other way.

(5) *Self actualisation*. For those people who enjoy their work either because of the work itself, or because it is a means of achieving what they regard as a worthwhile objective, a change may bring loss of satisfaction or even frustration. This can only be overcome by substituting equally acceptable roles or objectives.

THE MANAGEMENT OF CHANGE

In general it may be said that people will accept change if they perceive it as giving them a gain or advantage. Helping people to accept change therefore requires a manager to:

(1) Identify any real or psychological losses which each person will suffer

(2) Avoid unnecessary losses by assessing all the benefits in a person's present position and preserving as many of these as possible

(3) Ensure that people realise which losses will inevitably occur

(4) Make up losses by gains in kind wherever possible.

The best way of ensuring a climate receptive to change – assuming that the morale of the people involved is at a satisfactory level to start with – is to involve them in the process of identifying the *need* for change. Firstly this keeps people "in the picture", thus reducing rumour and uncertainty; secondly it makes them more aware that some "losses" are inevitable, and not the fault of the firm. A first class typist whose status and payment is based on outstanding typing speed cannot be blamed for resenting – and refusing to co-operate with – the introduction of word processors which enable unskilled juniors to produce equally good copy at the touch of a button. But if such persons – or representatives of their skill group – are asked to give an opinion to the most suitable replacement typing equipment, visits to Business efficiency exhibitions and showrooms will probably make them realise that the firm would be very foolish not to switch to word processors. They will realise the inevitability of the change, and in order to minimise their personal loss, will probably volunteer for retraining. The object of implementing change has been achieved.

«Environmental Changes, Ch. 2, p. 42»
«Group Decision Making, Ch. 5, p. 113»
«MbO, Ch. 5, p. 115»
«Participation, Ch. 11, p. 224»

Practice Exercises

(1) (a) Ask yourself, or anyone else who has left a job, why they did so.

    (b) Check whether the reason was a "satisfier" or "hygiene" factor according to Herzberg.

(2) What gives you most satisfaction at work? Which motivation theory does this fit? What does it tell you about yourself as a person?

(3) Try to identify what stimuli your colleagues would need for increased effort.

(4) What do the level of absenteeism and morale in your place of work indicate?

(5) When a change at work has been proposed to you, what was your first reaction? Why did you react like that?

(6) Have you ever been in a situation where you objected to a change? Why did you object?

From Chapter 8 you should have learnt:

There are numerous Theories of Motivation.

People are complex and are motivated in different ways.

People should be allocated to roles which will motivate them.

What is required for good performance.

Methods of job enrichment.

Changes in job design which do not improve motivation.

The significance of morale.

The factors which affect productivity.

The steps in managing change.

Stimuli applicable to individuals.

Stimuli applicable to groups.

External Factors which affect motivation.

Hygiene Factors.

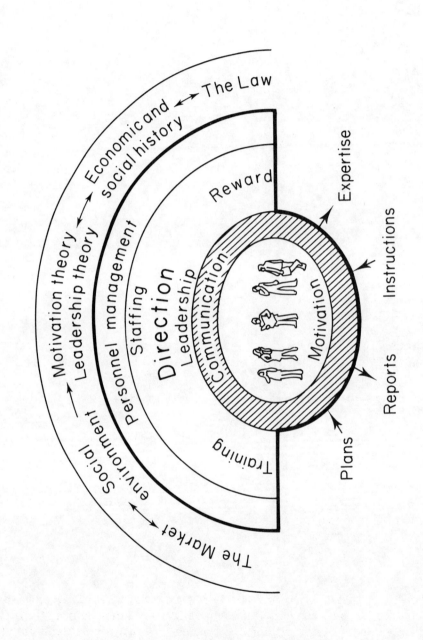

Chapter 9

Communication

DIRECTION

Direction is the element of management which is concerned with ensuring that the decisions made are implemented, that the routine work of any part of the business is directed towards achieving business goals, and that the efforts of the individuals in a section of the business are directed towards the goals of that section. Good communication between higher management and the section, between sections, within the section, and if appropriate with the environment, are essential for the process of direction.

A manager directing a business department needs:

(1) sufficient technical knowledge of its activities to understand what is happening and how it fits into the pattern of activities of the company.

(2) Decision making ability.

(3) *Communication* skills and a knowledge of the communication techniques available. This will ensure that he can obtain all the information required for the decision he needs to make, and for the process of direction itself.

(4) Leadership skills to induce his subordinates to act according to his guidance.

(5) Authority to insist on his instruction being carried out. Good leaders will seldom have to use this authority, but they must be prepared to do so if their subordinates do not obey agreed or group norms, if they put their own convenience or interests before that of the group, or if there is disagreement or conflict among subordinates.

In this chapter "communication" is examined more closely.

The relationship between a manager and his subordinates, and leadership are examined in Chapters 10 and 11.

COMMUNICATION

Communication involves transmitting a message from a source to a recipient. The basic unit of communication is a simple "channel" involving a one step transmission, normally illustrated as in Fig. 9.1.

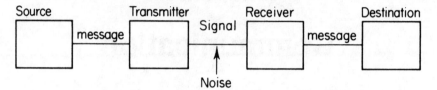

Fig. 9.1 A simple communication channel

COMPOUND CHANNELS

A compound channel of communication involves a message passing through a number of transmission and reception stages before reaching its destination.

It should be noted that the effect of "noise" may be to distort a signal (if not drown it altogether). Obviously the risk of this happening increases with the length of the channel of communication. Technically anything which changes the signal between transmitter and receiver is a "noise". Common examples of noise include:

- mis-routing of signals
- failure to pass on a signal (by accident or design)
- destruction or obliteration of the signal
- excessive delays

The communication channel illustrated above is a "one way" channel, whereas most communication is "two way".

PROBLEMS OF COMMUNICATION

It is important to distinguish between the source and the transmitter in a simple communication channel, because faults can arise at both points. In a person to person communication the transmitter is the voice. Voice problems are uncommon, but most of the problems mentioned on the next page may occur at the source – i.e. due to the personality, experience and ability of the speaker.

At the destination end of the communication the majority of the problems will occur at the "destination", i.e. the person receiving the message, rather than at the "receiver" which is simply his hearing mechanism.

However in a more technical situation – e.g. when the "source" is a computer storage disk and the transmitter is the VDU, problems can occur equally at both points.

In order to obtain good communications it is necessary to eliminate problems at all the stages in the channel. Problems can be grouped into three types:

TECHNICAL PROBLEMS

The noises listed above are examples of such problems. Other important examples of technical problems are:

(a) *Message formulation*
Many people have difficulty in expressing complex ideas, whether on a technical or abstract level, in message form. In the former case a "demonstration" may be an alternative and it should be noted that this is a communication using vision as the medium.

(b) *Understanding*
The ability of a recipient to understand the message plays a large part in its effectiveness.

(c) *Retrieval*
This is the problem of using information which is already in existence. Overcoming this problem requires knowledge by all concerned of the information storage systems available, and training in their use.

(d) *Psychological Problems*
These are similar to (c) in so far as they involve activating information already in existence in the cumulative store of knowledge and experience of the personnel within an organisation.

People tend to keep information to themselves because they want to retain the power which knowledge or experience appears to give them; because of shyness; because of embarrassment at being in possession of the experience; because of uncertainty of the accuracy of information, or of how it will be received; because of the fear of making a fool of oneself, and because they are unaware of the relevance or importance of their knowledge and experience.

TWO WAY PROBLEMS

Managers do not only have the problem of overcoming their own deficiencies in this respect but also that of inducing other people to communicate with them. Apart from leading by example and making people aware of the information needs, this involves the human relations skill of recognising other people's problems and changing their attitudes in an appropriate way.

SEMANTIC PROBLEMS

These problems concern the use of language and arise at several levels.

(a) National differences   (c) Levels of abstraction
(b) Local differences   (d) Occupational differences

LEVELS OF ABSTRACTION

There are considerable differences in the linguistic ability of different people. English is a very rich language which allows concepts to be expressed alternatively by "sophisticated morphemes accurately defining specific concepts" or "a number of simple words giving a general idea".

Relevant examples are the terms used for leadership:

e.g. autocratic   = *telling* people what to do
     missionary   = *selling* an idea
     consultative   = *asking* people what they think
     participative = *joining* in the decisions.

The range of words which people understand is based on their innate ability and education. Over a long period a person's vocabulary can be increased but in the short term good communication needs to take into account their existing ability to understand. It is a sobering fact that, when they leave school, less than half the population have passed O-level English.

This not only a question of the vocabulary but also one of concepts. The average person is capable of comprehending "concrete" topics – physical things which can be seen and touched. It is very difficult for them to communicate about "feelings" or "attitude", i.e. more abstract ideas such as "honesty", "sympathy", or "humour". Many highly abstract concepts such as "depreciation", "motivation", or "inflation adjusted discounted cash flow", will be totally outside their comprehension.

   In banking the staff normally all have a minimum of four O-levels. In terms of their linguistic abilities they are therefore above average and the problem of levels of abstraction is not as severe as in other industries. The problem will however have to be taken into account in any efforts the Banks make to gain the custom of the 40% of the population who are as yet unbanked because they are the ones who generally communicate on a lower level of abstraction. One of the reasons (among several), for the building societies' success in their market sector is because they have pitched their messages to the clients at an appropriate level.

PROBLEMS OF EFFECTIVENESS – OBJECTIVES

For economy of operation within an enterprise communications should only be undertaken if they have a purpose or objective. A list of possible objectives would include:

- providing information
- gathering information
- influencing action.

- seeking reassurance
- inducing action

A communication can only be regarded as satisfactory if it achieves the intended result – i.e. if it is effective. The problem of ensuring effectiveness involves:

(a) The choice of destination.
(b) Message formulation.
(c) Choice of medium.
(d) The appropriate method of delivering.

(A) CHOICE OF DESTINATION

It is important to decide carefully to whom a message should be directed:

(a) to ensure effectiveness – some subordinates will carry out particular tasks much better than others, their workload may be different, and they have different skills, interests and attitudes; some customers are more likely to use new services than others; some colleagues are more likely to respond to requests for help than others;

(b) to ensure economy. Unnecessarily wide circulation is a waste of resources;

(c) to ensure that the people in an organisation are not overwhelmed with the communication burden. If they are, they will either neglect other work, or communications will be dealt with selectively. Too many communications may mean much useless reading and memo-passing, while some important data is overlooked. Many more mistakes are also likely to be made.

(B) MESSAGE FORMULATION

Having identified the objectives of a communication and its intended recipient the message can be formulated in language and at a level of abstraction comprehensive to the recipient. The goal of effectiveness means that the psychological effect of message formulation must be taken into account. Some people will regard a request to do something as a sign of weakness in a manager and will only act on a firm "order", others will resent and obstruct "orders", but readily comply with "requests". In advertisements a sales message to women is often different to that for men.

In general messages should be kept as simple as possible, but where errors may result in serious losses, it is normal to build in "redundancy" i.e. saying the same thing in two or more different ways. Figures and words on a cheque illustrate this.

(C) CHOICE OF MEDIUM

The main media of communication used in business are:

- verbal
- written
- visual
- data processor based.

In practice there is a considerable overlap between these media – all written communication requires the ability to see, and one of the virtues of verbal communication is that it is reinforced by gestures and facial expressions. Visual communication often involves reading. Frequently, as in television, all three media are combined, but the one which is predominant attracts the ultimate label.

Written Communication

This label covers all communications on paper and its equivalent. Handwritten memos, cheques, typed letters, telex messages, computer print-outs, manuals, newspapers, posters, books, architect's or other drawings, graphs, are all regarded as "written" in this sense. In effect they can range from manual, i.e. handwritten, documents through various degrees of mechanisation, to those prepared automatically by sophisticated technology. The common factor is that the document prepared is permanent unless specifically destroyed. This is the main feature which distinguishes written from other forms of communications. The main indicator for written communication is therefore the desired "life" of the communication. Some messages, e.g. requesting audience from a superior, or informing a colleague that one is going to lunch, have a very short "life" – they are pointless an hour later and always verbal. Among long-life communications are all forms of records, standing orders, instruction manuals and reference materials. These should always be written.

- Management reports to superiors or from specialist departments

- project or decision making information

- customers' statements and activities

- orders to subordinates and specialist departments

- requests for guidance and information

- training activities.

All of these fall in an intermediate time period. Other factors may then determine the medium to use; as a general guide, any communication with a life of about a month or more should be put on paper.

Further advantages of written communications include the fact that there is a *record of the message*. This is important when errors may result in losses, and when there is a risk of dispute. The former factor indicates the use of written format for anything committing or involving money – purchase orders, money transfers and cheques are common examples, as are instructions for installing and maintaining equipment, where mistakes result in reworking or lost output; this is why contracts, agreements, minutes of committee meetings, reports on investigations into performance variances, and disciplinary warnings are put in writing.

Acknowledgements of the receipt of messages can also be recorded by a receipted copy being returned to the transmitter.

Accuracy. Complex technical details are almost impossible to describe except in writing. Drawings and photographs exemplify the complex detail that can be presented. Flow charts and mathematical models and calculations fall into the same category.

Add-on and correction opportunities. With written communications it is relatively easy to modify a message because a particular figure, paragraph or section of the original document can be easily identified, traced and altered. Similarly records can be updated and additional information included.

Noise in communication terms is anything which distorts a message after it leaves the transmitter, or anything which prevents it from reaching its destination. The most likely cause of noise on written communications is misrouting or misfiling of messages, causing delay, or complete non-delivery. If machinery is used, e.g. telex or word-processing, malfunction of the equipment may cause errors. However overall the risk of distortion in written communications is less than in other media.

Draw-backs of Written Communications

Formality is implicit in a written document. Such formality is often detrimental to good human relations. It is also difficult to put many abstract topics, particularly those concerned with attitudes and emotions, into formal words. Such formally expressed views are often misinterpreted and this probably accounts for the reluctance of most people to put personal thoughts on paper.

Feed-back. It is not automatically clear whether people have understood a written communication, and what their reaction to it is.

Data Processor-based Communications

The main features of data processors are the large storage capacity and easy recall, not only of the whole of the information but of any section of it. In this way this modern medium is superior to conventional information on paper. It also requires less room for storage. Because access depends on the correct knowledge of codes, confidential information is safer. On the other hand, because access is limited to authorised and trained users, there is a greater training cost involved, and there is a greater risk of people being excluded from the network, and therefore from valuable information, by default.

Verbal Communication

The basic form of verbal communication is a person to person conversation. This can be extended to form networks involving one person addressing a group of people, and meetings or conferences which are all channel networks. The scope of verbal communication can be extended by technology and in the shape of telephone, loudspeaker equipment, recording, and radio.

The two main advantages of verbal communication are immediate feedback, and the "all channel" facility. Feed-back may be important, even critical, for any type of communication. In providing information to superiors by means of verbal report, the adequacy of the report can be judged from the superior's reaction. When giving instruction to a group of subordinates their willingness to implement the instructions can be assessed. When providing customers with information about services, the customer may indicate different interests.

Training relies very much on feed-back to confirm what the trainee has learnt and in trying to change attitudes feed-back is essential to check the effect of a communication.

Any communication which requires immediate feed-back, where the reaction of the receiver is important, or where additional explanation may be needed, should therefore be verbal or have a verbal component.

Conferences or meetings are effectively communication techniques using speech as a medium. They are particularly useful when it is not certain who is interested in particular items of information, and who is in a position to contribute information, knowledge or judgement. People at a meeting can be selective as to the items they note, they are aware of what has been discussed and can join the discussion when their sphere of influence is affected. The range of awareness and speed of information transmission cannot be matched by any other media.

Attitudes and feelings are best communicated verbally, as is any "off the record" communication. This applies to many communications between a manager and his subordinates, covering difficulties, disciplinary matters, appraisal and reassurance. Discussions of problems among colleagues and the whole field of informal communications are also verbal. The main disadvantage of the verbal process is the risk of messages being forgotten and the fact that there is no record.

Visual Communications

In its simplest form, information can be supplied visually by means of signs and signals, e.g. the light above a counter free to serve customers. These are cheap, simple to understand and quick. In information gathering, visual assessment of attitudes, and of such attributes as cleanliness and overcrowding, are very effective. In training and changing attitudes visual displays –

e.g. models, lower the level of abstraction of many concepts to a level within the capacity of people who would not understand a verbal or written description.

Modern Developments

Communication technology is developing very rapidly and some of these developments affect the choice of medium.

Examples
Conference microphones simplify the production of minutes.

Radio paging has opened whole new fields of verbal communication.

Telex and facsimile transmission has speeded up written communication.

On line terminals can be used to up-date information and make it available instantaneously at geographically distant points.

Microprocessors enable "generalist" managers to use mathematical decision techniques.

Word processors edit and produce documents with perfect accuracy.

Photocopying makes it much simpler to pass identical information to intermediate numbers of recipients (i.e. between carbon copies and printing).

Microfiches reduce the cost of storing drawings etc.

Tape recording conversations provides a permanent record. Thus a major disadvantage is removed.

The absence of non-verbal signals in telephone conversations can be overcome by telephones incorporating vision.

Interactive video-discs increase the topics which trainees can learn at their own pace, or in places where classes are not available.

Decision Making Techniques, Ch. 5. pp. 119–122»
Territorial Structure; Centralisation; Decentralisation, Ch. 4, pp. 83; 87; 91»

Cost

This has to be a factor in any choice of medium. Each major communication system has to be considered on its merits as there is no general advantage for any one medium. The cost is affected by the length, life and complexity of a message and the number and spread of recipients.

Speed

Intrinsically speech is undoubtedly the quickest medium *provided that the recipients are available*, e.g. a manager can summon one or more of his staff for consultation. An aspect of the case for open-plan offices is that a person intending to speak to another person can choose a moment when he can see that the intended recipient is at his desk and not already talking to someone else.

As soon as the recipient is located outside the personal range of the sender, the risk of a long delay in contacting a person makes a written message preferable. The same applies if identical messages are to be sent to a large number of people, e.g. informing clients of a price change. A circular, apart from being cheaper, will reach more people in a short time than personal contact would.

Accuracy

Summarising comments made earlier: for technical or scientific information, written or visual media are more accurate; for abstract and psychological communication speech is less likely to be misinterpreted.

(D) THE METHOD OF DELIVERY

In written communications the importance with which an incoming message is regarded may well depend on how it is delivered. Something received by special messenger or recorded delivery will get more attention than a note deposited in the in-tray.

A formally delivered speech to a group assembled in a board-room will have a different impact to the same words spoken casually to a group at their work stations. Rhetoric, violent language, and persuasive logic all have their appropriate application.

COMMUNICATION NETWORKS

A number of one- or two-way channels of communication build up into a network. Three important types of network can be identified.

THE WHEEL

For straightforward communications this is a quick and effective network. From the personnel management point of view, its importance lies in the advantageous position of "A" whether by design, i.e. as manager of four subordinates, or by accident. Not only is "A" the only individual in the network to be in possession of all available information, but he is also able to filter or modify communications between the others. This puts him in a powerful leadership position. (See Fig. 9.2.)

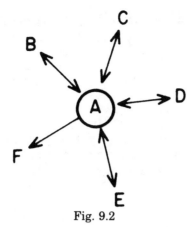

Fig. 9.2

A serious disadvantage of the wheel is the risk of overloading the person the hub by excessive numbers of communications or channels.

THE CIRCLE

Both the risk of overloading and the leadership situation are eliminated in the circular network. This network may, however, be slow and unreliable if any members of it are absent or inefficient. It is mainly used for the dissemination of information for future use. (See Fig. 9.3.)

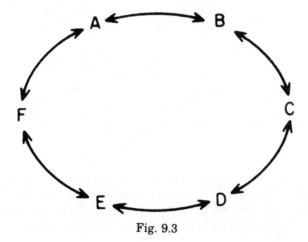

Fig. 9.3

THE ALL CHANNEL NETWORK

In this network direct communication between all members is facilitated and encouraged. It is very effective for two way communication and exchanges of ideas, as in a committee. It may however be expensive if for instance, people who are not involved attend meetings unnecessarily, or if there is an excessive proliferation of internal telephones.

REQUIREMENTS OF GOOD COMMUNICATIONS NETWORKS

Adequacy – the messages must go to all individuals concerned.

Adequate Channel Size

Channels which are too small for the load to be carried result in delays, mistakes, and often complete loss of the communication, which might well be a customer's order. If these faults are unacceptable an increase in channel size, duplication of the channel, or the adoption of queuing systems may improve the situation.

Economy

This can be achieved by ensuring that unnecessary communications and unnecessary destinations are eliminated. (See Fig. 9.4.)

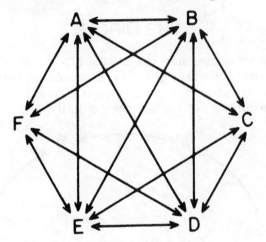

Fig. 9.4 All channel network

Efficiency

Technical efficiency of the system and proper training of the personnel involved results in economic running costs without loss of effectiveness. As an example – a well trained telephone switchboard operator can cope with many times the number of calls that an untrained person can handle.

Reliability

The originators of communications must be able to rely on the channel to do its work without constant supervision. The most important causes of unreliability are blocks and gaps in the lines of communications.

(a) Gaps – It is evident that communication will stop if a break occurs in the "line". Certain gaps will inevitably occur in any organisation, and a good system will allow for alternative routes to avoid the gaps. The absence of personnel due to sickness, holidays or business commitments is typical of this situation.

More difficult to spot, particularly in large organisations are permanent gaps which arise because of changing roles, or transfer of personnel, to which the system is not adapted.

(b) Blocks – A block in the channel of communication can occur accidentally or deliberately. The former are usually due to overloads either of the channel, the transmitter or receiver, or particularly of the persons originating communications or those for whom they are destined. Deliberate blocks are caused by people intercepting or failing to transmit or act upon information or other communications which are detrimental to their own interests, or which they consider to be wrong in form or purpose, or even which they regard as unimportant. This type of block is often difficult to detect and even more difficult to eradicate. Awareness of the problem and strong managerial action are needed.

«Personnel Services, Ch. 12, p. 247»

USE OF COMMUNICATION

Examples of typical activities involving communications are:

Communication Upwards

- Reports
- Work sheets
- Recommendations of solutions to problems
- Past experience
- Information transmission.

Communication Downwards

- Instructions and orders
- Training
- Advice
- Transmitting information for any of the above
- Informing subordinates of performance.

Communication Sideways

- Conferences and meetings with colleagues, customers, suppliers and external authorities
- Discussion of data and problems
- Information on progress.

Sideways communication tends to predominate in companies subject to rapid change, for example those involved with advanced technology, or those operating in a highly competitive market such as foreign exchange dealing. Much upward and downward communication is indicative of excessive centralisation.

The branches in territorially organised businesses such as Building Societies or banks have special communication needs because of their physical separation from head office. There is a danger that information does not get to them, or that it is not properly understood. Similarly their problems may not be appreciated at head office.

The branch manager is the official representative through whom most such information is channelled, but auxiliary channels are provided by specialists such as personnel officers who may visit the branch.

Briefing meetings held by the branch manager to pass on details of new products, policies, developments etc. are a common method of disseminating information from head office and obtaining feed-back.

Branch circulars are used for similar purposes for matters which do not require explanation or feed-back.

Branch manuals contain all the standing orders, regulations and routine information which may need to be referred to from time to time.

Conferences of Branch Managers or of specific types of branch staff, help to foster corporate identity and offer the opportunity of exchanges of view and experience between the branches.

SECRECY

It is often not realised that lack of communication not only results in the loss of the benefit of communication, but has a positively adverse effect in creating an atmosphere of secrecy. It has been said that "common knowledge unites – secrecy separates". Much of the gulf that exists in many British companies between management and workers is due to a lack of communication.

There is a tremendous amount of information which is withheld from people whom it concerns, ostensibly because it will cause jealousy or uncertainty. This does not prevent people speculating about the matters withheld. People's attitudes will therefore be formed by speculation rather than fact, and will probably be the worse for it.

Practice Exercises

(1) Describe Fig. 8.1 to a friend while keeping your hands in your pocket and get the friend to draw it without asking you any questions. Do not check the drawing.

Repeat the exercise but allow the friend to ask questions. Repeat it again using your hands in demonstration. Finally show him a drawing.

What does this tell you about written and verbal communication?

(2) Why do you telephone someone instead of writing?

(3) Why do you go to see someone instead of telephoning?

(4) Look out for "gaps" and "blocks" in communications. Can you identify their causes?

(5) List the communications you get from management and their purposes.

From Chapter 9 you should have learnt:

The parts of a channel of communication.

The effect of "noise".

The technical problems in communication.

The objectives of communicating.

The requirements for effective communication.

The advantages and disadvantages of written and verbal media.

Three basic types of communication network.

How to deal with gaps and blocks in communication.

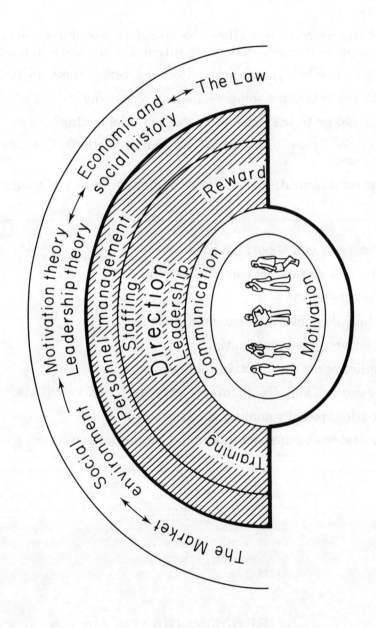

Chapter 10

The Manager/Subordinate Relationship

AUTHORITY

Authority may be defined as "the right to give orders or exact obedience". It may be personal or institutional. The most helpful classification is:

Legal authority possessed by public officials such as inspectors of weights and measures, taxes, or safety. This type of authority is also possessed by the directors and equivalent appointed officers of corporate bodies.

Managerial authority is held by a person by virtue of the role they have been assigned in an enterprise. Thus a "buyer" has authority to purchase on behalf of a firm, and managers in general should have the authority to choose and, if necessary dismiss, their subordinates.

Expert Authority. This is derived from knowledge, ability or skill. It is personal, as opposed to the institutional authority of the first two types, and it includes the ability to attract loyalty and support, which some people possess.

Usurpation of Authority. The possession of authority gives individuals a considerable power, and it is incumbent upon them not to misuse such power. Managers frequently do not realise the power of their position and may inadvertently misuse it. Usurpation of authority may occur when managers use the authority of their roles to promote personal or political ends, or go outside national or societal constraints to achieve the enterprise's objectives.

RESPONSIBILITY

The authority invested in a person carries the responsibility to use that authority in the manner and for the purposes laid down, and to the satisfaction of the person, group, or body who provided that authority – normally a person's immediate superior. Responsibility and authority must be congruent. This means that no person can be held responsible for events or performances without having the authority necessary to control such events or performances. Conversely authority always carries full responsibility.

DELEGATION

In practice managers entrusted with a task find that the task needs many people to complete it both because of the volume of work involved and also because much of it will require abilities, knowledge or experience not possessed by the manager concerned. In such cases the manager "delegates" much of the work and decision making to others, only reserving to himself those decisions and activities which cannot be carried out by his subordinates. He delegates some of the "authority" possessed by him. It should be noted that only institutional authority can be delegated; responsibility *cannot* be delegated. The subordinates concerned acquire a "new" responsibility to the manager, but the latter's responsibility to his own superior is unaffected.

Delegation frees managers for work which they are uniquely able to deal with. It is maximised by Fafour's policy that: "All authority not expressly and in writing reserved to higher management is granted to lower management".

SUPERVISORS

Supervisors are managers in charge of operators – i.e. in charge of non-managerial staff. The role of supervisors includes the same elements as managers at a higher level. Their task is made more difficult by the lower initiative, lower standards of skill in communication and in resolving conflict and limited enthusiasm for taking responsibility, which they are likely to find among their sub ordinates.

It is therefore imperative for the success of organisations that supervisors should have sufficiently high skill levels to direct their subordinates effectively.

PRINCIPLES OF DELEGATION

(1) If a manager can readily make a decision, or has already made it, there is no point in delegating, as worse, or inconsistent decisions may result.

(2) The manager must be certain of the effect of his decisions at lower levels. If obtaining such information involves time and therefore cost, delegation is preferable.

(3) Delegation should go to that level at which the decision can be most

efficiently made, bearing in mind the quality of the resulting decisions –
particularly where subjective judgements are required, and the cost of
decision making, including:

- the value of the decision maker's time

- the availability of information

- the cost of obtaining, transmitting and interpreting information.

(4) If consistency is *essential* delegation is undesirable.

(5) The ability of people to deal with abstract concepts varies, as does the
level of abstraction of decision. This limits the ability of people to deal
with decisions. Where a subordinate has persistent difficulty with making decisions, or makes them unsatisfactorily, delegation should be
withdrawn.

(6) Regular requests from a subordinate for decisions on the same issue
indicate potential for delegation, either by laying down decision rules, or
by training or developing the subordinate's ability to make the decision
himself.

The concept of delegation is very much concerned with ensuring that managers concentrate their efforts on what they are paid to do. A manager is part
of the team or "command" which is responsible to him. In the case of middle
and senior managers this includes their immediate subordinates, all *their*
subordinates and so on. All the employees share in the work of the department. The manager is paid at the highest rate. He therefore should concentrate on the work which only he can do. Anything else can be done at a lower
rate of pay.

Among the activities which cannot be delegated are:

(a) *Settling conflicts among subordinates and dealing with their problems.*
This particularly means identifying the conflict/problem in the first
place. A manager who waits for conflicts to be drawn to his attention by
one of the protagonists has allowed a situation to build up which, whatever his decision, may sour staff relations. By extensive delegation, he
should have sufficient time to exercise his communication skills – perception, listening, running meetings – to become aware early of any
conflicts and initiate action to eliminate them.

He should also be available to deal promptly with work or personal
problems pertaining to his subordinates.

(b) *Management of Personnel*
Ultimate responsibility for the proper staffing, appraisal, training and
reward of the people in his command rests with the manager. Most of the
work is often delegated to personnel departments but the final decision
should be the manager's. In a business with strong personnel departments some decisions may have to be taken negatively – e.g. by rejecting

unsuitable staff allocated to an office until the personnel department
sends more suitable ones.

(c) *Planning*
   Again some of the routine work involved in the planning process can be
   delegated, but the manager remains responsible for procuring the
   resources needed by the department, for identifying the need for change,
   for organising change and for implementing it.

(d) *Representing his Command*
   The manager himself is expected to represent his department inside
   or outside the company at any level equalling, or above, his own status.
   He must also monitor his subordinate's relations with outsiders.

(e) *His Responsibility to his Superior*
   The manager remains responsible to his superior for any work decisions
   which he has delegated. It is incumbent upon him to set up a control
   system within his command which makes certain that delegated work is
   completed correctly on time and that delegated decisions are made correctly on time. The manager must also ensure that subordinates to
   whom he delegates have the necessary attitude, ability and training to
   do the job satisfactorily.

(f) *Specific Duties*
   A manager may have certain duties delegated to him personally and
   specifically – e.g. decisions involving committing the company to expenditure within a given range, or personal contact with major clients.

In general a manager cannot delegate to subordinates anything which is not
within his own sphere of authority, or anything which requires his own
special skills to reach the required standard.

BARRIERS TO DELEGATION

It is generally accepted and should be evident from the above analysis that
the extent and quality of delegation is a major factor in managing
efficiently. Faulty delegation will reduce management efficiency, but in
practice the major problem is failure to delegate *sufficiently*. The reasons for
this failure can be grouped as being due to organisational causes, the subordinates and the manager himself.

Organisational Barriers

The way work is assigned to the command, will affect a manager's ability to
delegate – e.g. if he is given too many specific things to do himself, or if
methods and procedures are specified rigidly so that they are not within the
capacity of the manager's subordinates.

The company policy on allocating work and defining roles has an important
impact. The more rigidly the content of each job in his command is defined,
the more difficult it becomes for the manager to delegate.

«*Approaches to Organisation, Ch. 3*»

An excessive concern with status and seniority within the organisation inhibits delegation. This concern affects questions such as:

- Who is entitled to sign or receive documents?
- Who is included in the communication network?
- Who sits on committees for the department?

«*Communication, Ch. 9*»

Barriers Due to the Subordinate

Herzberg and several other motivational theorists hold that job interest is important for motivation and that responsibility is a major component in job interest. However the survey of motivation in Chapters 7 and 8 has demonstrated that people vary greatly. There are large numbers of people, particularly at operator level who are reluctant to accept more than a very minimum of responsibility. There is no future in forcing responsibility onto such people, and they should be placed in roles not requiring decision making.

Often, unfortunately, the reluctance to take responsibility is not an inherent characteristic of the subordinate but has been induced by the attitude of successive managers. Managerial actions which will cause unwillingness to accept responsibility include:

Setting unachievable goals and inducing a sense of failure in his staff.

Excessive criticism – many managers look for faults – they are not happy unless they find something to criticise even in a basically successful task.

Lack of proper briefing, i.e. the person is afraid he will not be properly told what to do.

Unwillingness to help the subordinate over his first difficulties.

Excessive punishment if the subordinate makes a mistake.

Lack of recognition of success in handling extra responsibilities.

All such managerial attitudes make the subordinate insecure and afraid of failure and therefore unwilling to take extra responsibilities.

Barriers Due to Managers

It has been shown in the preceding paragraphs that the attitude of the manager in respect of briefing and training subordinates and towards criticism and recognition creates barriers.

A further barrier is a *lack of trust*. This is difficult to eliminate if based on a realistic assessment of subordinates' abilities. For good delegation a manager must be confident that employees will report any difficulties to him immediately they arise. Whether they will do this depends on the attitude of the manager and the team spirit he can create.

Some managers, particularly when newly promoted, become intoxicated by the power of their position and do not delegate because they feel, incorrectly, that *delegation diminishes their power*.

Managers who are *promoted beyond their abilities* may find their new tasks distasteful or even frightening. They may take shelter in doing the work which they did successfully for years before being promoted, and which now should be done by their subordinates.

Perfectionism may be a barrier to delegation, especially if the manager is very experienced in the work of his subordinates. In view of the fact that he was promoted, his own standards of performance and decision making may have been much higher than would normally be expected. He may find it very difficult to accept that the benefits of delegation justify a somewhat lower general norm. It is also difficult, but essential, not to interfere when subordinates struggle and worry to make a decision which would apparently be much more easily and quickly made by the manager. But it is only by practice, even by making mistakes, that subordinates' performance will be improved.

It is one of the virtues of Key Results areas as described in Chapter 6 that they define both the areas where minimum standards are essential and those where employees can be allowed to experiment and make mistakes. Planning the work of a department by setting objectives in Key Results areas for each subordinate makes delegation much more practical. This is firstly because it reduces the opportunity for criticism and failures and secondly because the manager only has a limited number of activities to monitor, and therefore can be more confident of not overlooking anything important.

THE MANAGER/SUBORDINATE RELATIONSHIP

Managers are normally expected to be responsible for the resources under their command. If these include human resources – i.e. people, it means that the manager is responsible for the actions and performance of these people, she must therefore have full authority to correspond with her responsibilities.

The main spheres of decision making in this respect are:

- Choice
- Training
- Assessment
- Reward

In practice a manager's authority in this field is limited by law, by company policy and by the standards of society. Any such limitation must also apply to the manager's responsibility. It must, however, be reaffirmed categorically that success in man management depends largely on maximising the authority of individual managers.

CHOICE OF SUBORDINATES

Unless a manager can choose her subordinates her chances of success are very slim. The greatest problem arises when a manager takes over a department with its existing staff. She must then be given the opportunity to evaluate the staff before accepting the managerial role and the responsibility that goes with it. It is at this stage that any unsatisfactory staff should be identified with a view to replacement in due course.

With new employees the problem arises that they will not only be within the command of one manager but indirectly in the command of all that manager's superiors. These superiors should therefore be involved in the choice. An acceptable and common method of dealing with this problem is to have a selection committee comprising the manager, her immediate superior, and a staff specialist representing all other relevant managers. Alternatively a short list could be prepared by a staff specialist, and approved by the superior leaving the final choice to the manager herself.

«Selection, Ch. 13, p. 269»
«The Personnel Department, Ch. 12, pp. 243–244»

The right to choose also carries with it the right, in fact the obligation, to ensure that subordinates who do not meet minimum requirements are not "carried" by a department to the detriment of their colleagues, the department, and the enterprise as a whole. More often than not a person performing unsatisfactorily is trying to the best of their ability. In such circumstances dismissal from a "role" preferably involves the offer of more suitable employment elsewhere within the organisation, with appropriate training, if necessary, or even changing the role to suit a person who has given long and faithful service. These decisions involve higher and/or specialist managers, and a manager can, therefore, normally not dismiss her subordinates without reference to her own superior. This procedure also helps to ensure that the manager does not misuse her power of dismissal and that legal requirements are met.

TRAINING

Managers responsible for the performance of their subordinates are implicitly responsible for ensuring that these subordinates have the requisite skills and knowledge, and for arranging training to eliminate any deficiencies.

This is particularly important when staff are promoted or transferred into a position, and when there are changes in the requirements of the role. The latter situation is arising more and more frequently due to the rapid changes associated with modern society.

Training objectives and methods will be more fully dealt with later in Chapter 14.

ASSESSMENT

Managers should assess the abilities, knowledge and performance of their subordinates for a number of reasons satisfying the needs of the manager, the enterprise, and the subordinate himself.

The need of the manager is to fulfil the responsibilities of her role, by ensuring that decisions and tasks which have been delegated are being properly carried out. This involves appraising whether:

- adequate resources are available to the subordinate
- he has understood his instructions properly
- his authority has been defined clearly
- no conflict arises with the authority of other subordinates
- no responsibilities have been left unallocated
- the volume of work delegated is reasonable.

The need of the enterprise is for people's abilities to be used to the full. A manager's assessment of a person's ability and particularly his potential, are essential information for the planning of training schemes, recruitment and other aspects of manpower planning, and individuals' promotion and career structures. This involves identifying the individual's strengths. It also requires assessments to be standardised and recorded so that they can be retrieved for future use and correctly interpreted.

«*Promotion Policy, Ch. 13, p. 262*»

The need of individuals is for help in identifying and correcting their weaknesses, and in reassurance about their general performance. Insecurity and lack of confidence are a great hindrance to good performance. Managers who fail to discuss the performance of their subordinates with them, may actually create insecurity and lack of confidence. Managers who limit themselves to criticism undermine subordinates even more. It cannot be over-emphasised that regular, positive assessment interviews are essential for creating confident and enthusiastic staff with steadily improving performance.

Reassurance is particularly important after previous criticism.

METHODS OF ASSESSMENT

Subordinates should be assessed in the following spheres:

(1) Prescribed performance
(2) Discretionary performance
(3) Efficient use of resources.

Prescribed Performance

This includes all the compulsory components of a role and those where a specific level of performance is expected, whereas *discretionary* performance will include those things that are not essential, but which distinguish the best performers from the mediocre. Specific targets, and processing routine documents on time are examples of prescribed performance. Up-dating local organisational arrangements, or reporting to higher management on unexpected environmental events which *might* impinge upon the business are often discretionary.

Assessment of Prescribed Performance

This is relatively easy because actual performance can be compared to prescribed standards or targets, but when judging quantitative results, the following should be checked:

(a) How much change in method should the subordinate have developed in the way he does his job?

(b) Should he have been able to foresee any trouble that arose, and been ready with a solution?

(c) If *his* subordinates are of poor quality or have underperformed, is this due to the policy of, or interference by, his superiors or the company?

(d) Was the prescribed task realistic bearing in mind outside influences?

Assessment of Discretionary Performance

This is difficult to assess but gives a better picture of a subordinate's potential. He should be assessed in spheres such as:

Creativity in his own problem solving
Creativity in producing ideas for general or his colleagues' use
Innovation is his sphere of operation
Reaction to change
Relations with colleagues, other departments, etc.
Quality of his decisions and activities.

Assessment of Resources Used

The efficient use of resources tries to take account of some people achieving the same results as others with totally different use of resources. In two machine rooms with the same annual output the machines in one may need replacing after a year, while the others last for two years. On the face of it this would reflect on the machine room supervisors' control of maintenance and training of operators. In any case the first supervisor's depreciation cost is twice as high. It is also wise to take into account the extent to which a person makes use of the company's central services, and how much of his own manager's time he absorbs.

Assessment can be made on the basis of:

control reports
questionnaires completed by the subordinate

appraisal reports completed by the manager
individual interviews
group interviews.

It will be apparent that the choice of method depends on the immediate objective and that a combination of methods will almost certainly be required. Good control reports are, for instance, a simple way of assessing the performance of prescribed tasks but have little value in terms of building confidence.

APPRAISAL INTERVIEWS

Appraisal interviews should use the same concepts as selection interviews which are more fully described in Chapter 10. Above all the interviewer must be properly trained and prepared. The subordinate should, in this situation, be given advance notice that he will be appraised and ideally should either be asked to prepare a self-appraisal, or be given the opportunity to see his superior's assessment before the interview. He should be allowed to answer any criticisms.

One of the constant problems associated with formal appraisal is the fear of sub ordinates that their immediate supervisor is biased. The correct solution to this problem is undoubtedly to develop a satisfactory relationship between them, which is properly monitored by the supervisor's superior. The superior should also check the skill of the appraiser.

Three alternative solutions are however commonly used:

(a) The appraisal is carried out by a personnel officer in the presence of the immediate supervisor/manager. This does improve consistency of appraisal.

(b) The assessment interview is carried out by a higher level manager — e.g. the branch manager in a large branch, on the basis of an appraisal form completed by the immediate superior.

(c) An appraisal committee which visits different departments or sites. This gives great consistency but is only satisfactory if the immediate superior is co-opted on the committee.

All the above are more expensive because more staff are involved, but the need for and cost of training all managers and supervisors in assessment is reduced.

The whole assessment procedure depends for its success on appropriate action being taken as a result of the appraisal.

SPECIMEN ANNUAL APPRAISAL SHEET

APPOINTED OFFICERS

ANNUAL REPORT FOR THE PERIOD . . . . to 19

Name . . . .   Status . . . .   Salary . . . .

Time of present duties . . . . Grade . . . . . . Tier . . . . . .

	Mark
POTENTIAL Willingness to accept responsibility and to take decisions	
Initiative and drive	
Imagination (ability to question the present and to look ahead)	
Ability to develop a sound working relationship with: (a) customers and public	
(b) superiors	
(c) contemporaries and subordinates	
GENERAL Judgement	
Analysis of information	
Documentation processing	
PLANNING General understanding of bank activities	
Knowledge of local conditions	
Appreciation of support role	
TARGETS Lending – judgement and temperament	
New business including related services	
Commission income	

STAFF Induction	
Training	
Staff welfare and amenities	
Discipline and morale	
ORGANISATION Branch operation costs	
State of equipment/office	
Work flow and distribution	
Control of delegation	
PERSONAL Volume of work handled	
Technical knowledge and application	
Comment on health, attendance, punctuality	

Mark as appropriate from 1 to 4

(1) "Unsatisfactory"
(2) "Satisfactory"
(3) "Consistently Good"
(4) "Outstanding"

(1) Is this officer's job description correct? Do you wish to add or otherwise comment?

(2) Which personal characteristics or skills will be of the greatest value to this officer's advancement?

(3) Do you agree with this officer's comments on his/her training and development and in what ways can he/she be helped to improve his/her performance?

(4) What do you recommend as his/her next position?
How soon?

(5) Is there any alternative line of advancement to be explored in other divisions of departments?

CONCLUSIONS AND GENERAL COMMENTS

Signature . . . .
Position . . . .
Period of close association . . . . . .
Date   . . . .

PROBLEMS OF DIRECTION

There are of course many factors why management is not always up to the best standards. Most of these are dealt with under individual topics. There are however a number of general points to which attention may be drawn:—

Managers wrongly assume that problems to do with staff are the responsibility of the personnel department.

Managers wrongly rely on institutional authority.

Managers do not "develop" their subordinates.

Managers do not realise that staff will not carry out effectively orders which go against their own interest.

Managers assume that their subordinates will "pick up" skills and knowledge from fellow workers.

Practice Exercises

(1) On what type of authority do the managers in your office base their direction?

(2) Are there decisions which you think they should be delegating?

(3) Why do the managers in your office not always delegate?

(4) List the means by which you are assessed. Analyse the choice of method and comment on it.

(5) Who was responsible for recruiting you? What was your present manager's role in the choice?

(6) Who decides whether you need any training? How does he decide?

(7) Who arranges for your training?

(8) If you perform well – how is your superior performance rewarded?

(9) Who decides on penalties for employees who do not perform or behave well?

From Chapter 10 you should have learnt:

The different sources of authority.
When to delegate.
What to delegate.
What not to delegate.
The barriers to delegation.
The responsibilities of a manager in relation to his subordinates.
The importance and uses of appraisal.
● How appraisal helps a manager.
● How appraisal helps an employee.
● Why the personnel departments use appraisal.
● Different methods of appraisal.

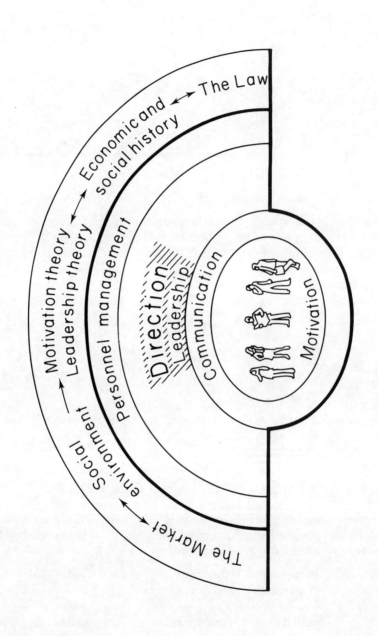

The Law ↔ Economic and social history

Motivation theory ↔ Leadership theory

Personnel management

Direction
Leadership

Communication

Motivation

Social environment

The Market

Chapter 11

Leadership

The effectiveness with which the management task is carried out has a major effect on the success of an enterprise. Because of this a great deal of work has been carried out to determine the factors which cause some managers to be much more successful than others. In this section the theory is examined, as well as the effect of some practical tools of leadership. Leadership is defined as the process of obtaining co-operation, interest, loyalty and participation.

STYLES OF LEADERSHIP

The theoretical experimental work can be grouped under four headings:

The Trait Approach
The Attitude Approach
The Group Relations Approach
The Contingency Approach

THE "TRAIT" APPROACH

Differences in leadership success were originally attributed to the traits or characteristics of the leaders concerned. Among the many characteristics cited as being important for good leadership are:

A high standard of personal behaviour
Fair judgement on personal matters
Firmness
The ability to identify and concentrate on key issues as opposed to trivialities
Calmness
Vitality and physical stamina
Persuasiveness

Decisiveness
Consistency
Integrity
Enthusiasm
Responsiveness (to attitudes and suggestions of subordinates)

Whilst many good leaders possess the above qualities there is ample evidence that none of them are really essential. Examples of outstanding leaders often showing diametrically opposed traits abound. Decisiveness and consistency, particularly in obeying his own rules are probably the most important. More recently the ability to anticipate subordinates' needs has been suggested as being equally essential.

Vanity, arrogance, and breaking one's own rules and procedures are suggested as the traits most likely to reduce the effectiveness of a manager.

Charisma

While it has not been possible to confirm the value of any of the traits mentioned there is no doubt that certain people have an exceptional ability to enthuse their subordinates and inspire them with courage or loyalty. This is however an innate characteristic of the individual and cannot be acquired or taught.

It may be more useful to focus on some of the *skills* which a good leader needs to possess. Those cited include:

● the *ability to take a helicopter view* – i.e. an overview of a problem as opposed to the details;

● the *ability to cope with the uncertainty* of longer term planning;

● "vision" enabling her to look further than her subordinates.

THE ATTITUDE APPROACH

This approach believes the attitude of a manager to his role to be the key to success. This approach is exemplified by Blake and Mouton's Managerial Grid, 1964.

Two main attitudes which distinguish management styles are "concern for people" and "concern for production". On the managerial grid the ideal is the 9.9 situation in which concern for both production and people is high. Failure of apparently highly motivated managers is attributed to a tendency to over-concentrate on task efficiency (say 9.1) or human relations (1.9). Blake and Mouton attempt to train managers by identifying their position on the grid and training them to move towards the ideal position.

Concern for Production

In banking terms this is concern for the work which goes into providing the bank's services to the customers. In the specialist departments it is concern

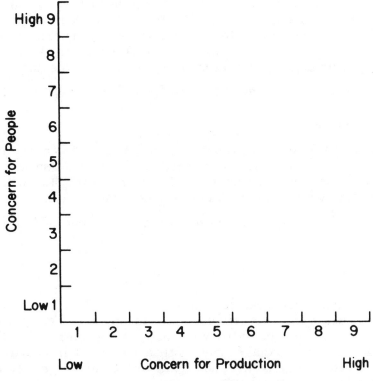

Fig. 11.1 The managerial grid

for providing the back-up services and advice which the operating departments require.

Concern for production involves:

(a) seeking all the information necessary for making plans and decisions;

(b) defining the department purpose and agreeing target;

(c) planning the work of the department and preparing workschedules;

(d) allocating tasks to subordinates and setting targets;

(e) setting group goals;

(f) controlling performance and initiating corrective action to ensure that the department as a whole and its individual members achieve the targets;

(g) ensuring that all activities in the department are aimed towards achieving departmental objectives;

(h) keeping discussions relevant;

(j) providing information.

Typically it is necessary to explain and clarify the plan and individual tasks to subordinates. Information received from higher management may have to be evaluated, interpreted and transmitted to subordinates. Colleagues and managers of specialist departments have to be kept informed of news of interest to them. Progress, suggestions, difficulties have to be reported to senior management. Often information has to be gathered, summarised and presented in a more suitable form.

(k)   Encouraging new ideas, checking their feasibility and the consequences of their introduction;

(l)   making decisions;

(m) innovating – this involves constant monitoring of methods and procedures to see whether improvements can be made. Changes in the task, the facilities and resources available, and in the staff will create opportunities for innovation even in the best run groups.

Many of these activities have been described in greater detail in Chapters 5 and 6.

Concern for People

The "Needs" of people have been described in Chapters 7 and 8. A manager's first task is to ensure that the "Hygiene factors" are satisfactory. In banking, salary levels and career security are outside the control of individual managers, but the bad manager can instil a feeling of insecurity in his subordinates by constant nagging and setting unrealistic targets. Insecurity is also created by showing behaviour opposite to that recommended in the "Trait" approach.

A manager needs to assess the extent of the "social" needs of his subordinates. Some people prefer to work on their own, others in groups; the manager should allocate the person to an appropriate role. In doing so he should also take into account other aspects of the person's "direction" of motivation, i.e. he should try to find him a role where the work fits his natural inclination.

The social need also comprises "recognition". By recognising and commenting upon good performance the manager will satisfy this important need.

Status needs can be met by a manager formally acknowledging the standing of individuals in terms of quality or quantity of output, or of other factors such as length of service.

Other individual needs which a manager should attempt to meet may include the need for:

Job satisfaction –   by assigning the right work to the right person, by proper job design, and by challenging but achievable targets.

Promotion prospects – by ensuring that people capable of promotion do get promoted.

Involvement –   by using an appropriate leadership style, but also by
                               keeping people informed about their progress and
                               that of the department, and about the company's
                               plans and policies.

Blake and Mouton's Managerial Grid is mainly used as a training technique. Managers study a problem and put forward proposals which are judged
by their peers in terms of achieving the best balance between concern for
people and concern for production. In this way managers are often per-
suaded that there may be a better alternative to their traditional methods.

More recently a three-dimensional grid has been put forward in which the
third axis is "Concern for effectiveness". This is an attempt to make the
hypothesis coincide more closely with observed situations.

«W. V. Reddin, *Managerial Effectiveness*, McGraw-Hill, 1970»

GROUP RELATIONS APPROACHES

A number of investigators have used this approach and have developed
similar descriptive models of the leadership process.

R. Tannenbaum and W. H. Schmidt in their article, "How to choose a Leadership Pattern" in the Harvard Business Review, Vol. 51, No. 3, 1973, suggest that there is a whole range of possible leadership styles from authoritative to participative. There is little doubt that this view is correct, but it is
useful to describe typical examples of the extremes and two intermediate
types. Thus four styles emerge – described as:

- Authoritative
- Missionary
- Consultative
- Participative

It will be noted that the styles described range from what might be considered the classical idea of a manager simply issuing orders which he expects
to be obeyed promptly and without question, to a high degree of involvement
in the decision-making process by those expected to contribute to the
implementation of the decisions.

«Motivation, Ch. 9, p. 190»

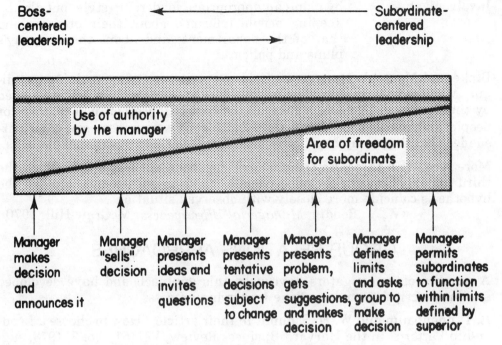

Fig. 11.2 Continuum of leadership behaviour

Participative Leadership

The "democratic" extreme means that only those courses of action put forward, or at least approved of, by the majority are implemented. This management style presupposes that the principles of democracy have been fulfilled, i.e.

● a majority tolerant of the reasonable attitudes of the minorities

● free expression of opinion

● unpressurized "voting"

● participants sufficiently well trained and "informed" to judge issues correctly.

This situation often arises at director and senior management levels, and in partnerships, but also at all levels in scientific or high-technology enterprises.

This leadership style also depends for its success on the willingness of employees to participate in discussions and take responsibilities.

Advantages of a Participative Style

Tasks in a modern business can be graded according to a number of criteria. Relevant to the topic of leadership are:

- the extent to which the success of the activity depends on the subordinate;

- the extent to which the volume of output depends on the subordinate;

- the extent to which quality of service depends on the subordinate.

In many routine, mechanised jobs the operator has no control over the level or quality of output. The operator's attitude to the job in such a case is not very important. On the other hand the quality and success of a training session depends considerably on the training officer in charge. If this officer thinks the session is unnecessary or ill-conceived, he is unlikely to perform well. Similarly the performance of a small branch depends upon co-operation between all employees at the branch. Co-operation cannot be forced on people – messages may or may not be passed, and it is easy to be too busy to help out someone else.

If subordinates are instructed, or asked, to carry out a task, they may do so enthusiastically – or they may not. Ensuring that they *always* carry out tasks to the best of their abilities is a key leadership objective and is very difficult to achieve. It has, however, been found that employees always do their best, if *they themselves* have chosen the task, determined the target, or decided on a policy. It is the likelihood of commitment from people participating in decision making, that makes participation an attractive management style.

In addition to the commitment of the participants, further advantages of participation are:

- It takes account of the practical experience of those involved in implementing decisions.

- It takes account of the opinions and attitudes of the participants.

- It improves co-operation because people learn to understand each other's problems.

- Discussion may create new ideas.

Disadvantage of the Participative Style

Cost and time are involved in distributing information for decision making.

Discussion may be protracted leading to *delays* and high costs in terms of time spent.

Agreement on a course of action *may not be reached*. Unsatisfactory compromises may result, or divisions and conflict created.

Powerful individuals may misdirect the efforts of the group.

Workload – Well-motivated subordinates are likely to be immersed in their own jobs and may well resent having to spend time participating in decisions which have no immediate relevance to them. This problem is least likely to arise if participation is recognised as a regular part of the job.

The Role of the Leader in the Participative Style

In the strict interpretation of the term the leader subordinates his views to that of the team making the decision. His role is still a very important one. He has to:

(a) *Choose the topics* which justify the relatively high cost of this management style, i.e. those which depend upon the commitment of the people concerned for their success, which are within their understanding, where there is ample time for discussion, and where he can anticipate that a concensus opinion will emerge;

(b) define the framework for discussion – i.e. time limits, location and organisation;

(c) organise the flow of information;

(d) handle meetings efficiently;

«Meeting, Ch. 3, p. 74»

(e) *avoid deadlock* by using his authority – if necessary by making a decision himself if no agreement is reached;

(f) *act as spokesman* and representative *vis-à-vis* other groups;

(g) *organise the implementation* of the course of action chosen.

(h) compensate the members of his staff for time lost through participation by reducing their remaining workload correspondingly, or by extra payment.

It should be noted that giving lip service to the participate style of leadership – i.e. involving people in discussion and then ignoring their conclusions – is counter productive. It alienates people from future discussion, undermines their confidence in the leader, and makes them obstructive to the course of action chosen.

Authoritative Leadership

Authoritarian or autocratic styles of management were originally based on the institutional and economic power of managers. It should be noted that on a world-wide basis this is still extensively exercised. In "western" type industrial nations the change in moral attitudes and power structure has limited this style of leadership to the management of crisis situations, e.g. the fire and para-military services, where speed of action supersedes all other considerations, and to situations where people willingly agree to accept orders.

Under such circumstances such a style is perfectly feasible. It may occur where, as in an investment department, subordinates have a high respect for the expertise of the manager, or where they accept – as in a foreign exchange dealing room – that speed of action is paramount and it is better to act on instructions and argue afterwards, than the other way round.

Paternalistic leadership is an authoritarian style where the leader is deemed always to act in the best interest of his employees. While still common in small companies, the size of a large corporation makes it impractical both owing to the variety of interests of employees and the difficulty of keeping in touch with what those interests are.

Consultative Leadership

On p. 224 the conditions necessary for a participative style are identified. Among these the ability of the subordinates to understand and evaluate the issues is important. "Consultation" may be used, when the co-operation and commitment of the staff is important and their knowledge and experience valuable, while either the whole issue, or important aspects of it, are outside their comprehension. The important difference between the participative and consultative style is, that in the latter the final decision is solely that of the manager, although he takes it after considering all the views put to him. This style is also advantageous if, for example because of continuity, it is felt that one person must be held solely responsible for implementation, or if there is a wide divergence of views among subordinates. The cost of consultative leadership and the time required for it is less than for participative leadership.

In a hierarchical structure formal consultation may involve a series of meetings at different levels. These may be time consuming and, by preventing staff from getting on with their jobs, effectively add to the workload. Without compensation or allowance this may lower motivation and morale. Informal consultation may be more successful.

«*Classical and Human Relations Approach, Ch. 3, pp. 52, 58*»

If employees do not wish to be involved in decision making – because of basic attitudes, pressure of work, or alienation, the consultative style is an alternative to participation.

Missionary Leadership

This is a further alternative to the consultative and participative styles, indicated when some commitment is necessary, but employees are unwilling, or unable to participate or where they are so committed to their own tasks that distracting them is counter-productive. It means that the manager takes decisions without prior discussion with his staff, but then "sells" them the idea by explaining the benefits to them, the department or the organisation. Other methods of persuasion may involve invoking the loyalty of subordinates or encouraging their competitive spirit.

THE CONTINGENCY APPROACH

In the survey of alternative leadership styles so far, there have been several comments regarding the effect of differences in staff or situations on the most appropriate style.

The "Law of the Situation"

This consideration was formally investigated by Mary Parker Follet in the 1920s and explained by the "Law of the Situation". She postulated that all individuals or groups have objectives which they are trying to achieve, and look for a leader who will help them achieve their objectives. Thus a different style of leadership would be needed, according to the characters and abilities of the staff, and the pressure upon them, and according to the type of situation. Typically, in a management team leadership often passes from one member to another depending on their respective experience of problems to be solved.

Importance of Correct Stimulus

When objectives are indeterminate or do not provide current incentives, a leadership style must be chosen to stimulate co-operation and interest.

Fiedler's Theory

More recently Fiedler has put forward the case for a style/situation interaction. He has identified the important situational variables as:

(1) The extent to which the leader is trusted and liked by his subordinates.

(2) The extent to which the tasks are spelt out in detail.

(3) The extent to which the leader has power to hire and fire.

Where each of these factors is favourable a task-oriented approach is said to be the most suitable. The same applies if *all* the factors are clearly unfavourable.

It is only in intermediate situations where the human relations approach is important.

«E. Fiedler, "Style or Circumstance – The Leadership Enigma",
Psychology Today, March 1964»

ACTION CENTRED LEADERSHIP (ACL)

It was noted in Chapters 7 and 8 that "group behaviour" is often different and/or independent from the behaviour of individuals. John Adair drew attention to the importance of leaders satisfying team needs as well as individual and task needs. He has designated these as the "Maintenance Needs".

In order to meet the maintenance needs a manager has to:

(a) set *group* tasks, goals and standards;

(b) brief the group on the above;

(c) maintain group standards and influence the rate and quality of performance;

(d) encourage and discipline the group;

(e) create a team spirit (see Chapter 7);

(f) identify conflict within the group and ensure that it is eliminated;

(g) maintain good communications within the group by setting a good personal example and by organising constructive meetings or other appropriate internal communications.

Dr Adair emphasises, like Blake and Mouton, that the successful leader is
the one who is able to "balance" the requirements of the team, the task and
the individuals. He illustrates this by means of the overlapping circles in
Fig. 11.3. These highlight the fact that some actions by the manager are
only relevant to one type of need – e.g. encouraging the career potential of
an individual. Others deal with two interacting needs – e.g. the ergonomic
design of a working position to speed up the work while its comfort and
smart appearance will add to the status of the operative. A few will cover all
three needs – a daily briefing meeting over coffee may improve control of the
job, encourage team spirit by establishing a group "ritual", and satisfy the
individual's "need to know".

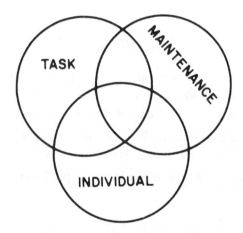

Fig. 11.3 Needs a team manager must meet

ACL is used as a training technique in some clearing banks, among others.
The training consists of about two days, based around leadership exercises.
The purpose of these practical exercises is to give an individual practice in
leading, at the same time giving the rest of the team participating roles, and
the rest of the course the opportunity to observe and to learn from the
leader's successes and failures. The leader is given as free a role as possible.

In addition to the practical exercises an ACL course includes periods for
tutor explanation, group discussion and group reporting.

LEADER'S CHECK LIST

KEY ACTIONS	TASK	TEAM	INDIVIDUAL
Define Objectives	Identify task and constraints	Involve team Share commitment	Clarify objectives Gain acceptance
Plan	Establish priorities Check resources Decide Set standards	Consult Encourage ideas/actions Develop suggestions Structure	Assess skills Set targets Delegate
Brief	Brief the team Check understanding	Answer questions Obtain feedback	Listen Enthuse
Support Monitor	Report progress Maintain standards Discipline	Co-ordinate Reconcile conflict	Advise Assist/Reassure Recognise effort Counsel
Evaluate	Summarise progress Review objectives Replan if necessary	Recognise success Learn from failure	Assess performance Appraise Guide and train

CONFLICT

Among a manager's most important duties is dealing with conflict in his command. He must remember that:

(a) he carries responsibility for failures caused by such conflict;

(b) unless conflicts are exposed, there is no way of knowing whether they are important, nor of preventing unauthorised compromise settlements;

(c) conflicts may be due to his own attitude, performance or instructions.

PERSONAL CONFLICT

Conflict between individuals or groups due to clashes of personality or objectives are the most damaging and at the same time the most difficult to settle. The main effort of managers must therefore be directed towards prevention rather than cure. This is achieved by:

(1) careful and correct selection of staff;

(2) avoiding instruction which may lead to clashing personal objectives;

(3) preventing managerial conflict from becoming personal;

(4) ensuring that incipient conflict is brought into the open.

EXECUTIVE CONFLICT

Executive or *managerial* conflict is said to occur when there is disagreement as to the correct decision or course of action when dealing with a management issue. Provided it is constructive, this type of conflict may be quite harmless, or even positively desirable. As previously explained it is the manager's task to see that a decision is reached within an acceptable time.

«*Group Decision Making, Ch. 5*»

INTER-GROUP CONFLICT

Group conflict occurs almost inevitably where there is a division of labour. It is also common as between management and employees. The severe problems created by inter group competition have been identified on p. 160. To avoid such conflicts

(a) There should be relatively greater emphasis on total organisational rather than group effectiveness. Groups and departments should be measured and rewarded on their contribution to the whole.

(b) Frequent and effective interaction and communication should be stimulated between groups and help given to other groups should be specifically rewarded.

(c) Rotation of staff between groups and departments should be organised to promote mutual understanding of each other's problems.

SETTLING CONFLICT

In settling disputes it is first necessary to ensure that the "real" as opposed to "apparent" difference is determined, that individual issues are separated from each other, and that differences are not due to communication problems. When the issue has been clarified it can be settled by:

● Domination
● Compromise
● Integration

Domination

One way of settling an argument is for one party to it, or the manager, to use his power to get his own way. Managerial authority, strikes, personality or influence may be used to impose a solution. Provided an individual or group has the necessary power and uses it for the enterprise's good, this may not be a bad thing in cases where there is no consensus of opinion or when the result of alternative outcomes is very uncertain. It is however important for a manager using domination to anticipate the other parties' responses and to consider whether such responses may adversely affect other issues.

Compromise

Compromise involves choosing an alternative which meets some but not all of the desires of the parties to a dispute. It is the basis of collective bargaining in the United Kingdom. It is bad in principle because it usually means that neither party is fully satisfied.

Integration

Integration means finding common ground between the parties and choosing an alternative which will, if possible, satisfy all their common desires. Very often this can be achieved by revaluing desires in terms of those which are important, and those which are not strongly entrenched. Integration is a very important managerial task requiring considerable effort and ingenuity. Integration is made more difficult by:

● The desire to dominate
● Inadequate implementation of agreed plans
● Language and communication problems
● Misrepresentation by the leaders of groups
● Lack of training.

The Desire to Dominate

This is a personality characteristic and one that should ideally be recognised before a person is recruited. People of this type refuse to back down from a position they have taken up and will not be convinced by rational argument. Even if it is to their own detriment they promote their view by threats, delaying and legalistic tactics and suborning others. Such persons may be good leaders in an authoritative situation, but make integration very difficult.

Inadequate Implementation of Agreed Plans

Where plans have been agreed after democratic discussion or consultation, and management then refuses to implement them, or implements them in a way which was not intended, those involved will be disillusioned. They are liable to refuse to reconsider their priorities and personal interests, which is an important part of the process of integration, because their experience tells them the other party will not keep to their side of the bargain. This is a form of alienation which takes years to eradicate once present.

Language and Communication Problems

Problems of levels of abstraction often occur in discussions between management and operators, or the unions representing them (cf. p. 190). Communication difficulties are also frequent between different specialist departments, or specialist and operating departments using terminology not mutually familiar. Although a well-known and easily identified problem, it is often an obstacle to settling conflict by integration. It can be solved by training in awareness and communication skills.

«Communication Problems, Ch. 9, p. 188»

Misrepresentation

Many disagreements are discussed by *representatives* of the groups concerned. They may be trade union representatives discussing redundancy policy with personnel managers representing the firm, or representatives from lending, security, money transmission, and marketing departments discussing the launch of a new credit card. It is very important to ensure that:

(a) the representatives accurately present the views of the interests concerned;

(b) that proposals are accurately reported back to the interests, with full back up information;

(c) that feed-back from the interests is again accurate and realistic.

Misrepresentation (apart from the language problem already mentioned) may be due to failure of the representatives to do their job properly, or because they are promoting their *personal* views or interests.

The latter is very common because people with strong views and personalities often realise that committees and other discussion forums are excellent media for promoting their causes. While genuinely representative members of a common interest group often regard committee membership as an undesirable additional chore, people with minority views are willing and enthusiastic to take on the job. Hence there is a genuine danger of misrepresentation by "militants" in industrial relations, or by managers with an axe to grind in executive conflict. This highlights the importance of an effective method of choosing representatives.

Failure to do the job properly may be due to lack of interest or ability. The former again requires proper selection and possibly compensation for additional workload, whereas the latter highlights the importance of training representatives properly.

Training

Integrating conflict requires creativity, and analytical decision making abilities of a high order. Lack of training in any of these may be an obstacle to integration.

«Committees, Ch. 3, pp. 71–74»
«Role of the Personnel Department, Ch. 12, pp. 237, 244»
«Collective Bargaining and Grievance Procedures, Ch. 16, pp. 310, 313»

Practice Exercises

(1) Identify the styles of leadership which your manager adopts.

(2) Does he use it in the right circumstances?

(3) Are there any issues about which you would like to be consulted?

(4) Would you wish to participate in any particular types of decision?

(5) When do you desire a manager to use his authority?

(6) How do you rate your Managers on the managerial grid?
(Try this exercise with several friends.)

(7) When a disagreement occurs in your office or at home, note down by which method it was settled. Would the settlement have been easier or better if the issue had been dealt with earlier?

From Chapter 11 you should have learnt:

A definition of leadership.

Four Leadership Theories.

What concern for production involves.

What concern for people involves.

The factors to be considered when deciding on how to lead.

The role of the leader when a participative style is adopted.

The meaning and content of ACL.

The significance of "constructive" conflict.

Three methods of settling conflict.

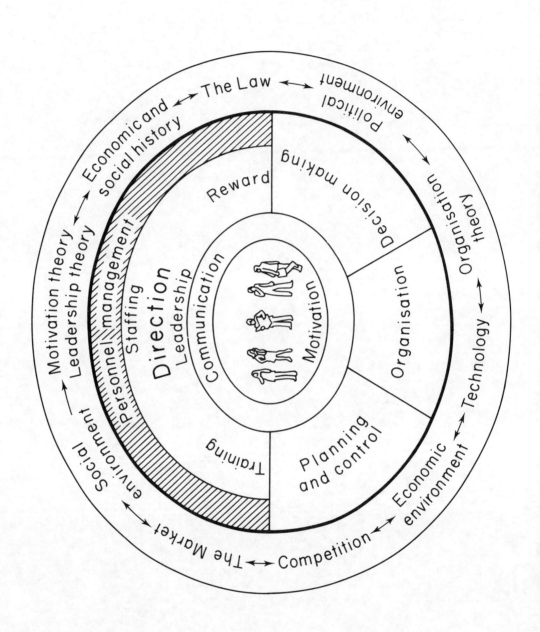

Chapter 12

Personnel Services

INTRODUCTION

The Management of personnel is the direct responsibility of the superior of the personnel concerned, and she must have the authority to deal with them. A separate personnel function or department is not intended to replace the manager's role in respect of her subordinates. The Personnel Department should concern itself with:

(1) personnel policy

(2) manpower planning

(3) providing advice

(4) providing services

(5) representing any other managers concerned with the same subordinates, as a group or individually and dealing with corporate personnel matters

(6) industrial relations.

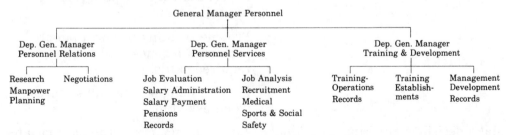

Fig. 12.1 Chart showing typical organisation of a personnel department in a clearing bank. Many of the departments will also be divided on an area basis

PERSONNEL POLICY

It is one of the important duties of the Chief Executive in any organisation that employs people as a major resource, to lay down guide-lines for how this resource is to be managed. These guidelines will become personnel policy. In large companies there will be personnel specialists responsible for advising the Chief Executive on the options available, and on their advantages and disadvantages. These specialists may be represented on the board by a Personnel Director, or indirectly by another Director responsible for a number of service departments; often they report directly to the Managing Director himself.

An important point to note is that the Personnel Department should not have the authority to *make* policy, it only advises on what the policy should be. The actual decisions on policy cannot be separated from the overall strategy of the organisation and must therefore be made at the highest level.

The *control* of personnel policy is, in large companies, also delegated to the personnel department.

To distinguish between the roles of operating management and the Personnel Department in personnel matters we can separate their duties as follows:

Operating (line) managers	Personnel Department
Decide Personnel Policies	Advise on choice of correct personnel policies. Recommend changes needed.
Implement Personnel Policies	Keep middle and lower level managers informed of personnel policies. Check that policies are being correctly interpreted and applied. Inform managers of how their performance compares with expectation and the performance of similar managers.
	Provide training in how to apply personnel policies, and in the required skills.
	Provide help, advice and service when asked for.
Make decisions affecting individuals, or groups within their own command	Advise managers at the appropriate senior level regarding decisions which affect large groups of employees.

Operating (line) managers	Personnel Department
Contact Personnel Department and request approval or criticism for any proposed decisions which might affect other departments, before such decisions are finalised.	Advise line managers of the possible impact of their decisions on other sections of the organisation. Inform higher management of possible embarrassing decisions about to be taken by line managers against the advice of Personnel Department. Propose rules to avoid embarrassing personnel decisions by managers.

MANPOWER PLANNING

Manpower planning is concerned with all the people in an enterprise. During their career people will work for many different managers, in different departments and even different divisions. Manpower must be examined as a whole. This necessitates a centralised effort which is normally carried out by the personnel department. It is part of the corporate planning effort and the work must be clearly integrated with other planning departments.

Planning has become accepted as an essential element of modern management. This is applied to all the resources used in an enterprise. The human resources are of great importance to the financial sector and planning human resources should therefore receive appropriate attention.

Manpower planning may be related as follows to the key questions asked in corporate-planning:

(1) What kind of business should we be in?
   What kind of workforce *should* we have at all levels?
   How does our present workforce differ – both better and worse – from what we should have?

(2) What market, production, technological, investment and organisational changes does (1) imply?
   What changes in skills and numbers does this require?
   What potential for these requirements does our workforce possess?

(3) What action is required to achieve the changes in (2)?
   What changes in manpower policies and programmes are required?

(4) On what parameters are the plans based and what effect will changes in these parameters have?

On what personnel and manpower parameters is the manpower plan based, under what circumstances might they be changed and what provision will have to be made for these possibilities?

«*Objective Setting, Ch. 1, p. 4*»
«*Planning, Ch. 6, p. 125*»

DEFINITION

A definition of manpower planning is "a strategy for the acquisition utilisation, improvement and preservation of an enterprise's human resources". In order to achieve this, the fundamentals required are:

● A time scale – usually in line with the strategic planning cycle of the company.

● A numerate approach – manpower planning is concerned with "quantities" of skills – rather than individual people. These two first fundamentals differentiate manpower planning from other personnel management areas.

● The commitment of resources to do the job properly.

● A systemisation of method, particularly with regard to personnel records.

● The use of a computer – in larger companies.

Planning does not mean trying to predict and control exactly what is going to happen in the future. It means being clear about what one is trying to achieve, how one intends to achieve it, and the assumptions which have been made about the performance of one's own company, and about outside events which may affect the people employed or to be employed by the enterprise.

A plan made on this basis enables one to monitor the assumptions and thus to react rapidly to any changes in them, to ensure that one is still able to achieve one's original objective.

SPECIFIC REASONS FOR MANPOWER PLANNING

(1) In many companies wages and other benefits represent a substantial proportion of turnover. This component of cost must therefore be carefully planned in the context of a corporate plan.

(2) Manpower of the correct type and quality is a scarce resource. Due to its relative immobility this may be so even in conditions of high national unemployment.

(3) Legislative as well as moral restraints limit the way in which manpower can be deployed, particularly in the short term.

(4) Retirement, promotion and recruitment interact in a complex way. If a staff structure is allowed to develop haphazardly imbalances may arise which may be difficult to correct.

(5) Because learning new skills, even if practical, is a slow process, changes have to be planned far ahead to ensure that necessary skills are available when wanted.

(6) The comparatively well educated and sophisticated employees of the future will expect companies to provide a rational career structure and controlled change.

DETERMINING THE MANPOWER OBJECTIVE

In order to determine a manpower objective, it becomes necessary to forecast both the demand and supply.

Demand for Manpower

The demand for manpower is determined from the organisation structure planned to meet the enterprise's objectives. This involves determining the workload and must take into account manpower utilisation which is inevitably less than 100%.

Demand then has to be aggregated for:

departments	part-timers
grades	function
shiftwork of different types	occupation
	skill

Supply of Manpower

The starting point for a supply forecast are the existing personnel records which should show each employee's:

department	occupation	experience	earnings
grade	skill	mobility	qualifications
function	age and sex	rating	length of service.

In the past the quantities of information involved have limited the detail with which analyses could be made. A large clearing bank employs 50–100,000 people. The record of each person has to be updated at least annually. Full computerisation of records will facilitate greater detail in manpower planning.

The Process of Manpower Planning

Attrition Process

This is the reduction which will occur in existing manpower levels if no corrective action is taken. It comprises:

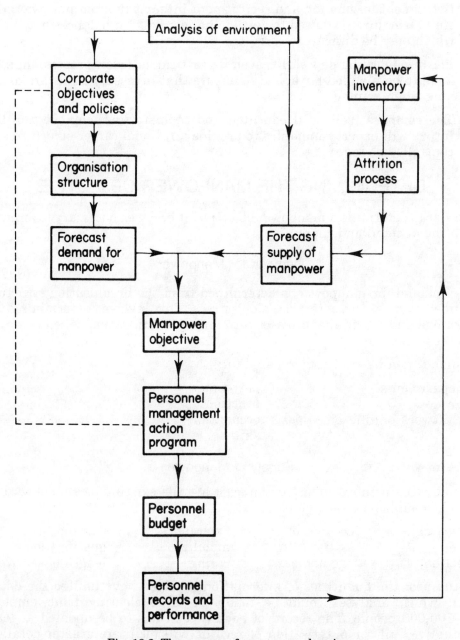

Fig. 12.2 The process of manpower planning

(i) *Retirements* – it should be possible to predict these accurately from the records.

(ii) *Promotions out* – personnel who are expected to be promoted out of a grade during the time scale.

(iii) *Transfers out* – many jobs are effectively stepping stones to others, so due allowance for expected losses must be made.

(iv) *Uncontrollable wastage* – there is a "normal" rate of wastage for different classifications, due to the personal circumstances of employees – e.g. illness or marriage.

(v) *Controllable wastage* – this is concerned with people leaving for other employment, depending on factors such as comparative wage rates, industrial relations and job satisfaction.

External Supply

In order to forecast the supply of manpower available from outside sources the planner must study the manpower which is expected to become available during the period of the plan in the catchment area of the enterprise. Output from educational and training establishments together with changes in social structure, e.g. school leaving age, are relevant, as are changes in social attitudes making some trades or skills more attractive than others. The pattern of national as well as local demand for people in each classification must be assessed, as well as their mobility. The enterprise's image will affect its ability to attract people from other firms.

Total Supply of Manpower

The combination of existing resources, attrition and external supply will enable manpower planners to forecast the extent to which the company's manpower balances, showing surpluses and deficiencies in all classifications. The manpower objective consists of correcting these imbalances by recruitment, transfer, training and if necessary redundancies.

Records

It will be appreciated that effective manpower planning relies heavily on accurate records relevant to the function.

ADVICE AND SERVICES

SPECIALISED KNOWLEDGE

The advisory function of a Personnel Department is not confined only to advising managers how to conduct their personnel affairs. It is also intended to make specialised knowledge available to line managers. Many incidents and occurrences which are rare in the context of an average line manager's experience are included in the education of personnel specialists. Personnel Managers should be specifically trained to have knowledge which the ordinary manager is not expected to have. Such knowledge would include the

(1) relevant sections of law,

(2) availability and function of welfare agencies and whom to contact,

(3) rating of different schools and colleges as sources of recruitment,

(4) selection tests available and their success as performance predictors,

(5) The comparative success of alternative reward structures and incentive schemes.

(6) Experiments and attempted innovations in personnel management in the company in the past.

(7) New developments being pioneered in all the above areas by government, educational institutes or other organisations in all the above fields.

SPECIALISED SERVICES

Line managers in a modern business are often appointed because they are highly skilled in specialised fields – e.g. systems analysis, selling or negotiating. A good line manager must have sufficient social skills to manage his staff, but he may be weak in some of the more specialised skills of personnel management, e.g.

- Formulating recruitment advertising
- Interviewing for selection
- Monitoring organisational health
- Counselling on personal problems
- Research into industrial relations
- Job Evaluation
- Training

The Personnel Department is responsible for ensuring that such skills are available in the business, are known to be available by those who might need them and *are* used whenever necessary.

There is no clear division between providing advice and services. Some parts of the personnel officer's job are purely advisory, some are routinely provided as a service. Between the two extremes advice often leads to a service being provided.

ECONOMIES OF SCALE

Even if neither service nor advice is necessarily required, some tasks are taken over by the Personnel Department purely because of economies of scale. Recruitment and training are the prime examples. Economies of scale also occur in personnel activities which have a corporate dimension – such as industrial relations, salary administration, centralised records and communication policy.

Corporate Personnel Services

Personnel Records

In other parts of this book properly kept records have been identified as the key to successful staff appraisal and manpower planning. Records of individual members of staff must be kept for salary administration and for a number of statutory purposes such as pensions and sickness pay. They are also needed to provide information for promotion purposes. In the aggregate staff records provide the basis for identifying training requirements and monitoring organisational health. To meet all the demands for information for these various purposes it is most practical to centralise personnel records. The case for centralisation is reinforced by the need to keep personal records confidential. A few people in charge of central records can ensure that information on an individual is only divulged to authorised persons.

«Centralisation, Ch. 4, pp. 87–91»
«Appraisal, Ch. 10, pp. 210–215»

Problems of Centralisation

The main problems about centralising records are:

(a) making sure that the correct records are kept. It is not unusual for some records to be kept for decades although they have never been looked at by anybody and never will be. Often this is because they are easily, perhaps automatically, recorded – e.g. a person's overtime payments. Other, quite important, information, may not be recorded at all because it is more difficult to obtain – e.g. why people leave.

(b) ensuring that information is up to date and complete. Incomplete and outdated information may cause ill-feeling and industrial relations problems, and makes good control impossible (cf. p. 135).

(c) making sure that records are accessible. Personnel records are intended to be used as management information. Many decisions have to be made by a deadline. Managers will only use the information if it is easily and quickly available.

One of the important benefits of computers is that the problems listed are considerably reduced. There is ample capacity for the records to be kept. Local terminals can be used for personnel officers – or even operating managers – to update information regularly. Data no longer required can be easily removed. Information on individuals can be called up at terminals by those supplied with confidential entry codes. Finally it is comparatively simple to arrange for management information to be extracted as required.

It is normally still necessary to keep certain documents, such as appraisal sheets, medical reports, or copies of disciplinary letters, in individual record wallets or files.

Data in Personnel Records

The data received would normally include:

Personal Details

Name and address	Medical history
Date of birth	Marital status
National Insurance	Number of Dependants
Educational and professional qualifications	Emergency contacts

Career Information

Position held	Dates from–to	Department	Salary Scale	Reason for Transfer
....	....	....	.....	....
....	....	....	.....	....

Appraisal Record

Date	Weaknesses (identified)	Action (proposed)	Review date
....	....	....	....

Date	Potential (identified)	Development (recommended)	Ready for Transfer to	Ready for Promotion to Grade
....	....	....	....	....
....	....	....	....	....

Training Record

Course attended	From	To	Passout Grade	Training Officer's Comment
....	.....	..	....	....

Disciplinary Record

Formal disciplinary warning		Written warning		Final warning		Action
date	Present	date	signatory	date	signatory	
....	....	....	....	....	....	......

Reasons for Leaving

The reasons for leaving are best determined at "Separation Interviews". At these interviews employees are often willing to make critical comments on conditions about which they would not normally complain. While single comments may be due to the employee not fitting in, regular comments of one type – e.g. work overload, or dissatisfaction with a manager, may indicate a serious management problem. Changes in the pattern of reasons for leaving are also useful indicators.

Reward Systems

It is necessary to have an equitable reward system in a firm to maintain a stable staff who will do their best to help the firm achieve its objectives. The reward system consists of a number of inter-related items known as a "benefit package", fully described in Chapter 15.

The personnel department will be responsible for administering several items in this package including Pensions, Holidays, Incentive Schemes and Fringe Benefits. Salary administration, including job evaluation, which is dealt with in Chapter 12 is usually also its responsibility, and in some companies even the payment of salaries comes under its umbrella.

Corporate Information

In order to integrate an intelligent work force into the organisation, and in order to keep in touch with their views and aspirations it is essential for information to flow freely where it is necessary. This is largely a question of organisation and of ensuring that managers are skilled in communication. The personnel department may advise in the field of industrial relations and will probably be responsible for the effficient running of consultative, grievance and disciplinary procedures.

Knowledge of company objectives and policies can be promoted by house magazines, notice boards and circulars but it is important that this is part of an overall communications policy. Operating managers must be briefed before information is passed to lower levels, to avoid undermining their credibility. In general the order in which various people in the enterprise receive information is very important. Much resentment is caused by information given in the wrong order. New problems and opportunities and the effect of action taken in parts of the business, should be communicated to others who might benefit. Senior management should be kept informed of changes in mood or attitude at lower levels.

The department is also well placed to draw attention to blocks and gaps in the communication system.

«Problems of Communication, Ch. 9, pp. 188–190»

There is an ACAS Code of Practice which, subject to various reservations, makes it obligatory for employers to provide the following information to employees' representatives:

(i) *Pay and benefits:* principles and structure of payment systems; job evaluation systems and grading criteria; earnings and hours analysed according to work-group, grade, plant, sex, out-workers and homeworkers, department or division, giving, where appropriate, distributions and make-up of pay showing any additions to basic rate or salary; total pay bill; details of fringe benefits and non-wage labour costs.

(ii) *Conditions of service:* policies on recruitment, redeployment, redundancy, training, equal opportunity, and promotion; appraisal systems; health, welfare and safety matters.

(iii) *Manpower:* numbers employed analysed according to grade department, location, age and sex; labour turnover; absenteeism; overtime and short-time; manning standards; planned changes in work methods, materials, equipment or organisation; available manpower plans; investment plans.

(iv) *Performance:* productivity and efficiency data; savings from increased productivity and output; return on capital invested; sales and state of order book.

(v) *Financial:* cost structures; gross and net profits; sources of earnings; assets; liabilities; allocation of profits; details of government financial assistance; transfer prices; loans to parent of subsidiary companies and interest charged.

Industrial relations is another important corporate personnel activity which is dealt with in chapter 16.

«Management of Conflict, Ch. 11, pp. 230–233»

Employee Services

Physical Conditions

Physical working conditions generally have to be maintained at a level in keeping with accepted standards; these vary between different parts of the country. In areas of low unemployment the place of work must be sufficiently attractive to ensure adequate recruitment and avoid employees leaving through dissatisfaction with their surroundings. When no more positive motivation to work can be provided people will move from one firm to another to obtain better physical surroundings.

Social Facilities

Canteens (and even more so sports facilities) contribute to the atmosphere of a department, but also serve the much more important purpose of creating a social climate in which primary groups can be formed. Here employees can fill their needs of companionship, loyalty and status. These facilities are therefore especially important in departments where no other opportunity of meeting these needs exists. Large Giro or credit card centres are typical.

Morale

The working conditions in terms of the atmosphere, systems and procedures in the firm are not normally within the authority of the personnel department. It should however, be the responsibility of the department to advise operating management of the importance of morale and how to monitor it. It should also collate, interpret and draw attention to comments from employees which may make specific complaints, or those who leave particular departments of the firm.

Welfare

It is being increasingly recognised that employees not free from serious personal problems are unlikely to devote themselves properly to their work – and whether a problem is serious depends on the attitude of the employee – not of anyone else. At operator level personal worries tend to show themselves in absenteeism, lateness, increased accidents and bad workmanship, whereas at manager levels mistakes, neglect, and deteriorating relations with colleagues, superiors and subordinates are common symptoms.

The good operating manager should identify these situations and is often in the best position to offer advice. Where there are wide spans of control, or frequently recurring problems of one type, reference to a specialist is probably more effective. Many of these problems can be solved by the provision of employee services, ranging from full educational, medical and housing services by companies undertaking projects in out of the way places, to hairdressing and counselling facilities. These services should not be confused with benefits such as luncheon vouchers or medical insurance subscriptions, which are just alternatives to money-wages.

Health

One example of personal problems is ill health, either of the employee or one of his relatives. The function of the company welfare services is to make it easier for employees to take the right action without jeopardising their jobs. Health at work can be considered from the point of view of legal or welfare requirements. The government health regulations include those which have become part of the cultural pattern, such as the prohibition of night work for women, and a wide range of minimum standards for temperature, cleanliness, overcrowding etc. Legal standards are normally below the levels which constitute acceptable working environments. It is one of the functions of the Health and Safety section of a personnel department to keep operating managers informed of any changes in the regulations, and to provide initial training for new incumbents of roles. Equally important, they should ensure that managers are aware of the standards maintained in other companies and industries.

CONTROL

One of the most important functions of a personnel department is to ensure that individual managers do not take decisions or actions which have a detrimental effect on other parts of the business. This is why many personnel matters are centralised. Unfortunately some of this centralisation is undertaken for the wrong reasons – e.g. because it enhances the power of the personnel department, or because it is much easier and more practical to make a "rule" apply to everybody, than to make decisions in individual cases. The correct procedure is for personnel departments to monitor the result of the managers' actions and if these show an unsatisfactory trend to report this both to the manager and his superior. The department should then be available to advise on corrective action or provide help if needed.

«Control, Ch. 6»

Illustration

Personnel department finds from labour turnover figures that this is higher in Mr Hoskins' office than in other similar offices. A report is sent to Hoskins with a copy to his superior. The superior requests an investigation by the personnel department with recommendation for action.

Methods of Control

«Ch. 6, pp. 136–141»

In the typical large company within the financial sector personnel departments are located away from many of the operating sites. Control mainly relies on monitoring performance indicators from the various branches and departments. Some of these are direct indicators, e.g. whether the required reports are received at all. Examples of reports which are normally expected include reports of:

Appraisals
Informal disciplinary warnings
Grievances upheld by grievance officers
Summary Dismissals
Commission or bonuses earned
Separation interviews.

Just as important are indirect indicators derived from monitoring management information which is not specifically gathered for personnel purposes, or by accumulating personnel management information, analysing and interpreting it.

The former involves studying the extent to which departments achieve their objectives and implement change, and considering whether failure to do so may be due to personnel policies not being applied. The number of complaints from customers also comes under this heading.

Indicators such as

absenteeism
labour turnover
number of grievances
sickness claims
industrial disputes

are indirect in the sense that they only become useful if the figures are accumulated regularly to show trends, and analysed for comparison between departments, branches and periods. Labour turnover is described in greater detail below.

Just as it is important to control the proper implementation of personnel policies, it is perhaps even more important to control whether these policies are the correct ones. It must be remembered that personnel policies are designed, not as an end in themselves, but to help the company achieve its objectives. A reward structure which is so attractive that no employees ever leave, may become very embarrassing in a period of technical change when natural wastage could save forced redundancies. Non-transferable pension schemes were originally introduced to stop employees changing jobs. In many cases they have since proved detrimental to both employees and employers.

When considering the meaning of the direct and indirect indicators listed above, the personnel department must distinguish carefully between attributing the cause to ineffective application of a policy or to the policy itself. Personnel policy can also be checked by comparing a firm's performance with that of firms using different personnel policies. Special control methods such as Staff Attitude Surveys are also available.

It should be noted that when the Personnel Department exercises control it does so on behalf of and as a service to senior management.

LABOUR STABILITY

Labour stability is the extent to which a labour force of a company remains the same over a period. There are situations where labour stability is not important. If there is a plentiful supply of labour and the work to be done requires no skills beyond those which the people in the labour pool have in any case, labour stability is not important. If a person leaves, a telephone call to the Job Centre or an agency will obtain an immediate replacement.

In practice there are few of these situations. In this country, cleaners, who are often part-time, and are probably required to work on their own, are probably the most general example. In the finance sector even this does not apply. Because of the need for security, the previous history of the cleaning staff has to be vetted. This involves management time and therefore cost, which is wasted as soon as the person leaves. People who are sufficiently trustworthy are scarce, there may be a delay in obtaining a replacement and the job is therefore not done. This again is not terribly significant in a cleaning job. In a job which is part of an operating process it may cause delays or a loss of output, and if customer contact is part of the job as well there may be a loss of goodwill or even business because customers like continuity.

Many roles cannot be filled properly unless considerable sums have been expended on training. All of this is lost when the employee leaves. So is any experience which he has gained during his work; experience affects output, efficiency and error rate; experienced employees also need much less supervision.

Where there is interdependence between the work of a number of employees, the work of all of them is affected if one leaves and is not immediately replaced by another of equal calibre. Where people work as a team, or where there is good group spirit, the atmosphere will also be disrupted. Repeated departures will lower group morale and may lead to the break-up of a group or team.

From the foregoing it is evident that staff stability is desirable both from the point of view of keeping costs low, and of the positive benefits derived from a team spirit and the feeling of being satisfied in one's job.

To achieve labour stability the hygiene factors as outlined by Herzberg must reach acceptable levels. Among these, management systems, management style and the nature of the work may be singled out for special mention, because they are less clear than the remainder.

"Management systems" refers to the organisation of the processes and management of the company. The reader is referred to Chapters 3 and 4 for the explanation of various organisational formats ranging from the bureaucratic to organic. To maintain labour stability the type of organisation must be matched with the people employed. Those wishing to use their initiative and creative ability will be unhappy in a bureaucracy, and may leave; while those who prefer following detailed instructions will leave an organic environment.

The same concept of matching, but on a more local and individual scale applies to management style as described in the Contingency Approach to leadership in Chapter 9 of this book. An unstable workforce in a particular department or branch may well be due to the manager not adapting his style as the people, the situations and the occasions demand.

We know from motivation theory that if people are doing work which they consider worthwhile, and where they can see a result of which they can be proud, they will be positively motivated. There are few jobs with that degree of job satisfaction in the financial sector but the *type* of work – e.g. analysing documents, dealing with accounts or foreign documentation, does give sufficient satisfaction to most people for them not to wish to move.

G. J. Cohen in a survey of AIB students in the London area found that job satisfaction was mentioned by 67% students in 1983 as ranking next to or higher than pay in their benefit packages.

Correct Job Design and Job Enrichment (Chapter 3) will also help in increasing stability.

Lack of promotion prospects is a reason frequently given by staff who leave their jobs. This is more likely to happen in a small office such as the London branch of one of the smaller overseas banks than in a large organisation, where there is an attractive career structure. Even with a proper promotion policy some people will still feel they are being overlooked, or have gone as far as they can in a particular company, and will therefore leave.

Measures of Labour Stability

There are a number of ways of measuring the stability of a work-force, or alternatively of the wastage of labour.

Labour Stability Index

This is defined as:

$$\frac{\text{Number with more than one year's service}}{\text{Total employed 1 year ago}} \times 100$$

Labour Turnover Index (BIM Index)

$$\frac{\text{Number of leavers in the year}}{\text{Average employed during the year}} \times 100$$

Average Length of Employment

$$\frac{\text{Sum of the length of employment of each person leaving}}{\text{Number of leavers during the year}}$$

Illustration

In Westown the bank employs 300 people below grade 6. During the year 30 people leave and are replaced.

In Eastown the number of employees at the beginning of the year is the same. By the end of a month twelve people have left. These are replaced, but 10 of the 12 leave by the end of another month. Of the 10 second replacements 8 leave after a month and are again replaced with a better group who stay. Compare the labour stability in the two branches.

BIM Index

$$\text{Westown } \frac{30}{300} \times 100 = 10\%$$

$$\text{Eastown } \frac{(12 + 10 + 8)}{300} \times 100 = 10\%$$

Labour Stability

$$\text{Westown } \frac{300 - 30}{300} \times 100 = 90\%$$

$$\text{Eastown } \frac{300 - 12}{300} \times 100 = 96\%$$

It will be noticed that the BIM Index does not differentiate between the two situations, whereas the labour stability index does. The latter is also more positive as it highlights good rather than bad performance.

A certain amount of staff wastage is inevitable. This is known as uncontrollable wastage and consists of staff who:

(a) leave at retiring age after a lifetime of service

(b) die in service or retire prematurely due to illness

(c) leave for family reasons – e.g. marriage or re-location of other members of the family

(d) leave for other reasons unconnected with the firm.

The total wastage for the above reasons is unlikely to be less than 6–7%.

It will be noted that the uncontrollable wastage impinges differentially on various groupings of employees. Those who leave for family reasons will be mainly (although of course not exclusively) women between 20–30. Retirement will have virtually no impact on the same group.

This highlights the fact that the value of all the measures of wastage depends on how well the group they are applied to is chosen. The smaller and, above all, the more homogeneous a group is, the more likely it is that turnover figures will provide meaningful management information. The groupings used will be largely the same as the ones listed for manpower planning.

Two other important forms of comparison are periodic and external ones.

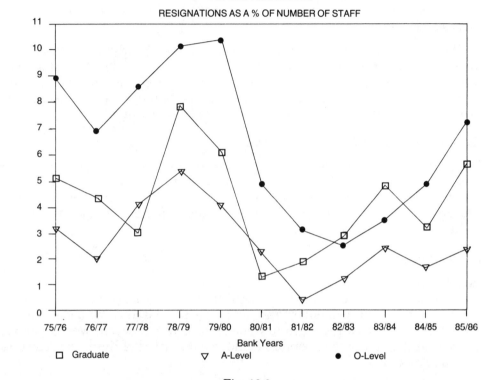

Fig. 12.3

Changes in turnover over a period draw attention to possible managerial problem areas. Unless otherwise stated turnover, wastage, or stability figures are worked out on an annual basis, but there is no reason why they should not be applied to shorter periods if this were to be considered useful – say to analyse seasonal fluctuations.

Comparison of figures with other companies in the same industry are useful to ensure that personnel policies and practices are not falling below the norm. They do not necessarily have to be the same as other companies but any differences should be explicable and justifiable.

Employers Federations are often able to provide industry-based statistics without divulging confidential information on individual companies.

Similar information on commerce and industry in general is available from government statistics and bodies such as the Institute of Personnel Management.

Controllable Wastage

Controllable wastage occurs when employees resign or are dismissed from a company for reasons which the management could have avoided. Some of this avoiding action may be short term, say agreeing different lunch hours or re-allocating work, but most of it is concerned with medium or long term policies and strategies, not only in the personnel field, but in other aspects of the business as well. Detrimental changes should therefore be spotted as early as possible.

A change in one of the wastage measurements is only an indicator that something is happening to cause the change. It does not tell management *what* is happening. By refining the indexes to apply to specific groups or departments the location of the problem can be found. It is then necessary to look at the factors which *might* have caused the change.

Factors Which Affect Labour Turnover

These can be divided into external and internal factors. In Chapter 8 Herzberg's Hygiene/Motivation Theory shows that the hygiene factors are those which a firm must provide to a level acceptable to the employees in order to prevent them seeking employment elsewhere. In many cases the level is dictated by external factors.

External Factors

(a) *Pay and other benefits.*
    The latter includes such pay equivalents as cheap mortgages, health insurance and pensions, and employees take into consideration the effort in time (working hours per day, days per week, weeks per year) which they have to expend to achieve a standard of living comparable to their peers.

(b) *Job Security.*
    If the security of their job is threatened by the company losing market share or market standing, or being in a trend of declining jobs, employees will look elsewhere for jobs.

(c) *Unemployment levels.*
    These affect the availability of alternative employment. Quite small changes in unemployment, which can of course occur locally or regionally, affect labour turnover accordingly.

Fig. 12.3 shows Labour Turnover at a large central London financial institution (not a clearing bank) over a period of years. It will be noted that among A Level and graduate staff there is a much higher labour turnover among women than men. For O level entrants the reverse is true if scale 1 women are excluded. Over the period as a whole, labour turnover was much higher when unemployment was low.

(d) *Changes in the structure of employment in the area.*
    Recruitment, redundancy and changes in pay offered by other firms will have an effect.

(e) *Travel patterns.*
   Travel patterns affect labour turnover because people count the cost of travel and put a value on their travelling time. This applies also to time spent travelling to shopping, leisure and educational facilities. A branch which is close to shops, a college or sports centre, may therefore be more popular despite lack of parking or easy transport connections.

(f) *Lack of promotion prospects.*
   This often causes people to switch jobs. In the case of smaller companies this may be regarded as uncontrollable wastage. Employees in large companies are often moved between functions or departments to gain experience. The employees of smaller companies not having these options available, have to find their experience elsewhere.

Internal Factors

(a) Within a company the first factor to be considered is the *selection process*. People often change jobs either because they are not suited to the job or the job does not suit them. Good selection tries to avoid both these difficulties. Money saved on the selection process may be lost several times over, if the wrong person is picked. Turnover is higher among first time employees than among those who have had previous jobs, because they are more likely to misunderstand what the job entails.

(b) *An Induction Crisis* occurs when people first take up a new job. They fear not being able to do the job properly or not liking the work. They fear that their new colleagues or the manager will dislike them and be unpleasant. They do not know their new surroundings and the system, and fear getting lost or otherwise making fools of themselves. It is a period of great insecurity with which many people cannot cope, unless there is adequate "induction training" to help them. The induction crisis has by far the greatest turnover.

«Induction, Ch. 14, p. 281»

(c) *The type of work* affects labour turnover. Some jobs are intrinsically less interesting than others, and specialisation for cost reasons makes some jobs very repetitive and boring. The wastage rate may be a good indicator of the attractiveness of particular jobs. In making such an assessment the effects of promotion prospects must be remembered, as these may cause people to stay in otherwise unattractive jobs.

(d) *Work organisation.* Chapters 3 and 8 introduced the value people put on working in groups. People also get positive pleasure out of working in an efficient, smooth running, and helpful environment. This is partly promoted by group organisation, but good communication and control and simple but effective organisation also play a vital role. The work force in such an environment will be much more stable than where the quality of organisation is lower.

(d) *Management Style.* In Chapter 9 the contingency approach to leadership described the importance of matching the leadership style to the abilities and needs of subordinates. If people's need for leadership is not met, or worse still if a conflicting style is adopted, dissatisfaction, often leading to people quitting their job, will be caused.

(e) *Physical Working Conditions*. These rank relatively low compared to the other factors. They include temperature, noise, crowding and extra facilities such as canteens. They are only likely to make a difference if all the other factors are equal.

It must again be emphasised that wastage rates are caused by differentials. it may well be that a physical environment, or a journey to work, may have been acceptable for years, but ceases to be so when work at another place, with better conditions or easier access becomes available.

Practice Exercises

(1) What authority does your departmental manager have over you and your colleagues?

(2) What authority does the personnel department have over you?

(3) What services does the personnel department provide to your office branch?

(4) Ask the personnel department for a look at your own personnel record. Where is it kept?

(5) What welfare services are provided by your company? What benefit do you gain from these? Does the firm gain anything?

(6) List the communications which pass between the personnel department and
(a) you personally
(b) your branch or office.

What is the purpose of each communication?

From Chapter 12 you should have learnt:

The roles of a personnel department, see chart on p. 236.

The division of authority between line and staff

The advantages of centralisation of the personnel function

The components of the process of manpower planning

What personnel records should contain.

Useful personnel management indicators

Method of measuring labour turnover and their features.

The factors which affect labour turnover.

The differences between controllable and uncontrollable wastage.

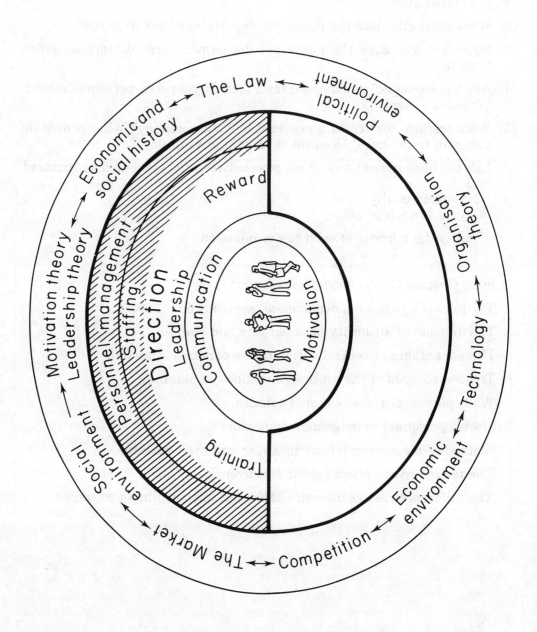

Chapter 13

Staffing

STAFFING

"Staffing" or "employment" is concerned with identifying immediate needs of the enterprise, finding or selecting applicants for employment, and training them.

Vacancies occur because occupants of a job leave, retire or are promoted, or because new posts have been created, or because an increase in work load has been identified. Banking staff change jobs within the organisation an average of every five years. This alone means 15,000–20,000 vacancies have to be filled annually in one clearing bank. It is up to the manager in charge of a department to ensure that his vacancies are filled with people who

(1) are *capable* of filling the role successfully

(2) are *willing* to make the necessary decisions and do the necessary work

(3) will stay in the job for an acceptable length of time

(4) fit in and co-operate with their fellow employees.

PROBLEMS OF STAFFING

From this analysis some of the problems which the staffing process has to overcome, become apparent:

(a) *The problem of defining the role or vacancy.* It has previously been noted that in modern business few roles remain static for long. Yet most people have only a limited work capacity and a limited range of abilities and interests. It has been described how "teams" of people can be used to overcome the flexibility problem. The staffing process thus often becomes one of replacing team members rather than filling an individual post. Often, when a member of a well integrated group leaves, the group loses some particular quality – e.g. the ability to stand firm under pressure, or how to deal with unexpected problems, and ideally the replacement should have similar qualities.

(b) The problem of how to define whether a job is done successfully – this is known as the "Criterion Problem".

(c) *The problem of knowing whether a particular person is going to fill a role successfully.* The major difficulty here is, of course, lack of knowledge. Unless relatively long and elaborate, and therefore expensive, selection processes are used, many wrong appointments may be made. Selection from within the organisation minimises this aspect of the problem, but it is still important to base selection on "future potential" rather than "past performance", for any job which involves different qualities or abilities, or a job requiring the same skills but at a higher level.

(d) *The problem of ensuring that candidates for jobs are fully aware of what the job entails.* If possible they should have an opportunity of meeting the people with whom they will have to work. This is especially important for managers taking up new appointments.

In any business which depends on the quality and performance of its staff, the staffing process must reach a high standard. Many good operating managers do not have the qualities or time needed to deal with some of the problems enumerated above, and personnel specialists are provided to assist them. There are also considerable economies of scale available, when recruitment is carried out centrally on the basis of manpower planning. A strong personnel department is also necessary when promotion from within is company policy.

It is the personnel specialists' task to provide services where economies of scale or specialist knowledge and/or skill will improve the process. This covers tasks such as:

Advertising vacancies
Guidance on job analysis
Guidance on staff availability
Preliminary assessment of application
Interviewing
Psychological Tests

RECRUITMENT AND PROMOTION POLICY

One of the fundamental personnel policy decisions which has to be made is how individual posts should be filled.

(1) By advertising each post and choosing the best applicant regardless of previous service with the company.

(2) By giving preference to *acceptable* applicants from inside the company even if better outsiders apply.

(3) By only advertising externally those posts for whom there is no internal candidate.

(4) By confining all promotion to staff already in the firm. This is known as single level entry, because all staff are recruited at the lowest level and promoted from there.

ADVANTAGES OF INTERNAL RECRUITMENT

The opportunity of promotion has been seen to have an important motivating role. A policy of promotion from within therefore contributes to high morale.

Reduced labour turnover results from employees being able to progress their careers without leaving.

Selection is more reliable and simple as records of skills, abilities, behaviour and attitudes are available, and the way employees fit into existing "groups" is known.

Induction training requirements are reduced because the number of new entrants is smaller, and simplified if the number of entry levels is less.

DISADVANTAGES OF INTERNAL RECRUITMENT

Training and Development for new roles may be more difficult and expensive than recruiting a fully trained outsider. This particularly applies to small firms.

It is difficult to predict accurately the quality and number of recruits required at lower levels to meet promotion requirement. Frustration will result if promotion potential is not used.

Excessive internal promotion may perpetuate old fashioned ideas and prevent new methods being introduced. Such an organisation can be become very rigid and have difficulty in adapting to change.

Most of the above difficulties can be met by a policy of aiming at promotion from within but insisting that this only applies if the necessary talent and experience is available and that a minimum proportion of outsiders is recruited to bring in fresh ideas. The degree to which such a policy should be applied will depend on how specialised the enterprise is and particularly on the importance of creativity and innovation.

EXTERNAL RECRUITMENT

Important sources of new recruits to a company are relatives, friends and acquaintances of existing staff. Provided that proper standards of selection are maintained, i.e. in meeting the requirements of job specifications, such recruits have effectively been vetted for achievement, reliability and specially for compatability with existing staff, by employees who have a vested interest in not being blamed for a bad choice.

Records may also be kept of casual, unsolicited applications for posts. This can be an important advantage in maintaining a good company image, which may attract candidates with initiative.

RECRUITMENT POLICY IN CLEARING BANKS

The clearing banks originally adopted a policy of single level entry. Recruits were chosen for:

- a pleasant appearance
- speech free from impediment
- practical and social interests
- a helpful manner
- integrity

As far as their intelligence and aptitude is concerned, the equivalent of four passes at O-level was set as a minimum. In an age when free schooling ended at the age of fourteen, it was assumed that a random intake of recruits at this level would provide sufficient people with the abilities and qualities for all the management needs of the company. No preference was given to candidates with higher education and promotion prospects were equal for all. This provided very strong motivation. In view of the size of the banks their intake was large enough for this system to work very well. The main disadvantage was "Organisational Moulding", i.e. the complacent assumption by people who have worked for a company all their lives that *their* methods, procedure and ideals are uniquely right. This was not too dangerous in a stable environment.

«Motivation Theory, Ch. 8»
«Assessment, Ch. 10, p. 190»

Ironically the introduction of free secondary and university education meant that many potential high fliers preferred further education to joining a bank after O-levels. The banks were starved of recruits with senior management potential and had to introduce offering preferential treatment to older school- and university-leavers to compete with other industries. In order to preserve the advantages of single level entry, those coming in under special schemes enter at the same level, but are considered for training, promotion and development more frequently and rapidly than the rest.

The spread of the interests of clearing banks into fields where they are minority employers – e.g. computers and insurance, and their needs for a limited number of specialists such as economists or valuers, means they now also recruit some mature staff. In London they may also have to replace mature staff who switch careers to the many overseas banks. Both these factors are useful in reducing the amount of institutional moulding.

STEPS IN THE STAFFING PROCESS

The staffing process is made up of a number of clearly defined steps as follows:

(1) Identification of the staffing need
(2) Person specification
(3) Advertising or publicity
(4) Selection
(5) Induction
(6) Control, evaluation and validation

(Students should note this as an example of the decision making process described in Chapter 5.)

It must be stressed that staffing decisions and therefore the staffing process cannot be properly made unless all these steps are undertaken and in sequence.

IDENTIFYING THE STAFFING NEED

There are two methods of identifying the staffing need:

(1) Manpower planning
(2) Job Analysis.

Manpower planning has been described in Chapter 10. For each of a number of broadly defined types of jobs – e.g. general clerical, middle management, computer specialists, manpower planning will yield the number of people required, either in the coming year or later. By comparison with the existing staff and their career patterns, the numbers which need to be recruited from other grades within the company, or from outside, can be determined.

It should be noted that some of the information required for manpower planning is obtained through Job Analysis.

Manpower planning is the basis of obtaining new recruits in single level entry system.

Job Analysis

Whenever a vacancy occurs at a level above the ones filled by new school leavers, a detailed analysis of the role to be filled is required. This is known as Job Analysis. Job Analysis comprises two steps:

1st *Job description*, concerned with the work and the responsibilities that go with it, and the position of the role in the organisation structure

2nd *Person specification*, concerned with describing the type of person who is required to fill the job successfully.

In large companies the job description and person specification are standardised for jobs which are the same throughout the organisation.

Uses of Job Analysis

Whereas the principle function of Job Analysis is as a basis for recruitment, the information gained is important also for the following:

Organisation

The job description helps to ensure that job content is suitable for the level of the role. By matching the description of different roles, role conflict is avoided and it can be confirmed that all necessary decisions and tasks have been included somewhere.

Manpower Planning

The job descriptions can provide the internal information on current manpower requirements.

Training

A comparison between the job descriptions and the actual attributes of job incumbents or applicants will identify those skills and qualities in which further training is required.

Transfers

Both parts of the analysis make it easy to identify roles to which candidates for transfer can be allocated.

Job Description

This is a written statement of the constituent tasks or decisions of a role. It should include the authority vested in a role and the position of the role in the organisation structure by defining relations with superiors, other operating and specialist departments, and outside groups, such as suppliers or customers. The area of autonomy, and the degree of supervision to which a job is normally subjected.

It should also define the sphere of subordinate operations and decisions covered. All the above are often described in detail, although it is better to highlight key activities. The trend is to concentrate more on defining the limits of discretion as this allows greater scope for individual intiative in the way jobs are carried out.

Another trend is to highlight the *results* to be achieved rather than the action or decision areas. The "Key results area" combines definition of the results areas with "Performance standards" to be achieved, and the "control data" by which these are judged.

In other job descriptions there may be differentiation between the managers duty to "act, recommend, or delegate".

Skills Analysis

This is a particular type of job analysis specifically dealing with operatives, whose work was divided by Honey into:

Mechanistic Knowledge: knowledge about things and techniques, facts.

Organic knowledge: knowledge about people – facts and particularly opinions.

Mechanistic Skills: skills with things and techniques.

Organic Skills: skills with people.

Illustration

Job Description of Branch Manager in a Clearing Bank

Responsible to regional director for all aspects of the business and organisation of his branch. He is also the banks' representative in his own catchment district.

Objectives

(1) To increase profitability by cost containment and higher productivity.

(2) To protect existing business through his own actions and the conduct of his junior managers.

(3) Planned growth of business by identifying and developing profitable areas for expansion.

He will always act in line with the policies of the bank and will strive to enhance its reputation.

Key Results Areas

(A) Deposits

(1) To maintain the branch's existing deposits

(2) To increase market share. He will always be aware that the protection of the depositor's money is a banker's main concern.

(B) Lending

Maintaining and expanding a highquality loan portfolio, within the terms of the bank's lending policy and any government constraints.

(C) Marketing

Have a planned programme to achieve these results

(1) More related services sold to existing customers
(2) Existing related services sold to existing customers
(3) New services sold to both customers and non-customers.

Where favourable opportunities arise for marketing, outside the planned programme, alert his regional director so that the necessary back-up can be obtained.

Other Responsibilities

(A) Good Customer Service

Motivate the staff responsible for routine operations. Try to emphasise the importance of day-to-day administration, e.g. telephone, correspondence, statements, counter, standing orders, enquiry desk.

Investigate all customer complaints and ensure that mistakes are not repeated.

(B) Community Relations

Take part in local activities e.g. treasurerships of local associations, so long as this does not conflict with business commitments.

The manager should also become known in circles which contain local "opinion formers" by joining organisations such as chambers of commerce, Trade Associations and luncheon clubs.

(C) Charges

He should monitor these regularly to see that fair and adequate remuneration is obtained for bank services in appropriate cases. This remuneration should be in line with published tariffs and any internal directives. If a fixed tariff basis does not apply, try to apply an equitable standard for all charges made. Whilst interest and commission should be reviewed periodically to take inflation into account, the manager should remember that business customers in a close-knit community may give the manager an undesirable reputation if charges are raised too steeply and on too widespread a basis.

(D) Premises

The internal and external appearance of the branch should be kept at a high standard relative to the local environment. The manager is responsible for ensuring that the structure of the branch enables business to be dealt with efficiently.

Regular fire drills should be carried out and safety rules made known to all staff. The provisions of the Health and Safety at Work Act should be familiar to the staff and they should also know where the accident book is kept.

The need for security of the premises, e.g. alarm systems, passwords etc. should be emphasised as well as the standard rules on protection of the staff in the event of an armed attack.

(E) Staff Control

The manager should undertake regular monitoring of all work inside his branch without usurping the functions of the Administration Manager/Sub-manager. He should plan staff training and development, with a view to every member of the staff reaching their full potential.

The manager should maintain sufficiently firm discipline for the smoothest and most efficient running of his branch. At the same time he should seek to keep staff morale high and also look after the welfare of all staff members.

(F) Audit

Carry out periodic supervisory checks to ensure that there is no risk of loss through maladministration or fraud. The manager is also responsible for signing all the returns required by the auditors and certifying their correctness.

PERSON SPECIFICATION

The purpose of the job description and Skill Analysis is to identify and define what sort of person the firm is looking for. Rodgers' 7 point plan, as described in Chapter 7 is a model of a person specification, and examples of the qualities required for recruits have been given above.

It is also important to note the ambition and potential of candidates because it affects how long they will be prepared to stay in a particular job.

Illustration

One of the problems of staffing in branch systems is that branches are small units where each person's contribution is vital. At the same time the branch is a training ground for general management, and specialist and head office staff. The need of each unit has to be balanced against the company's overall need. This implies an interference with the authority of local management, who cannot then be blamed for loss of efficiency due to staff being sent to them who will leave again shortly after training, and perhaps not fit in while they are at a branch.

ADVERTISING AND PUBLICITY

This is concerned with finding people to fill roles which are new or about to become vacant. These people can be looked for inside or outside the organisation. This is an area where a properly formulated and consistently applied policy is essential for success.

Sources of Employees

The best source of new employees depends on the type and level of skills, etc. required. In the following examples there is, of course, a considerable overlap:

Unskilled Labour	DES Job Centres
Temporary Clerical Labour	Employment agencies
School Leavers	Local Authority Careers Service; Schools
Skilled Labour	Trade Unions
Graduates	Universities and Colleges*
Specialists	Professional bodies
Managers	Executive Search and Selection Consultants

Recruitment by Advertising

Advertising for recruits depends for its efficacy mainly on message formulation and media selection. The successful advertisement will result in enough applications to give the firm a choice, while ensuring that unsuitable people are not induced to apply. Unskilled people will not normally move outside their locality while senior management nowadays may be recruited internationally. The distribution of the advertising medium must therefore relate to the catchment area of the potential recruits. The cost factor influences the choice because it is advisable to choose a medium which concentrates exposure of the message to audiences incorporating a high proportion of potentially suitable applicants, e.g. trade magazines.

SELECTION

Once an adequate supply of candidates for vacancies has been ensured the next stage of the staffing process can proceed. Selection will involve one or more of the following steps:

*The "Milk run" involves large employers touring the Universities each year to interview students about to graduate.

Written applications
Short Lists
Interviews
Selection Tests
Medical Examinations
Checking References
Confirmation of Employment
  (and advising unsuccessful applicants).

Before looking at the specific selection steps a number of general points, which may apply to all of them, should be considered.

Cost of Selection

If all the above steps, including perhaps a number of interviews, are carried out and the time of the managers involved is taken into account, the cost of selection may be very high. Many companies therefore take short cuts by not going through all the steps, or applying them in a superficial way, or by using untrained staff for selection. While such savings may be justified in certain cases, they must be set against the cost of selecting unsatisfactory people. Faulty selection may not only result in multiplying recruitment and training cost, but in waste, rejects, losses of output and indirect costs due to lowering of "morale" and performance.

Efficiency of Selection

The object of the process is to ensure that a role is properly filled. This means that applicants must:

(a) meet the job specification
(b) fit into the existing team
(c) fit the manpower plan.

The selection criteria must be based on these factors and not on subjective assessments of the "quality" of applicants and particularly not on the personal attitudes and opinions of the selectors (except when they will later have to work together). This requires social skills of a high order and it is essential that selecting staff have been properly trained and their abilities developed to the necessary standards.

Reliability of Selection

Many of the qualities considered in the selection process, such as motivation or disposition, are elusive. This creates major problems of:

(a) grading in relation to the job specification
(b) recording – e.g. appearance of candidates
(c) comparing with other candidates
(d) balancing various characteristics to reach a final choice.

To overcome these problems it is necessary to structure selection methods by planning, in detail, the questions to which answers are sought, their sequence, how answers are to be judged and recorded, and how they are weighted. The standard application form is an example of a structured questionnaire.

A disadvantage of the structuring technique is that it assumes that the job is specified, firstly, in much more detail than is generally practised, and secondly in the only possible way. In practice a candidate with different, perhaps unexpected, qualities, may perform equally well. The structured statement or interview may well not identify such a candidate.

It is customary to allow candidates to supply additional information by reserving a space for such information on an application form, or by having a more general conversation before or after a structured interview.

Short Lists

When the number of applicants for a particular post is large it is normal to select 4–12 people for fuller consideration. The list is usually chosen from the written application, although preliminary interviews are also used.

Written Applications

Information provided in writing is least costly to obtain and provides details of:

The candidate's person for purposes of identification, location and records

The candidate's circumstances, education attainments, occupational training, experience and success.

The candidate's special aptitudes and interests.

Four of Rodgers' seven points can therefore be covered. This information may be recorded on forms ranging from very brief and simple forms for unskilled staff to six page highly structured forms for some senior posts. Information in letter form may be preferred when the candidate's initiative, creativity and ability to express herself is valued. Many structured forms provided limited space for some form of self-expression.

Selection Tests

It is generally accepted that psychological tests properly administered can be of considerable use in forecasting success, or failure, particularly the latter, of a candidate at a particular job. They can also be used for placement, assessment and measuring the effectiveness of training schemes. Most of them, however, require specialist staff for proper administration.

Intelligence Tests

These are attempts to measure abilities such as inductive reasoning, verbal comprehension, numerical facility, memory and speed of comprehension. They are highly developed but difficult to relate to the needs of jobs and therefore may easily be misleading.

Special Aptitude Tests

Manual dexterity, neatness, and hand and eye co-ordination tend to be inborn, and can be reliably tested. Numerical and clerical aptitude tests can be used and applied to roles where these abilities are needed, usually at operator level. Aptitude tests can also indicate the type of training from which candidates are most likely to benefit and therefore which roles they will be able to fill.

Achievement Tests

These tests are used to recruit candidates who are already trained or experienced in a particular skill. They often take the form of a work situation, such as operating a machine.

Personality Testing

These tests include:

● Personality Inventory tests where candidates answer a series of questions or, choose from a series of phrases those he believes describe him most accurately.

● Projective Tests where the candidate's reaction to a theoretical situation is evaluated.

● Situation Tests in which the candidate is asked to do something about a real life situation.

The self-confidence of candidates can be assessed by comparing their performance on home ground with that of unfamiliar test centres.

Interviews

The main purposes of interviews are:

To confirm and enlarge on written information. Because of shortage of space it is inevitable that written statements are brief. Without discussion it would be impossible to judge the relevance of a potential area sales manager's experience in his previous post of "sales manager". This would depend on the type, volume and value of product previously handled, the staff and directors and the authority of the role, among other factors.

To attempt to explain any inconsistencies or gaps in the information provided, e.g. spare time interests conflicting with work attitude.

To obtain information which cannot be conveyed in writing – specifically Rodgers' points of "Physical Make-up and Disposition".

The less structured the interviewing technique is, the higher are the demands on the interviewer's objectivity, and communication and psychological skill. A stress component is often introduced to assess candidates' behaviour under such conditions.

Problems of Interviewing

Many failures of the selection process can be attributed to the problems of interviewing. Even if interviews are well-prepared, structured and recorded, and if interviewers use correct rating scales to reinforce genuine objectivity, there are serious additional problems, e.g.

The difficulty of judging abstract traits such as "integrity".

The "Halo Effect" which causes interviewers to overlook the deficiencies of candidates in some fields because they are exceptionally good in others.

"Contagious Bias" – resulting in the candidate giving answers based on opinions expressed earlier by the interviewer.

Errors of logic in deducing the candidates characteristics from historic information.

The problems can only be reduced fully by training managers in interviewing, provided they have the necessary basic ability. Many managers will never possess the necessary skills or objectivity. Personnel specialists should carry out interviews on their behalf, in the manager's presence if desired.

Interview Methods

One applicant by one interviewer.
One applicant by a panel of interviewers
One applicant by a succession of interviewers
Several applicants by one or more interviewers.

It has earlier been explained that in most managerial situations at least three people: the applicant's future superior, a senior manager, and the personnel manager would be concerned. If the former's interviewing technique is dubious and the demands on their time make a succession of interviews unattractive, a joint interview conducted by the personnel specialist would probably be chosen. This might also apply when applicants have to travel some distance for interviews.

The one-off, one to one interview should be confined to posts from which promotion or transfer is unlikely, or where the person's general utility is more important than his relationship with a particular manager or group.

Several applicants are interviewed at a time when recruiting for teams or similar situations concerned with assessing the candidate's reaction to each other.

Group Selection

This is a relatively expensive technique involving a one or two day course where interviews, discussion groups, and intelligence tests are combined. A written report on the course is often expected from the applicants, and their behaviour at meals and in their "spare" time is noted. One of the main advantages of this method is that applicants who may be able to maintain a facade to hide their true nature for a short interview, are unlikely to be able to do so for a full day or more. Group selection is used by several of the larger Building Societies and by several overseas banks.

Medical Examinations

These are relevant to pension and insurance schemes and where specific physical abilities are required. In some cases they are applied early in the selection procedure to avoid unnecessary costs.

References

The relevance of references depends on the importance of reliability, trustworthiness and interpersonal factors in the role, but they are also useful for confirming the candidate's record.

INDUCTION

In the description of labour turnover, p. 257, it was noted that turnover was highest in the initial or induction stages. The recruitment and selection process is expensive and continuity is important. Ensuring that candidates selected stay in their posts for a reasonable period can be said to be part of the staffing process. Proper induction is most important for new recruits to a company, but even with established employees, who are promoted or transferred to a different department or geographical location, the quality of induction will have a marked impact, certainly on relations with other staff, and possibly on ultimate performance levels.

Induction is a combination of establishing social contacts and providing factual information. A new incumbent should be welcomed to a department by his superior. The superior may then delegate a member of the new-comer's department team to continue the induction process over several days (or even longer) as only a limited amount can be absorbed at a time. Apart from introductions to the people with whom the newcomers are to work, and their geographical surroundings, they should be acquainted with local customs and practice, team history and ritual, and any "norms" of behaviour.

The factual aspects of induction are dealt with as part of training.

CONTROL

It is important to keep a check on the efficiency and effectiveness of the staffing process as on any other management processes. Some companies favour a system of probationary appointments, under which the appointment is only confirmed if the new incumbent has reached a certain level of success. This makes it simpler to correct mistakes in selection and it ensures that a review of the new appointment takes place at the end of the probationary period.

Control should also be exercised on the performance of interviewers, job analysts and others involved in the selection process.

Labour turnover figures may be helpful for indicating changes in the efficiency of the staffing process.

Practice Exercises

(1) Check on the entry qualifications required by your employer.

(2) Do they ever engage mature staff? Try to determine why.

(3) Prepare a job description for your own role.

(4) Prepare a skills analysis for your own role.
     Prepare a person specification for your own role.

(5) When you have identified the qualities/skills needed for your role, grade
     yourself and some of your acquaintances for these qualities/skills.

(6) Try to devise a "test" for the key skill in your role.

From Chapter 13 you should have learnt:

The advantages and disadvantages of internal promotion.

The steps in the staffing process.

The difference between job analysis, job description and person specifications.

The uses of job analysis.

The contents of job descriptions.

The advertising and publicity media required for filling vacancies of different types.

The steps in the selection process.

The types of test available to help selection.

The purpose and types of interviews.

The difficulties encountered when interviewing and how they may be overcome.

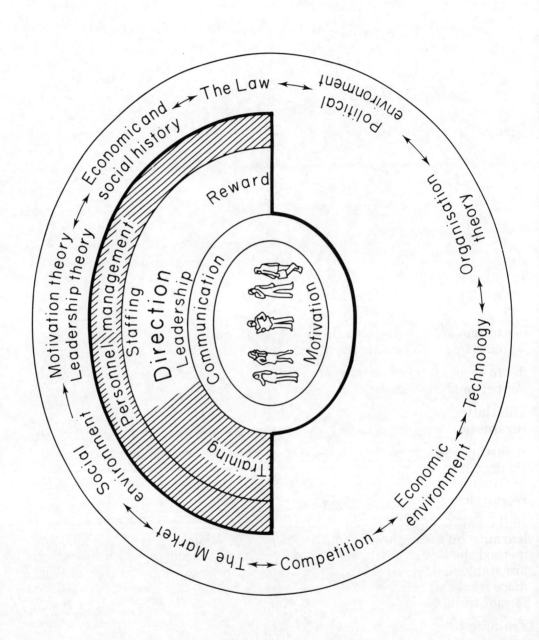

Chapter 14

Training

TRAINING OBJECTIVES

Training may be differentiated from "education" by its emphasis on the knowledge and skills applicable to a particular "role". Its purpose is two-fold:

(a) to maximise the economic value of an employee to the enterprise by ensuring that he fills his role at maximum efficiency;

(b) to ensure that the best is made of each person's abilities; this is known as personnel or manager "development".

This latter purpose also provides a direct benefit to the employee who regards it as a way of increasing his job satisfaction and his career prospects.

A further important benefit is the cost saved in reduced labour turnover. Inadequately trained employees are liable to leave because of dissatisfaction or frustration. This results in costs due to undermanning, and unnecessary recruitment and re-training.

In the past training has largely consisted of giving people an opportunity of learning by association with an experienced senior colleague. While this method should not be discounted it is mainly applicable to situations which are stable and where there is little change in products or techniques. The more frequently and rapidly these need to change, the greater the need for formal training.

Training by example is another informal approach which still has a pre-eminent part to play in modern management. While it is not preferable to formal training in most fields it is outstandingly effective in setting and maintaining subjective standards, e.g. of behaviour, exchange of information, manager/subordinate relations, customer relations and reaction to criticism.

A beneficial side-effect of training is that it can be used to provide a common bond between persons of different background and experience. It has been explained in notes on group psychology and motivation, that the more people have in common the more likely they are to form well-integrated groups. On the other hand, the performance of an enterprise is more likely to be progressive and lively if its members have diverse experience and backgrounds. This conflict can be successfully solved by superimposing common bonds on diverse characters by appropriate training methods.

ORGANISATION OF TRAINING

The stages of establishing a training programme are as follows:

(1) There must be a proper manpower plan, showing long, medium and short term requirements in terms of general and specialist skills and distributed according to age, departmental, or other relevant divisions.

(2) There must be a defined, rational, and comprehensive training policy, with clear objectives covering such factors as depth of skill, promotion policy, cost-benefit requirements and whether training should be internal or external; make use of standard or specially tailored courses, or be administered by operating or specialist managers.

(3) Overall responsibility for carrying out the training policy must be allocated to a suitably qualified person, together with the necessary authority and resources.

(4) Quantitative training needs must be established based on deficiencies identified from the manpower plan allowing for:

> labour turnover
> retirements
> new systems

Appraisal reports and counselling will identify further change.

(5) Decisions must be made on the type of training required to meet the training objectives.

(6) Organisational arrangements must be made to administer the training services successfully.

(7) Competent instructors or suitable courses must be selected.

(8) A system of controls must be introduced to check:

(a) whether the results of the training of individuals achieves the set standards within the cost limits determined;

(b) whether the overall training objectives are being achieved within the anticipated resource allocation;

(c) whether the training strategy adopted, including the objectives and resources allocated, are meeting the needs of the enterprise.

In the larger organisations in the financial sector training is well organised, but this is not typical of industry as a whole.

Encouraging staff to plan and control their own training may be a way of enriching the jobs of employees of large companies.

«Job Enrichment, Ch. 8, p. 176»

INDUCTION TRAINING

Induction training is concerned with introducing individuals into new roles. It is therefore applicable to those joining the firm, a branch, or a department for the first time whether they are operators, supervisors or managers. The impression gained by new employees during their first period at work will tend to establish their behaviour for a long time. During the first weeks of any new job, employees will feel very insecure. Guidance and help at this stage will have a high impact on labour turnover.

Induction training should cover:

(1) the *history* and *objectives* of the enterprise.

(2) Its *policies* as far as they affect the trainee, including safety, security, salaries, holidays, training.

(3) The *objectives and policies of the trainee's department* and how they contribute to those of the enterprise.

(4) *The firm's services*, procedures and technical jargon.

(5) The customers and markets of the enterprise.

(6) The *future plans* of the enterprise and the trainee's department's contribution to them.

(7) *Sources and channels of information* applicable and available to the role the trainee is to fill.

(8) The existence, purpose and composition of *informal groupings* within the enterprise.

Bearing in mind the differing characters, history and future needs of trainees, it is clear that induction training cannot be standardised and must be tailored accordingly. Company reports, for instance, while valuable to a new accountant, would be useless at operator level. Operators starting a new job will be concerned with the systems and arrangement within a department, whereas a manager, although the departmental systems are obviously important, will be equally concerned with being inducted into the external relationships of the department.

«Labour Turnover, Ch. 12, p. 256»
«Selection, Ch. 12, p. 269»
«Environment, Ch. 7, p. 146»
«Teams, Ch. 7, p. 161»

TECHNICAL TRAINING

In the branch banking field training will cover the book-keeping and computer systems, operation of computer terminals and the procedures for opening
and closing various types of accounts.

Training Procedures

In big organisations where there is annually a very large intake of trainees,
a major problem of monitoring and evaluating arises. It is an important part
of the branch and departmental manager's role to ensure the success of his
trainees and to identify those with potential for promotion. This potential is
then confirmed at "assessment" courses.

The training at branches is carried out by colleagues and in-branch training
material, supplemented by formal courses at training centres.

Day release or part day release is almost universal in the financial sector for
recruits who are expected to take the professional exams. One of the
problems of releasing new recruits is that many of them may not stay in the
industry. Many firms have introduced either a probationary period before
employees get study leave, or they expect them to take one or more stages in
evening classes or by correspondence course before the time off is granted.
The Scottish banks offer block release at later stages of study.

Logistically it is not possible for colleges to provide teaching except in the
larger towns. The advent of distance learning – including modern techniques of inter-active computer and video learning – is greatly facilitating
training at branches in less densely populated areas.

TRAINING METHODS

Among methods used in the financial sector are:

Lectures: particularly useful for the large groups at bank training centre.

Case studies: involve discussion by a group of background information
needed for decision-making. The members of the group are able to practice
and improve their perceptive, analytical and decision-making abilities, and
derive principles from their own investigations. The group format helps
them appreciate alternative approaches and attitudes and present their own
case.

Business Games: These are an extension of the case study where several
groups handle a series of the same case studies in parallel. This makes it
possible for the competitive element of real life businesses to be introduced.
Each group's decisions are analysed by a referee who promulgates the effect
on the environment and a new set of data for the next stage of the game.
Business games particularly develop the ability to work as a team and to
make decisions under conditions of uncertainty.

Role Playing: There are many situations where it is inadvisable for managers to practice unfamiliar skills in real life situations, e.g. disciplinary procedures, union negotiations or complaints servicing. In such a role-playing exercise different trainees will take the role, for instance, of manager, person to be disciplined, union representative and personnel officer. In these situations role playing can bring the manager concerned to an acceptable standard before becoming involved in a real life situation.

In-tray Exercises: Involving dealing with the random matters arising in a role, under supervision of a colleague. The manager being trained becomes aware of various tasks in the role, and their relative importance. He learns to determine priorities and to plan his day.

Programmed Instruction: This is useful for imparting knowledge and perfecting routine procedures to clerical staff. After being shown the correct procedures, the trainee does a test. If unsuccessful he is given further instruction; if successful he passes on to the next stage of the programme. The method is ideal for instructing the large number of staff scattered among branches, at various levels of attainment. Programmed learning with interactive computer programmes and interactive video-discs is being rapidly introduced.

ACTION CENTRED LEADERSHIP

This technique of team management is used as training for leadership of teams. See Chapter 9 for a more detailed description.

CREATIVITY

Creativity is an important quality which is basically developed by providing a liberal environment where managers are encouraged to experiment and failures in innovation are not penalised excessively. This management style is, however, not suitable for all types of business and it is sometimes necessary to develop the creative abilities of managers in other ways. Apart from specialised methods such as lateral thinking, two popular techniques are "value analysis", also used as a design and cost reduction method, and "brainstorming". The latter is used for problem-solving and involves trying to break down people's innovative inhibitions by getting them to jot down ideas at once, before thinking about the snags.

COMMITTEE MEMBERSHIP

Creativity, broadening of outlook and understanding can also be improved by membership of *effective* committees. Apart from management committees those dealing with innovation are particularly useful, but co-ordinating and planning committees may also be used.

THE LEARNING PROCESS

The two basic approaches to learning are known as the "whole" and the "part" method. The former involves completing the task in its entirety at the beginning of the training period and gradually increasing speed and proficiency. The latter involves breaking the job down into several simple parts each of which is learnt to a planned level of proficiency before the trainees proceed to the next. This method is used for large or complex tasks while the "whole" technique is more suitable for simple tasks. It is important to stimulate learners, keeping them active, varying method and providing practice.

MANAGER DEVELOPMENT

It has been mentioned earlier that manager development is concerned with individuals rather than training for job requirements, which is the purpose of management *training*. It is intended to help managers realise full innate potential by correcting weakness and developing strength, whilst at the same time helping them along a career which utilises these strengths. Many of the training methods fulfil this function at the same time as providing job training, but development techniques also include:

  guided reading
  studying for formal qualifications
  planned promotion
  group dynamics.

Manager Development is becoming more important in banking as the banks need to adapt to a more rapidly changing environment and managers need more or different skills from those they have succeeded with in the past.

GROUP DYNAMICS

This is a term covering a number of techniques for personal development. All of these are based on bringing people together in groups. In such groups individuals learn how different people – including themselves – react to situations. Some people demonstrate natural leadership, some are followers, some objectors. Mutual interests become apparent or conflicts may be generated.

The technique is useful for developing interpersonal skills dealing with:

  individuals and groups   Chapter 12
  communication   Chapter 9
  causes and characteristics of conflict   Chapter 10
  leadership and conflict   Chapter 11

MEASUREMENTS OF EFFECTIVENESS

Training is a costly activity which must be justified by one or more of the following:

Increase in profitability through more efficient operations.

Increase in customer satisfaction shown by growth in market share or reduced complaints.

Increase in job satisfaction and staff morale.

The effectiveness, as opposed to the value of training can be measured at five levels:

(a) Reaction of the trainee – whether he found the experience rewarding and relevant to his job.

(b) The learning effect – what skill or knowledge has been acquired?

(c) Job behaviour – what is the trainee doing differently in his job since training?

(d) Organisational effect – has there been a change of attitude of the staff, the work pattern at branches, or the behaviour of other employees?

(e) Ultimate Value – were the improvements identified in line with the firm's objectives?

Practice Exercises

(1) Write down what induction training you received in your first job.

(2) If you have changed jobs – why did you change?

(3) Do you know the objective of your section/department and how it fits in with the higher level objective? If not, ask your superior at your next appraisal meeting. (Say this book suggested it.)

(4) By what methods were you trained in your technical skills?

(5) Assess the effectiveness of the next training you receive under the headings shown above.

(6) Note how training is affected by:

   organisation   (Chapter 4).

From Chapter 14 you should have learnt:

The purpose of induction training and what good induction training involves.

The scope of technical training.

At least ten methods of training and their purpose.

How to measure the effectiveness of training.

The role of training in:-

   Motivation   (Chapter 9)

   Spans of control   (Chapter 3)

   MbO   (Chapter 5)

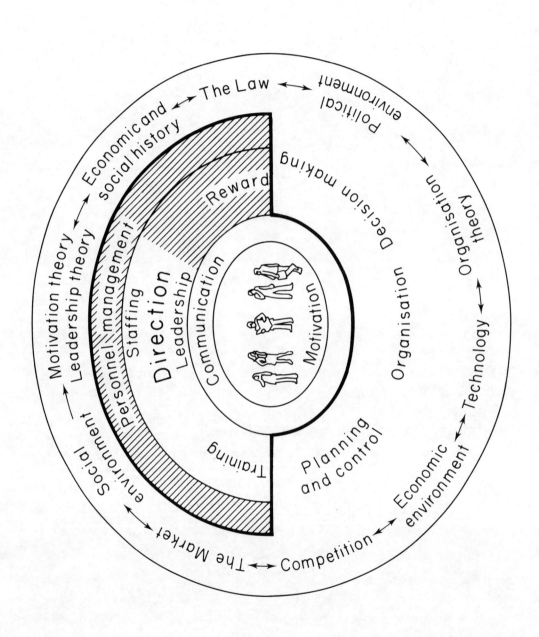

Chapter 15

Rewards and Benefits

THE REWARD SYSTEM

The Personnel department is responsible for advising the Chief Executive on an equitable reward system throughout the company. Possible systems range from rigid salary structures based largely on length of service to individual small subsidiaries having independent reward systems, or payment by results.

In all cases it must be remembered that the permanence and quality of service which employees give will depend on the employees evaluation of the benefit package which he receives.

The benefit package normally includes:

The nature of the work – people who have jobs which coincide with their personal interests will forego extra money to continue enjoying the work.

The working environment – particularly if friends and the working group fill an employee's social needs.

Working period – "unsocial" hours have to be offset by higher payments.

Salary – the basic hygiene factor.

Bonuses and incentive payments. These are only valued to the extent to which the employee feels confident of earning them.

Pensions are regarded as very important by older employees, but as of little worth by most younger ones.

Holidays and opportunity for time off (This includes the way the working week is arranged.)

Opportunity to travel

Fringe benefits In banking the ability to obtain cheap mortgages is regarded as one of the most important benefits by young employees. In a survey by G. J. Cohen over half of AIB students quoted this among their three most important benefits. In 1984 its popularity dropped sharply in favour of job security.

PAYMENT SYSTEMS

It has been explained in Chapter 8 that wages are a hygiene factor. If they are too low, the employees concerned have difficulty in maintaining what they regard as a reasonable standard of living. This problem will be foremost in their minds and they will take the first available opportunity to switch to more remunerative employment. Even if such employment is not available the problem of unsatisfied needs remains and will distract employees from their work and possibly lead to low work norms, demarcation disputes and other restrictions of output.

DIFFERENTIALS IN PAY

The first objective of a payment policy is thus to establish a payment level which eliminates the burden of unfilled basic needs. The second objective must be to avoid friction between groups of employees who consider their rewards to be unrealistic in relation to each other. Employees at all levels are very concerned about payment systems being fair. The problem of differentials is very complex because of the differing nature of work in various roles. Feelings among employees on this topic become so bitter that there is a strong temptation to keep wages and salaries for particular roles secret. This may, in turn, cause an atmosphere of suspicion. Secrecy is in practice not effective, especially if bargaining is collective.

DIFFERENTIALS IN JOB CONTENT

Where wages for various roles are published, the problem is simply diverted to differences of opinion about the "value" of roles. Employees may not be aware about difference in job or personnel specification which form the bases of differentials, while on the other hand they often know of differences which managers fail to appreciate. Co-operation between line manager, subordinates, employee representatives and personnel specialists when evaluating jobs can be particularly fruitful in reducing the problem.

PERFORMANCE DIFFERENTIALS

Although establishing proper base pay levels and differentials are the two essential objectives of payment systems, the systems may optimally be used as incentives for improved performance. It is useful to distinguish four performance levels:

(1) *Minimum performance* may be defined as the lowest performance which can be maintained without incurring dismissal.

(2) *Standard Performance* is a level capable of being achieved by employees without significant effort. This is the standard usually determined by organisation and methods techniques and used in incentive schemes. It could more appropriately be termed *basic performance*.

(3) *Normal Performance* is the level to be expected from employees of average calibre and motivation who are interested in their work in a favourable environment. It is substantially higher than Standard Performance.

(4) *Premium Performance* is at a higher level than the previous three.

It is this latter premium performance level which employees do not normally maintain unless there is some specific incentive in addition to the base pay. This incentive most frequently consists of enhanced monetary reward.

JOB EVALUATION

If an equitable relationship is required among the incomes earned by the employees occupying the various roles in an enterprise it is necessary to establish a system for the grading of these roles. Job evaluation is a systematic technique which can be used to arrange the jobs in an organisation in order of relative value (note: the jobs are evaluated, not the people).

An essential pre-requisite of evaluation is job analysis which provides the facts about job content, responsibilities, supervision, environmental factors and requirements of skills, experience and knowledge for each role, and how roles differ from each other in these respects.

PURPOSE

Job evaluation is not concerned with the person doing the job. Appraisal procedures have been described in Chapter 9 which can be used to assess the performance of employees in relation to their role's requirements. They can also provide a basis on which superior performance can be rewarded according to the wages or salary policy of the firm. These appraisals are in addition to, not in place of, job evaluation.

POINTS SYSTEMS

This system of job evaluation comprises:

Selection of *job factors*

Determining the "level" or *degree* at which each factor is present in the job

Assignment of *points* to establish the value of the degrees

Weighting of each factor to establish its importance in the role

Totalling the weighted points for each factor

Grading the jobs according to the number of points obtained.

Job Factors

The factors selected for a points system must be common to most of the jobs being evaluated and usually fall into three types:

Personal Requirements

e.g. Education   Physical effort
      Experience   Social skill

Responsibilities

e.g. Decision making   Supervision
      Planning   Concern for quality

Working Conditions

e.g. Value of equipment
      Safety
      Noise levels

The degrees in each factor need not be the same, nor do the degrees have to be allocated an equal number of points. The weighting of factors must be so arranged that the total adds up to 100% – i.e. a number of jobs may be composed of a different percentage of the same factors.

Each job grade will consist of a number of points. By determining the number of points in a job the grade is therefore automatically determined.

It will be noted that subjective judgement is required in the selection of the factors, selection of degrees, assignment of points to degrees and weighting of factors. This requires a high degree of skill, specialist knowledge and knowledge of the jobs; together with ample time for careful analysis. Outside consultants are therefore needed and the high cost of installation tends to limit this method to companies with specialised jobs on which large numbers are employed. Provided however that the system is properly installed in the first place, and degrees etc. clearly defined, it is then reasonably easy to use, explains role differences numerically and cannot easily be manipulated.

Ranking Systems

With this method jobs are ranked from highest to lowest by a subjective comparison of duties, responsibilities and requirements. A formalised organisation structure provides a good framework for this approach. It is often used for higher and middle management where organisation charts are available. In a refinement of the system, "paired comparisons" are made. Each job is compared with all the other jobs, with two points awarded for superiority and one point for comparability.

The evaluation can be carried out by any independent person provided that they have the help of the employees concerned. The need for specialist analysis is thus eliminated while at the same time equity is demonstrated. Ranking can also be applied quickly to new or changed roles.

The main draw-back, apart from its subjectivity is the danger of ranking the job incumbent rather than the job itself.

The Classification System

In this system a number of job grades are described covering, for instance:

Description of work (in general terms – e.g. "work of a recurring nature")

Requirements of the person filling the job – i.e. education, experience, skills and knowledge

Examples of types of work included in the grade

Typical jobs in the grade.

A number of such classifications are provided by professional and similar bodies and it becomes relatively simple to determine into which grade a particular role should fall. It is however important to select a classification which fits the type of organisation and its work, and these may not always be available.

The Factor Comparison System

In this system key jobs are considered, which have easily identifiable factors and well known standards of remuneration. By selecting at least as many key jobs as factors it is possible to determine the proportion of the salary attributable to each factor. Other jobs are evaluated by comparing them, factor by factor, with the key jobs. Having assessed the proportionate salary attributable to each factor, these are added to find the total salary.

This system differs from the previous ones described as it is evaluated directly in terms of money rather than points. It also takes into account market scarcity of certain factors, because it uses the existing salaries of the key jobs as a base. Whether this is a permissible approach is a topic of argument between those who hold that job evaluation should be a "pure" analysis of the job itself, and those who hold that it is only a means to an end, and a realistic final salary is more important than a theoretical analysis. The method is often difficult to explain to employees and its fairness may be questioned.

Specialised Systems

A number of proprietary systems of analysis, evaluation and grading have been developed by consultants. These are either more sophisticated versions of the methods described, or systems specially prepared to suit particular organisations. When first setting up job evaluation the use of consultants may well be advantageous provided that the precautions which should always be taken when employing consultants, are adopted. They are that:

The consultants can prove their system works satisfactorily in a comparable enterprise, or that they can prove success in developing and installing special systems;

the time and cost of installation are agreed and properly programmed;

the programme includes de-bugging and follow-up maintenance for a reasonable period;

the programme includes training of staff to maintain the system.

The HAY/MSL Guide Chart Profile method is an empirical approach which has been adopted by several of the clearing banks. The method has two principle characteristics.

First it evaluates jobs on the basis of their contribution to the achievement of the objectives of an organisation, i.e. it is "purpose" orientated.

Secondly, it employs elements of job content which are common to all jobs, whether in senior management, specialist departments, or operating branches. These common elements are:

"Know-how"
Problem solving
Accountability.

(1) *"Know-how"*
This is defined as the total of every kind of skill required for standard job performances. It has three dimensions:

(a) *Technical requirements* e.g. computer terminal operation, book-keeping, analysing lending proposition.

(b) *Managerial requirements* for know-how in integrating and harmonising elements involved in managerial situations e.g. a personnel manager balancing the demands of different branches, training requirements of staff, and training resources available.

(c) *Human relations* requirements for "know-how" in motivating people.

(2) *Problem solving*
This is defined as the "self-starting" thinking required for decision making, including analysing, evaluating, arriving at and making conclusions. It is the use of "know-how" in identifying, defining and resolving problems. It has two dimensions:

(a) *the environment* in which the thinking takes place, e.g. the amount of specialist back-up available and the efficiency of the companies' information system.

(b) *the challenge* presented by the thinking to be done e.g. ranging from simple choices based on repetitive experience – how to deal with common errors made by employees – to the development of new concepts in uncharted areas of knowledge.

(3) *Accountability*

This is the extent to which persons are answerable for their actions, the consequences of those actions and the measured effect on end results. Accountability has three dimensions, which are, in order of importance:

(a) *Freedom to act*, which is measured by how much the person's performance is guided or controlled by his superior or by company policies or procedures. The less freedom a person has, the lower the evaluation of the job, in this element.

(b) *The impact on end results* which the person's performance has e.g. the performance of the branch of a bank is affected more by the Branch Manager than the Branch Accountant.

(c) *The magnitude of the end result area* primarily affected by the job, generally expressed on an annual money basis e.g. the Branch Manager's job is valued according to the turnover of the branch.

The three elements and their dimensions are used in a chart form. In addition the method employs a number of balances and checks to test the validity of evaluation. When establishing this system the consultants rely on committees of people in the organisation who are knowledgeable of the work environment as well as the evaluation method.

REMUNERATION POLICY

Job evaluation is concerned with determining a value for different jobs; it is not concerned with how well or how or how fast the job is carried out. It is necessary to establish a policy, either for a whole enterprise or for groups of jobs, to enable decisions to be made regarding the remuneration of individual employees.

The first matter to be decided is whether employees should be paid according to the value of their jobs regardless of their standard of performance, or whether the latter should be taken into account. "Time rates" or "Incentive rates".

TIME RATES

This method of payment includes salaries, day work, flat rate payments and hourly pay. It is the most commonly used method and by it employees are effectively paid for spending time at work. Provided they reach the minimum acceptable performance level the quality or quantity of their work does not affect their pay.

SALARY SCALES

Clearing Banks use time rates as their remuneration method, in the form of salary scales. Job evaluation determines the grade on the scale to which each job is allocated. Some jobs can be allocated to several grades, to enable length of service to be recognised by a movement to a higher point on the scale.

An advantage of salary scale of this type is that people of different abilities can move through the system at different rates.

INCENTIVE SCHEMES

A policy of incentive payment necessitates guidance as to whether payment should be based on effort or success. There is frequently a major problem of defining effort or success, of measuring it, and of setting reasonable standards. The requirements of a good incentive payment scheme are:

(a) The reward must relate to effort or success.
(b) It must be just to employees and employer.
(c) It must be mutually agreed, clear and simple.
(d) It must have worthwhile and attainable objectives.
(e) No upper limit.
(f) Non-standard conditions must be allowed for.
(g) Reward should not be affected by outside matters, e.g. profit of the company.
(h) Reasonable permanence.
(i) Changes only introduced by changed conditions.
(j) It must tie-in with supervision and costing.
(k) It boosts morale.
(l) It promotes positive response to change.

MEASURES OF EFFORT OR SUCCESS

The most commonly used measures are output and sales, but in principle incentives can be used to improve any measurable attribute such as bad debt percentages, profit or market share. Schemes can be based on short or long term performance, and applied to individuals or groups.

GROUP SCHEMES

Group incentive schemes, where practicable, are almost invariably more effective than individual ones, because they have the following important advantages:

(a) Lower administrative costs.
(b) Fostering of team spirit.
(c) Ability to move employees between jobs within the group.
(d) They avoid jealousy between operators.
(e) Indirect workers such as maintenance and transport staff can be included.

DECLINE OF SHORT-TERM INCENTIVES

Since the original rapid spread of short-term incentive schemes of all types four problem areas have caused them to drop out of favour:

(a) *Specialisation* has reduced to very few the number of jobs in which a particular individual or group can be credited with complete products.

(b) *External factors.* A more educated workforce is aware of the impact on incentive earnings of many factors outside their control and insists that these should be allowed for. These two factors increase administrative problems to a level which may outweigh the benefit of increased output.

(c) *Levels of earnings* are higher than the "hygiene" needs of the average operator and more money is often no longer an incentive.

(d) *Incentives on secondary work* may distract staff from their mainstream duties.

MERIT RATING

In attempts to draw back from the problems which developed from the over-sophistication of incentive schemes, merit rating has come to the fore. It involves agreeing a number of levels of pay for a given role. If three levels are chosen these could be an "introductory" level, a "standard" level coinciding with the pay determined by job evaluation, and a "merit" level. "Agreeing" on this approach is the operative word because the problems of incentive schemes are the over-concentration on trivia which results in endless argument and bitterness about working conditions and factors affecting output. Reversing this attitude means that pay is based on acceptance of the validity of a more general standard. Management does not penalise staff for trivial variations in work, and employees do not demand additional compensation for insignificant or temporary extra effort.

Objective Merit Rating

Merit rating can be applied to quantitative targets determined by time and motion study and similar techniques, but payment is based on a broad range rather than on specific achievement. Alternatively, merit ratings can be assessed by superiors. The key to its successful operation lies in firm administration, particularly when it is necessary, perhaps only temporarily, to down-rate personnel with normally high performance.

Subjective Merit Rating

One of the difficulties faced when laying down payment policy is that there are a large number of roles, whose output cannot be easily defined. If payment policy is to differentiate between levels or quality of performance, this may be done by personal assessment. While many managers dislike such a subjective approach because of the dangers of abuse and misapplication, others hold that, if firmly and systematically applied under the supervision of personnel specialists, it may be much more realistic than a rigid scheme which may, for practical purposes, be based on identifiable quantitative components of a role, rather than its key areas.

Figure 15.1 shows an example of a salary "range" which has been developed by HAY/MSL for use in conjunction with HAY/MSL Job Evaluation. It is an example of subjective merit rating.

Maximum	————————————————————————120%
	Outstanding: This zone is normally reserved for those whose distinguished performance is clearly obvious to all. It would normally be expected that such a person would soon move to a bigger job.
	————————————————————————112%
	Superior: Zone for seasoned employees whose performance is noticeably better than "acceptable".
	————————————————————————104%
Mid point	*Standard:* Standard performance on the job entirely satisfactory 100%
	————————————————————————96%
	Incomplete: Zone for employees whose performance comes close to being "acceptable", but the need for further development is recognisable.
	————————————————————————88%
	Marginal: A provisional zone for inexperienced newcomers and others whose performance is below the accountability level. Such persons should either move up in the range or out of the job in a relatively short time.
Minimum	————————————————————————80%

Where an individual is paid within his salary range depends on a number of factors, not least length of time in the job, and performance in it.

Fig. 15.1 Anatomy of a salary range

Personal assessment is also one of the few ways of rewarding effort as opposed to results.

An alternative to merit rating is to make once and for all rewards – e.g. extra days' holidays, for special effort. This is a useful counter to the loss of authority often suffered by operating managers in a company with a strong personnel department.

FRINGE BENEFITS

These may range from luncheon vouchers through Health Insurance subscriptions to large cars. They originally came into fashion to avoid high tax rates. Their main disadvantage, as tax rates became lower, is that they are inequitable as many employees may not want the benefit or may not be able to use it. The administrative costs may also be high. On the other hand some fringe benefits – by external appearance or by creating a common bond – may serve to improve corporate identity.

PRODUCTIVITY

Productivity is the ratio between output and the resources used to achieve that output. In discussions on the comparative "productivity" between different companies, industries or countries, interest normally centres on what is only part of overall productivity – e.g. labour productivity.

Labour productivity is of major importance in industries where staff costs represent a significant proportion of the total. In making comparisons, even within one company, it is, however, essential to compare like with like – both in terms of environment and non-labour resources used for the output.

Illustration

(1) In the savings market the potential for increasing the deposits in a particular area will vary according to the affluence of the population and the amount of competition. A branch manager trying to attract deposits in a poor area where both banks and building societies are well established, will inevitably have low productivity.

(2) A cashier with an automatic cash dispenser can deal with more clients than one who has to count manually – but the productivity of one cannot be compared to the other.

In order to maximise productivity management has to combine and balance three approaches:

(1) To address itself to overall productivity by providing the best organisation, methods and equipment, and ensuring – through participative or consultative leadership and productivity schemes – that these are adopted by all employees.

(2) To ensure that the hygiene factors and motivators as described in Chapter 8 are correct.

(3) To provide further monetary incentives where individual or group success makes this appropriate.

PRODUCTIVITY DEALS

One of the most modern approaches to pay administration favoured by companies with successful progressive industrial relations is time rates with or without merit differentials combined with productivity development schemes. These aim to create greater profits by higher labour productivity. The greater profits are then shared by the company and its employees, who receive their share in better wages, pensions, reduced hours etc.

The use of the productivity development schemes is favoured because they help to achieve several objectives:

(a) Increases in employee benefits based on real gains in wealth.

(b) Overcoming resistance to change.

(c) Promoting free discussion of productivity.

(d) "Buying out" restrictive practices resulting from past management fail-
     ures.

Success of Productivity Schemes

Such schemes must be carefully managed to be effective. The criteria for
success are:

(a) There must be adequate data on present performance, cost and results.

(b) There must be specific changes in method or practice making direct
     contributions to increased productivity.

(c) There must be an agreed method of sharing gains between shareholders,
     employees and the enterprise.

(d) There must be a clearly defined policy regarding foregoing present gain
     for future gain – e.g. by lowering charges to customers.

(e) Social responsibility objectives must be met, e.g. providing services in
     rural areas.

(f) Benefits must be distributed *after* being earned.

(g) Benefits must allow for changes in capital employed, supervision,
     services, etc.

Practice Exercises

(1) Obtain a copy of your firm's salary scale.

(2) If your firm does not have one, why do you think this is? Does the firm benefit from not having a scale? Do the employees?

(3) If your firm does have a scale, what do you gain from it?

(4) Does it encourage

    (a) effort,   (c) innovation,
    (b) performance   (d) loyalty?

(5) How is the salary for your work decided? Who decides? Is it fair in relation to other salaries?

(6) What would your firm have to do to make you do your work better?

(7) Rank the benefits you receive in order of preference.

From Chapter 15 you should have learnt:

The contents of a benefit package.

Why differentials create difficulties.

How job evaluation works. Which of four types of method are suitable in particular conditions.

The advantages and disadvantages of individual incentive schemes.

The advantages and disadvantages of group incentive schemes.

The effects of different payment policies.

The purpose and procedures of productivity deals.

The role of payment policy in:

Organisation	Chapter 4
Decision making Implementation of decision } MbO	Chapter 5
Control	Chapter 6
Motivation	Chapters 7 and 8
Authority of managers	Chapter 9
Labour turnover	Chapter 12
Collective Bargaining	Chapter 16
Conflict	Chapter 11

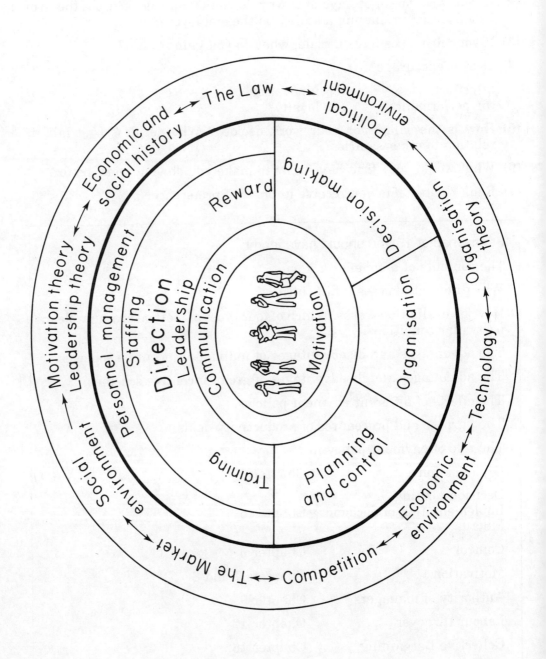

Chapter 16

Industrial Relations

Many of the matters dealt with by managers when fulfilling their personnel functions can concern either an individual subordinate or a whole "grade" or "class" of subordinates. The latter situation would normally be referred to as industrial relations. This covers such activities as collective bargaining for wages, conditions of work, disputes involving groups of employees, and joint consultation into matters of interest to managers and employees.

PURPOSE

From the manager's point of view industrial relations attempts to ensure consistency in the areas outlined above, to ensure fairness both for its own sake, and to avoid discontent between employees or groups of employees who consider themselves to have been treated less well than others. From the employee's point of view this same parity can be obtained more easily by powerful combinations of employees.

THE REPRESENTATIVE SYSTEM

Individual managers can only deal with issues concerning their own subordinates. When the issues involve large numbers of operators it becomes necessary in practice to have a representative system where groups of operators have representatives to deal with these issues on their behalf.

The purposes of a representative system should be:

(a) to keep managers informed of the attitudes, goals and problems of employees.

(b) To keep employees informed of company, industry and economic trends likely to affect them.

(c) To enable managers to give advance notice to employees of any changes in plans, organisation or company strategy.

(d) To enable common objectives to be maintained in the enterprise.

(e) To educate employees to enable them to participate in democratic decision-making.

It should be understood clearly that in all except very small companies a representative system is not only desirable, but in most cases essential to the long term success of an enterprise. The need is least when top decision-makers are in close contact with employees at all levels, and at the same time are very sensitive to their views. This situation is in practice very rare.

TRADE UNIONS

The basic form of representative system is confined to one particular enterprise. This has the great advantage that discussions between managers and classes of employees are not distorted by issues irrelevant to the enterprise. To be recognised as "unions" under the Industrial Relations Act such systems must be "registered" and prove independence from management influence.

The term "union" in this country is generally applied to a combination of workers from a number of different enterprises. The officers of these unions still represent their members but in this country also indulge in substantial political activity. Some of this has certainly been instrumental in obtaining valuable benefits for the membership, but there is a danger of a confusion of roles which can seriously affect a union's effectiveness in its main function.

Craft Unions

These are the earliest forms of unions whose original purpose was maintaining standards of skill and levels of income by limiting apprenticeships. They are still very effective for this purpose, but through their reluctance to adapt to changing skill, cause great problems to industry and their own members through restrictive practices and demarcation disputes. The latter are to some extent being reduced by the amalgamation of small craft unions into larger groupings.

General Unions

These were formed by workers not having any training or occupational qualifications and include Britain's largest unions – the TGWU and NUGMW. They tend to have considerable power – both industrially and politically – by their very size. At the same time, however, it makes it more difficult for them to represent accurately the variety of interests of their members.

White Collar Unions

These include clerical and administrative workers in offices, and specialists and managers in industry. They have grown rapidly in recent years to help their membership maintain their status relative to manual workers.

Industry Unions

These cover all the grades in one industry including unskilled, skilled and managerial employees. They therefore have the advantage of size, with the greater resources and power which this brings. They are also still representatives of a common interest group, which facilitates discussion with managers about issues relating to the industry. In addition they largely eliminated the problems associated with craft unions, although demarcation problems may still arise between unions, e.g. between the NUR and the TGWU regarding the transport of cars.

The unions also provide welfare benefits, e.g. for old age, sickness, accidents or unemployment, legal assistance, group benefits such as insurance and travel, and may even deal with disciplinary, employment and redundancy issues. These activities are more highly developed in countries with a less elaborate welfare system than the UK.

THE GROWTH OF WHITE COLLAR UNIONISM

From the survey of Trade Union development it is evident that trade unions were originally developed to protect the interests of so-called blue-collar workers, who comprised mainly manual activities, although very often to a high level of skill. It should be noticed that social status was never a bar to trade unionism, as groups such as doctors and journalists have been organised from an early stage. It should also be noted that many comparatively highly paid groups of workers, e.g. computer technologists, enthusiastically embrace unionism, whereas industrial clerks and other low pay groups steadfastly resist joining formal organisations.

One of the significant changes in the structure of society has been the increase in proportion of non-manual workers. Mechanisation has replaced more and more unskilled jobs by machines. An increase in standards of living has resulted from the increased productivity. Much of the higher spending power of the population has been diverted to services which have a higher non-manual content.

At the same time the management of plant and machinery has increased the proportion of each firm's employees engaged in non-manual specialist departments such as planning, quality control, accountancy, and O & M.

Overall the proportion of white collar workers has risen from 18.7% of the working population in 1911 to 49.1% in 1979. During this period the membership of white collar unions grew proportionately.

Since 1964 there has been a dramatic increase in the proportion of white collar workers who have joined unions. G. S. Bain, in analysing the causes of this change, has identified three main ones:

(1) Concentration of industry
(2) Company attitudes
(3) Government policy
«G. S. Bain, *The Growth of White Collar Unions,* Clarendon Press, 1968»

CONCENTRATION OF INDUSTRY

Concentration of industry has already been examined in Chapter 2. From the industrial relations point of view, the result has been that large groups of employees with similar interests are now working on single sites. Many of these employees are doing routine work which is demoralising and alienating. They often feel remote from the senior management which makes decisions affecting their work, careers and standard of living. Such employees will perceive a need to enhance their power and influence (see Chapter 7) and any invitation to join an established power group such as a union is likely to be accepted gratefully.

From a union's point of view it is economically and practically much easier to recruit members at a site where several hundred people are working than where there may be only a dozen or less. Even large unions only have a small number of full time officials in any one area. The rate at which these can recruit depends largely on how many people they can deal with in one visit.

ATTITUDE OF GOVERNMENT

The government, directly through Government departments, and indirectly because of its influence on Nationalised Industries, is by far the largest employer in the country. A number of governments since World War Two have been strongly in favour of unionisation and have encouraged recruitment among their employees. Not only by accepting union membership but by positively insisting that collective bargaining should take place with recognised unions.

In addition numerous pieces of legislation have extended the privileges and rights of trade unions compared to more informal representative systems. Some of this legislation is designed to make unions more democratically responsible. This has overcome the objections of some people reluctant to be ruled by a minority of militants, as well as the fear which some managers have of dealing with such a body. Meanwhile the legislation has also had the effect, which much legislation is intended to have, of causing people to accept that the law of the land is a reflection of the view of society. In this case many managers with anti-union views have been influenced by the legislation to regard unions as acceptable organisational formations.

COMPANY ATTITUDES

The influence on managers of legislation has just been noted. Perhaps an even greater influence, in conjunction with the increased size of company, has been a recognition of the need to have some sort of representative system to keep in touch with the feelings and attitudes of large numbers of employees. Communication between policy making levels and operatives is inevitably tenuous both because of the numbers involved and their physical dispersion. Even local management is physically out of contact with the head-office-departments. The need is particularly felt by the new generation of senior managers who have entered the bank at graduate level, who have been taught the principles of Industrial Relations, but who have never themselves had real experience of working as operatives.

In addition to the main reasons identified by Bain, it is also true that Unions have become generally more socially acceptable. The switch from blue collar to white collar work has meant that many clerical jobs have been filled by people whose parents were probably blue collar workers and where trade unionism was not only acceptable but encouraged. These people have, as it were, spread the gospel, and dispelled the belief that unions are necessarily militant or destructive.

Differentials in conditions of service have changed in the last few decades. Blue collar workers have gained many of the benefits which were previously the preserve of white collar workers. Monthly notice has replaced one hour's notice, payment is continued during sickness, holidays have lengthened and pensions have become commonplace. The white collar worker has made no equivalent advances, so that differentials have been eroded. Many attribute this to the power of the blue collar unions and aim to regain their differentials by similar militancy.

Finally technology, in the form of automation and computers, is now creating the same problems for clerical workers as mechanisation has in the past for manual workers. Lost skills, the need for re-training or re-location, and the risk of redundancy, all reinforce the potential benefit of seeking the protection of a powerful group.

THE FINANCIAL SECTOR

The description of the growth of white collar unionism has been closely paralleled in the banking sector. Early in this century there were a large number of banks which have now been reduced to about ten.

The English banks employ nearly 300,000 employees of which about one-third are in London, mainly head office departments. A typical office will house 1,000 staff, most of them on similar work. Of the 65,000 Building Society workers, 37,000 are employed in the six largest societies who also have large head offices. The large foreign banks have huge office blocks, and

there has been a spate of amalgamations among other financial organisations. The conditions for people to want to join a union, and for ease of
recruitment are therefore in existence.

These conditions may be reinforced if the current boom in financial services
abates, or if the growth in employment shown in figure 16.1 is overtaken by
mechanisation. During the last three years growth in employment has been
about 1% per annum, which is much slower than the previous 20 years.

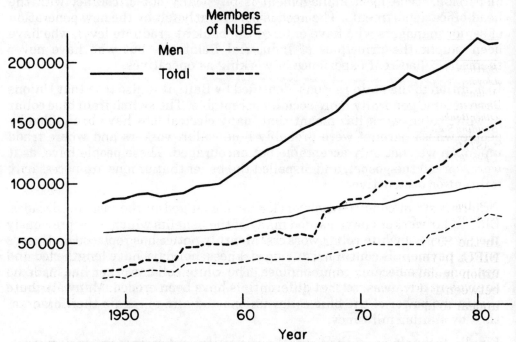

Fig. 16.1 English clearing banks: number of full time employees

The only employers' body active in industrial relations in the financial
sector is the Committee of the London Clearing Banks. This has for a long
time provided a forum for the discussion of staff matters. In particular
competitive bidding for new recruits in the tight labour market of the 1960s
was avoided by agreeing percentages for the annual pay awards. In 1968 an
employers' body was formed to combat a series of one day strikes. In 1972
the Federation of London Clearing Bank Employers was reformed as a
result of the Industrial Relations Act 1971 (now replaced by the Employment Acts 1980 and 1982). Ever since then it has been encouraging the
banking employees to form a joint body with whom it can negotiate.

In response the Staff Associations of the big four clearing banks formed a
Confederation of Banking Unions (CBU) for national negotiations. They
were however not able to agree on joint negotiations together with the
Banking Insurance and Finance Union (BIFU) thus making national
negotiations very difficult.

Most of the major Building Societies have Staff Associations which are certified as Independent Trade Unions but Societies do not have a joint negotiating association. Some of the Staff Associations belong to a Federation which agrees on what their attitude to benefits and conditions of service should be. They claim about 85% membership among the Societies staff.

Staff Numbers and Union Membership in the Financial Sector – End 1986 (approximate figures).
employees belonging to

	Staff	BIFU	Staff Association
Barclays	82,000	19%	57%
Lloyds	48,000	28%	47%
Midland	47,000	44%	4%*
Natwest	73,000	28%	47%
Other Banks	70,000	N.A.	N.A.
Building Societies	65,000	2%	79%+

*ASTMS
+ Feb. '87

[Fig. 16.2]

N.B. Due to different group structures the figures for the 4 major clearing banks are not strictly comparable.

In the Scottish Banks and the TSB nearly all employees are members of BIFU. In the rest of the banking sector, as shown in figure 16.2 the level of union membership is surprisingly level at about 75%, but the balance between BIFU and CBU varies widely in different banks. There does not appear to have been a dramatic change in representation in recent years.

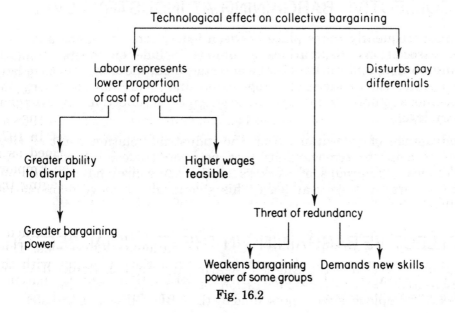

Fig. 16.2

New technology means that within each bank there are now groups of specialists – e.g. systems analysts, whose specialist training was received outside the bank and a great part of whose experience has been gained outside. They are therefore more closely allied to their own speciality than to the bank. Their Salaries have to relate to salaries they can receive elsewhere rather than in the bank. This may cause anomalies compared to the salary and career structure within the bank and cause non-specialists to join a union to redress the balance. At the same time the specialists are more mobile and therefore more likely to join a union such as ASTMS.

COLLECTIVE BARGAINING

As a result of a Royal Commission in 1869, the legality of trades unions was established by the passing of the Trades Union Act in 1871. This brought in its wake the development of voluntary collective bargaining which is now well established in this country. It means fixing wages, conditions of work etc. by the representatives of a number of firms on the one hand and a number of groups of workers on the other hand.

One of the main problems of "collective bargaining" is its divisiveness in splitting members of one enterprise into two "sides". Historically this resulted from managers not taking account of the legitimate "goals" of operators. This provided the "stimulus" for operators to combine to obtain their goals in alternative ways. Hence we now have a conflict situation which is not mirrored by countries, such as Japan, where managers have traditionally been more concerned for their employees' needs.

«Nature of People, Ch. 7, p. 156»

COLLECTIVE BARGAINING AT INDUSTRY LEVEL

This most frequently takes place between federations of unions and employers' associations. Federations of unions include engineers, printers, building workers and workers in the entertainment industry. These federations areintended to increase co-operation and co-ordination among the trades unions in order to increase their strength in collective bargaining at industry level.

The advantage of federations from the industrial relation point of view is that it helps to remove anomalies between trades, inherent in the craft unions, e.g. groups of workers in the same firm having different working hours. In theory at least, this should also remove demarcation disputes.

COLLECTIVE BARGAINING IN THE FINANCIAL SECTOR

At National Level 3 of the English Clearing the English Banks have one representative body – The Federation of Clearing Bank Employers – whereas the employees are represented by the CBU, BIFU and ASTMS.

The main items in the national negotiations are:

(a) Salaries of the four basic clerical grades (approximately 70% of clerical staff)
(b) Minimum salaries for branch managers on first appointment
(c) Territorial allowances
(d) Safety of employees
(e) Working hours
(f) Overtime
(g) Holidays of unappointed staff

It is agreed that the matters listed above should be negotiated nationally. Obviously the necessity to reach agreed terms in each area, while negotiating with three different unions, makes the negotiating process extremely complicated, time consuming and long winded. This unsatisfactory state of affairs is exacerbated because each union wants to prove to its members that it can obtain better terms, hoping thereby to increase its own membership. The members' long term interests are therefore likely to be sacrificed to the shorter term interests of the union itself.

BIFU has an added interest in obtaining good terms from the clearing banks because these tend to be pace-setters for the Insurance and Finance sector.

ASTMS normally accepts the deals negotiated at national level by the other two unions as it is more concerned with conditions of technical staff.

In recognition of the problems of national collective bargaining, and to retain some of the advantages of collective bargaining as such, bargaining in the financial sector takes place at two levels below the national one – i.e. "domestic" and "local" bargaining.

DOMESTIC COLLECTIVE BARGAINING

In banking, The Midland Bank negotiates separately with its staff association all the matters included in the national negotiations mentioned above. For all the banks additional matters such as the salaries for higher clerical specialist and managerial staff are negotiated domestically.

In the Building Societies there are no national negotiations because there is no employers' joint negotiating body. All the major Societies have Staff Associations which are registered trade unions and belong to the Federation of Building Society Staff Association.

The matters negotiated are:

Salary, Fringe Benefits and Pension.
Discipline and Grievance.
Safety, Security, Health and Welfare.
Application of new Legislation.
Reorganisation especially related to new technology.
Job evaluation, work load and manning level.

Some Societies have a set annual salary review for which a typical time table would be;

5 months before review date:
   Questionnaire sent to all S.A. members to obtain their priorities and expectations.

3 months before review date:
   Regional Council make proposals to National Council on salary claim.
   Draft claim prepared by National Council, making allowance for comparative data gathered, and the society's overall performance.

2 months before review date:
   Society's response considered by negotiating committee.
   Possibly several negotiating meetings before.

1 month before review date:
   Agreement on terms to be prepared for implementation on review date or Implementation of conciliation or arbitration procedure.

GRIEVANCES

A grievance arises whenever persons or groups feel that they are being unfairly or improperly treated. Note that it is this feeling which is initially important, rather than the facts of a situation. In many cases groups react vigorously to defend the positions of individuals.

Disputes

If a grievance develops to the extent that action is taken by one of the parties concerned, a dispute arises. Such disputes may take the form of:

Strikes

Here groups of workers withhold their labour. This involves the workers and employers both losing their sources of income. A strike is designed to put pressure on employers. Parts of union dues are devoted to building up "strike funds" to replace at least partially, the income lost by workers. When this "strike pay" is made available the strike is said to be "official". In an "unofficial" strike there is no such compensation for the workers so that there is substantial inherent pressure for unofficial strikes not to occur. Their actual occurrence indicates serious grievances and a high level of frustration by workers, probably due to lack of management reaction to long standing grievances, or inadequate representative systems. Sometimes such situations are exploited by agitators concerned with non-managerial issues.

Unfortunately the result of strikes may well be the weakening of both parties to the dispute, and a deterioration in the availability, security and reward of work.

Lock-outs

Where employers refuse to provide work, usually by refusing workers access to premises. The basis of lock-outs is the reverse of that applying to strikes.

Go-slows

The normal rate of work of operators is greater than the minimum which employers would be prepared to accept. By working at the minimum level, and taking advantage of all concessions generally used only in exceptional circumstances, employees are able to put pressure on employers without weakening their own position.

Working to Rule

Industries which are stable can be managed by laying down rules governing the tasks and action of employees. Changing circumstances tend to make such rules out of date very quickly. By invoking them employees are again able to apply pressure on employers without short term disadvantages to themselves.

GRIEVANCE PROCEDURES

Many disputes arise because grievances are not settled either because of the ignorance, intransigence or lack of power of first line managers, or because workers do not know how to get something done about their complaints.

Grievance procedures are intended to avoid a build up of frustration among employees. Particularly among those who do not have much initiative or ability to express themselves and to fight their own battles. All individuals should know who the "grievance officer" for their branch or building is. The person to whom grievances are to be reported should also be readily available. In the larger companies in the financial sector it is likely to be a personnel officer. The exact details of a grievance procedure are less important than the need for it to be known and fully understood by every employee. It should be included in initial training – not to encourage grievances – but to ensure that minor grievances are dealt with before they become major disputes.

Time Scale

The second most important aspect of a grievance procedure is the time element. Very often major grievances build up from minor ones, perhaps appreciated by managers but not cleared up because of pressure of work or lack of authority. A grievance procedure should therefore include time limits after which the next step in the procedure is activated. These limits should be as short as practicable. The time schedules are particularly important where large companies or unions use committees to decide industrial relations issues, as the non-availability of committee members on suitable dates may cause interminable delays.

Appeals Procedure

The third essential of a grievance procedure is the "appeal" element. This means that an aggrieved party not satisfied by a decision, whether at supervisor or company level, has the *facility* to get the situation reconsidered, if necessary at national level.

JOINT CONSULTATIVE COMMITTEES

The causes of many grievances are decisions which may affect companies or groups of employees where the needs and wants of those affected have either not been considered at all, or invalid assumptions have been made about them.

When large groups are involved, consultative committees are a method of dealing with this problem. These committees can be very effective if used by all the members in a genuine effort to discover, and to take account of, the views, worries and goals of the others, or the groups whom they represent.

Due to the above mentioned time which can be consumed in committee meetings, consultative committees can easily be used as a delaying device or to avoid action. In such circumstances they impede, rather than promote, good management and industrial relations.

DISCIPLINARY PROCEDURES

The need for discipline was accepted within management from the earliest times. It was included as one of Fayol's principles of management. It is a need which arises partly because it is a way of standardising activities to improve efficiency and reduce the risk of accidents, and partly because undisciplined behaviour patterns are likely to cause conflict.

Most financial services activities take place at a relatively leisured pace, there is normally ample space and little physical movement, so the risk of accidents due to "horse-play" or carelessness is small. However, the risk of disagreement and conflict between members of staff, and between groups of staff is no less than in other industries and this is often due to different views as to the proper way to behave. It thus becomes desirable to define behaviour patterns in critical areas.

Critical areas are those where people's behaviour affects others. Good behaviour in relation to others involves consideration of the feelings and needs of others, sometimes at a disadvantage or inconvenience to oneself.

Most people are prepared to put themselves out for the general good, *provided everyone else* is prepared to do likewise. The purpose of discipline is to define what the standard of behaviour should be, and to ensure that people who are selfish and inconsiderate do not gain an unfair advantage over the rest, and do not spoil a satisfactory working environment.

Unfortunately some managers tend to misuse their power by trying to enforce behaviour patterns in areas which are not important, or, even more to be deprecated, by enforcing discipline inequitably. They allow some people to break the rules quite regularly while others are pounced upon for the occasional minor breach. There is no doubt that personal favouritism sometimes occurs, but often managers are afraid of offending subordinates with long experience or high expertise, while they are positively pleased to make life difficult for subordinates whom they consider to have been unhelpful.

The severity of punishment meted out to offenders against discipline is often arbitrarily varied. Another common grievance is that people are punished for actions and omissions which they were not aware would arouse the manager's displeasure.

All these problems highlight a need for some measure of control of the use of authority by managers. In order to apply controls it is necessary to have a standard. The standard for this purpose is a formal "Disciplinary Procedure" against which the actual performance of managers can be judged.

A good procedure should be in writing. The reason for this is that in a well run office it may be only seldom required. If a manager relies on his memory he may, in fact, create the very problem that the procedure is designed to avoid, by treating a case differently from the last time it occurred. Often a similar problem has never been faced by the manager; if he simply uses his judgement, it may differ from that of his predecessors, or colleagues in other offices. It is therefore necessary for him to have a written procedure to which he can refer. This is also useful to show to employees, to demonstrate to them that they are not being unfairly treated. The procedure should be available for study by all employees and should ideally be issued to them as part of their contract of employment. It should make clear which employees are covered by it.

A good disciplinary procedure has the following essential components.

(1) All offences which lead to some form of punishment should be *specified*.

(2) *The forms of penalty* which a manager is authorised to use must be specified. Forms of penalties in use range from losses of privileges through losses of bonuses or holiday or training entitlements, to suspension and dismissal. Normally managers are not authorised to dismiss staff without at least prior approval by a superior or a senior personnel specialist. This is partly because of the responsibility of the firm for ensuring fair treatment and partly because unfair dismissal is an offence under the 1980 Employment Act.

(3) *The penalties, which different offences carry must be specified.* This is especially important where dismissal is a possibility.

(4) *The procedure for disciplining staff must be stated.* A procedure for dismissal is recommended in an ACAS Code of Practice.

    (a) *An informal verbal warning.*
        A major purpose of this step is to avoid misunderstandings. It is found that many breaches of rules only occur because the employee is unaware of having done something wrong. A word in his ear and the problem is solved. Note that this is in any case the proper procedure from the point of view of management technique, which is not

to punish but to ensure correct behaviour in future. This informal step is not recorded.

(b) *A formal verbal warning*.

If the employee does not react to the informal approach a similar warning is given formally. This means it must take place in the presence of a third party, and a note is usually made on the employee's record. In the case of a minor offence the "third party" may simply be another employee. If it is an offence liable to dismissal it is normal for a representative from the personnel department or the staff association, or even both, to be present.

(c) *A formal written warning*.

Only one written warning is required by law to precede a dismissal, but some firms write a second, and final, warning letter. The written letter goes onto the employee's record and is often at least vetted by, and sometimes even issued by the personnel department. A copy of the written warning is sent to the employee's representative.

(d) An arrangement must be included giving the employee the *right of reply* to a complaint. His answer or excuse should be included with the relevant records.

(e) *Time limits should be specified*. It is not fair to ignore a breach of discipline initially and then bring it up at a later stage. On the other hand where a breach occurs in the heat of an argument there is a case for a cooling-off period. The length of such a period should be specified, but, bearing this cooling off period in mind, disciplinary action should be as prompt as the other duties of a manager allow. A time limit should be set within which the matter must be concluded.

(f) *Appeals procedure*.

To eliminate the risk of unjustified disciplinary action, the alleged offender must have the right of appeal. This is normally to the manager's immediate superior.

A procedure on the above lines should avoid the disciplinary problems discussed earlier. It will be varied according to the seriousness of the offence. In minor offences step (e) may not be considered necessary. It is also desirable that the time for which an offence is kept on record is specified.

In addition to a clear disciplinary procedure setting out the basis of action, the critical factor in maintaining proper discipline is that offences must not be *condoned*. Condoning offences which justify dismissal is one of the grounds for claiming unfair dismissal. The principle applies equally to less important breaches of discipline. Managers must not lull their subordinates into a false sense of "laissez faire" and then unexpectedly apply strict discipline. If some of the time breaches of discipline go unpunished it means either the manager is not doing his job properly or the rules should be changed to make it a non-punishable breach.

Illustration

Non-attendance at day release classes, although taking the time off work, may be punishable by withdrawing the day release privilege.

1st: the manager will point this out informally
2nd: the manager will discuss it in the presence of the training officer
3rd: a letter will be sent as described in the procedure
4th: day release will stop

but for this procedure to be effective it is incumbent on the manager (or the training officer) to check the very first week after each warning that it is being heeded, and then to follow this with regular checks.

TRAINING

When managers are first appointed to a post giving them authority to take disciplinary action they must be trained to understand the "spirit" of the procedure, the detailed content, and also the method of dealing with employees in disciplinary matters.

DISCIPLINARY INTERVIEWS

The range of disciplinary problems with which a manager has to deal is so wide that no set interviewing pattern can be prescribed. Two important principles should guide the way discipline is enforced.

(1) The underlying objective is to bring behaviour up to the standard accepted by all, rather than to punish.

(2) Justice must be seen to be done.

The first of these principles has as a corollary the maxim "Praise in public, admonish in private". From this follows the idea of the "informal warning" which should therefore always take place in private. This "interview" is designed to "help" the employee. The emphasis is therefore on a friendly and relaxed atmosphere. Ideally not in the manager's office, which would put the subordinate at a disadvantage, and preferably immediately following some other dealings between the manager and subordinate.

With more persistent offenders the manager must assert his authority by summoning the offender to his office. Here privacy is maintained, although it is possible to meet the second requirement by ensuring that the rest of the staff are aware of the summons. In more serious cases the presence of the offender's friend or representative also ensures that the staff know undisciplined behaviour is not being tolerated.

ROLE OF THE PERSONNEL DEPARTMENT

The Employment Act 1980 includes protection against Unfair Dismissal. Unfair dismissal is in any case against the personnel policy of most companies. The personnel department therefore often has the sole authority to sanction dismissal. In order to maintain discipline and not erode the authority of operating managers, it is the latter who should carry out disciplinary interviews. All offences which carry the risk of suspension, dismissal or transfer, should be reported to the personnel department, if they are repeated after an informal warning. This gives the department an opportunity to advise the manager concerned on acceptable alternative courses of action before the formal disciplinary interview. By also being present at the interview the personnel officer can ensure a proper hearing of the offender, eliminate the risk of embarrassing or legally improper action by the manager, and emphasise the seriousness of the offence to the employee.

At the next stage of the procedure the department will be able to provide examples of legally acceptable written warnings. It will also ensure disciplinary matters are included in the employee's records, and in due course removed.

"Summary dismissal" refers to immediate dismissal without notice or further investigation. In our society it is only acceptable in specific circumstances. e.g. "insolence with violence" towards a superior, or when an employee is *caught* stealing. Managers must be clearly briefed whether, and in what circumstances, they may summarily dismiss a subordinate.

Practice Exercises

(1) Find out whether you are represented in discussions with management.

(2) (a) Who is your representative?

(b) How was he elected?

(c) Did you vote for him?

(d) Who voted for him?

(e) Is he similar in outlook, attitude and background to you and your Colleagues?

(3) Are you a member of a union? What are your reasons?

(4) If you are working in a branch, get a friend at H.O. or in a department to answer the same questions and compare the answers (or conversely).

(5) Has any new machinery been introduced into your office? What effects has it had?

(6) Read up details of your firm's grievance and disciplinary procedures. Ask your personnel officer, if necessary; say that you want them for study.

From Chapter 16 you should have learnt:

Why representative systems are needed.

Why white collar unions have grown in recent years.

The effect of technology on collective bargaining.

The advantages and disadvantages of collective bargaining and the levels at which it can be carried out.

The difference between a grievance and a dispute.

The effects of various types of disputes.

The use and workings of grievance procedures.

Why discipline is necessary and what the essential features of a disciplinary procedure are.

Index